Education and the State

A Liberty Press Edition

Professor Edwin G. West received his Ph.D. in economics from the University of London. Now Professor Emeritus at Carleton University, Ottawa, Canada, he has been a visiting scholar at the University of California at Berkeley, Virginia Polytechnic Institute and State University in Blacksburg, Emory University in Atlanta, and the University of Chicago. He is author of over a dozen books and approximately one hundred articles in scholarly journals. *Education and the State* was first published in 1965 by the Institute of Economic Affairs in London, England. Dr. West is also the author of *Adam Smith: The Man and His Works,* published by Liberty Fund in 1977, and of *Education and the Industrial Revolution* (1975). His main areas of interest include public finance, the economics of education, public choice, and the history of economic thought. Among his latest writings are *Adam Smith and Modern Economics: From Market Behaviour to Public Choice* (1990) and "The Benthamites as Educational Engineers: The Reputation and the Record," *History of Political Economy* (1992).

LIBERTY FUND
STUDIES IN EDUCATION AND LIBERTY

Teacher in America

By Jacques Barzun

Education in a Free Society

Edited by Anne Husted Burleigh

Education and the State:
A Study in Political Economy

By E. G. West

E. G. WEST

Education and the State

A Study in Political Economy

Foreword by Arthur Seldon
Introduction by Myron Lieberman

Third Edition, Revised and Expanded

LIBERTY FUND

Indianapolis

1994

This is a Liberty Press Edition published by Liberty Fund, Inc.,
a foundation established to encourage study of the ideal of a society of
free and responsible individuals.

The cuneiform inscription that serves as our logo and as the design motif
for our endpapers is the earliest-known written appearance of the
word "freedom" (*amagi*), or "liberty." It is taken from a clay document
written about 2300 B.C. in the Sumerian city-state of Lagash.

Originally published by the Institute of Economic Affairs.
© 1965 and 1970.

Third Edition, Revised and Expanded © 1994 by Liberty Fund, Inc.
All rights reserved.
All inquiries should be addressed to
Liberty Fund, Inc., 8335 Allison Pointe Trail, Suite 300,
Indianapolis, Indiana 46250-1687.
Printed in the United States of America.

Library of Congress Cataloging-in-Publication Data

West, E. G., 1922–
Education and the state : a study in political economy
/ E.G. West. — 3rd ed., rev. and expanded.
p. cm.
Originally published: London : Institute of Economic Affairs, 1965.
Includes bibliographical references (p.   ) and index.
ISBN 0-86597-134-X (hard : acid-free paper). — ISBN 0-86597-135-8
(pbk. : acid-free paper)
1. Education and state—Great Britain.   2. Education—Economic
aspects—Great Britain.   3. Education and state—United States.
4. Education—Economic aspects—United States.   I. Title.
LC93.G7W4   1994
379.41—dc20   94-3918

10 9 8 7 6 5 4 3 2 1

CONTENTS

vii

LIST OF TABLES

xi

FOREWORD

Since it was first published in 1965, Edwin G. West's pioneering study of the origins and economics of both state and private education in his *Education and the State* has become something of a classic in modern scholarship. The first edition of the book represented a direct challenge to the conventional misinterpretation of history which held that state involvement in education in 1870 was necessitated by the rudimentary patchwork of private schooling (much maligned in the fictional works of Charles Dickens). Ironically, the enlarged second edition of *Education and the State* was published in 1970, as British politicians and the educational establishment were celebrating 'the centenary of state education'. In the ensuing years, Professor West has continued to strengthen and refine his analysis of the history and economics of education.

This new third edition is especially timely, as the continuing failure of state education becomes increasingly evident on both sides of the Atlantic. This edition presents telling evidence that there is an almost precise parallel in the misinterpretation of history in both the United States and Great Britain; and it analyses the vain attempts made to introduce market techniques as a remedy. Professor West has extended Chapter 12 to bring up-to-date the history of the failure of state education in Britain; and he has added Chapter 17 to demonstrate an almost identical failure in the United States.

The government in Britain has given the new power to 'opt

out' of the state system to the producers of schooling and denied it to its consumers. In public-choice terms, as Chapter 12 demonstrates, the structure of power and self-interest in state education has led central and local government officials and teachers to resist the transfer of power to the consumers of education. The state's refusal to return taxes (indirect as well as direct) to parents so that they might pay fees in a free market for education reflects the propensity of the bureaucracy to protect state schools from competition from better private schools. This practice thus suppresses the 'supply-side' effect that occurs when school officials respond to consumer demand.

The American experience, as shown by nineteenth-century developments in New York State, produces comparable evidence that vindicates the central theme of *Education and the State*. Although private education had been growing impressively since the early 1800s in both Britain and New York, officials misread the evidence in both localities. Moreover, the growth of state education was buttressed by the now familiar (and false, as Professor West shows) claims of external benefits that required state supply of education. In both countries, the growing faith in the state replaced the old view, reflected in the classical liberal teachings of such thinkers as Adam Smith and Nassau Senior, that parents should be encouraged to pay for education. In economic terms, the concentrated interest of the politicians, bureaucrats, and teacher suppliers overcame the dispersed interests of the consumers in a free-market system. And the argument heard in Britain that the poor could not pay was supplanted in New York by the assertion that only the state could pay for all children.

The lessons gleaned from *Education and the State* can be broadened to apply to the conduct of democracy as a political system. Adam Smith taught that it was the instinct of every man to better his condition. The world has painfully learned that free markets, and *not* state monopolies, are the institutions required to fulfil this instinct. Professor West's studies of education in Great Britain and the United States point to the conclusion that because it is more sensitive to organised educational interest groups than to unorganised students and parents, representative democracy often frustrates the instincts of every consumer of education because it leads away from the free market and toward state monopoly. This is the ultimate contribution and achievement of Professor West's scholarship.

Arthur Seldon

Arthur Seldon is a Founder President of the Institute of Economic Affairs in London. He is the author of *Capitalism* (1990) and *The State Is Rolling Back* (1994).

INTRODUCTION

Education and the State is a comprehensive indictment of public education or, more precisely, a powerful repudiation of the idea that education should be a government service funded by tax revenues. Even proponents of public education are likely to agree that West's rigorous analysis invites a radical rethinking of the rationale that underlies the creation of state-run education and calls for the continuation of government schools in the United Kingdom and the United States. At bottom, this book raises the fundamental question of whether the education of our youth is a proper function of government. *Education and the State* argues persuasively that, except for the truly indigent, government financial support for education is neither essential nor desirable.

In debunking the myths of public education, West challenges the false assumptions upon which it was originally established in the last century. He demonstrates the fallacies in the claim that government schools were needed to protect minors. He also thoroughly discredits the so-called "neighborhood effects" argument, which held that government schools were necessary to reduce crime, increase equality of educational opportunity, inculcate the common values of a democratic society, and achieve economic growth.

In his historical analysis of the antecedents to the creation of government schools in England, West shows that there was an extensive system of private education before 1870 and that the vast majority of children were receiving at least a primary education. The high levels of literacy that preceded compulsory education and government schools in England will surprise many readers. A government commission that reviewed the situation at the time recommended strengthening the existing system, *not* replacing it with government schools. Why, then, did Parliament, in 1870, enact educational legislation establishing government schools? West explicitly argues that misleading government reports, along with an abundance of studies done by educators with more than a modicum of self-interest involved, played a critical role in the decision. This is hardly surprising, of course, given the fact that government agencies and government officials throughout history have frequently disseminated reports that are heavily biased in favor of programs they espouse.

Unlike so many critics of modern education, West insists upon taking into account *all* of the consequences of public education. This leads him to point out that government provision of education has greatly weakened the educational activities of private voluntary organizations, especially religious groups. Although government schools were supposed to increase the opportunities of the children of low-income families, they did not emphasize the long-range versus the short-range consequences of human conduct. Voluntary denominational schools, more than public schools, emphasized the importance of hard work and delayed gratification and encouraged the young to take the long view. Therefore, the poor have had the most to lose with the decline of private denominational schools, and many poor children would probably have been better off had government schools never been created.

The decline of voluntary denominational schools also raises

several interesting questions. When the first edition of *Education and the State* was published, almost 90 percent of the private schools in the United States were denominational; and of those almost 90 percent were Catholic schools. A question arises: If government reduced its support of education, would denominational schools regain the commanding position they once held? Undoubtedly, they would experience an expansion of some sort, but it is questionable whether they would ever achieve the dominant status they once enjoyed. Nevertheless, private schools of the future may foster some of the moral values associated with a religious point of view. This would seem especially likely if government schools are replaced by schools for profit.

A nagging question in the debate over the retention of government schools concerns the fate of the poor. How would the children of the less fortunate members of society be educated if public schools ceased to exist? As West points out, in England the funds for public education were raised largely by consumption taxes—regressive taxes that fell most heavily on the poor. In emphasizing this little-known fact, West challenges the conventional wisdom that the poor could not afford to send their children to school without government support. *Education and the State* suggests that most low-income families in England and the United States could afford private schooling if they were relieved of the regressive taxes for government schools.

This new edition of *Education and the State* is being published at a time when the decline of the extended family is both cause and effect of the tendency for government to usurp more and more the functions of the family. Before government schools became a monopoly, families tended to take care of their own, whether indigent, disabled, or retarded. Today, however, pressures mount for government to expand its family support role. Each government expansion weakens individual and family responsibility; and, in turn, each decline in individual and family responsibility seems to increase the pressures for government intervention and support. West explains how this interactive process has led to the enormous expansion of government schools in Great Britain and the United States. The reader will note, however, that West does not suggest a strategy for reversing this erosion of family responsibility. *Education and the State* points to the *fact* of erosion and shows how it happened, but West stops short of discussing a strategy for restoring producer and consumer incentives to educational services; this task is beyond the scope of West's book.

Education and the State is a book whose insights transcend the particular era or circumstances in which it first appeared. In this, and in many other ways, it is a landmark in the field of modern education. It is today, as it was in 1965, an appropriate point of departure for thinking about the future justification for government schools, compulsory education, and a host of other issues pertaining to educational reform. Given the fact that West wrote most of this book when the school choice movement was intellectually impoverished and politically feeble, his achievement is all the more timely, prescient, and remarkable. Indeed, *Education and the State* is actually more relevant today than it was when it was first published, for in 1965 the deleterious effects of public education were not so apparent as they are today. Educational achievement has declined in Anglo-American society since the first edition of this book was written. The question is not whether the public schools have deteriorated, but why. It is precisely at this point that

Education and the State is most relevant and most valuable in understanding where we went wrong and how we may begin to recover.

Myron Lieberman

Dr. Myron Lieberman, an educational consultant and writer, is Senior Research Scholar, Social Philosophy and Policy Center, Bowling Green State University. His books include *The NEA and AFT: Teacher Unions in Power and Politics* (1994), *Public Education: An Autopsy* (1993), and *Privatization and Educational Choice* (1989).

PREFACE

We may look forward, as I said before, to the time when the labouring population may be safely intrusted with the education of their children; but no Protestant country believes that this time has come, and I see no reason to hope for it until generation after generation has been better and better educated. The Report must admit that, while legislating for what remains of the nineteenth century, we ought not to be diverted from the conduct which we think most beneficient now, by our wishes or by our hopes, as to what may occur in the latter part of the twentieth century. So far as we are influenced by those wishes or hopes, we ought to try and prepare the way for their realization, by giving to the present generation an education which will fit them to educate still better another generation, which, in time, may further improve a third, until England becomes what no country has ever yet become, an Utopia inhabited by a self-educated and well-educated labouring population.

Nassau Senior[1]

Why should the state, or government, educate? Do we believe that others cannot be trusted? What is the real basis of the common assumption that if the state withdrew from education and reduced taxes accordingly, most children would be worse off? Even if it is established that the state should have the last word, is the present method of intervention (the public provision of schools) the best available procedure? Do most people believe

1. *Suggestions on Popular Education*, John Murray, 1861, p. 5.

xxiii

that education is really free? Does the average parent on the other hand approve of the present system only because he or she thinks that other (richer) people are paying for most of his or her child's education? Or does each parent continue to support the present arrangement in the belief that most *other* parents would be negligent if the state did not continue to do their educational spending for them? How many people today still share Nassau Senior's hopes (above) that once we reached the latter part of the twentieth century most people would have been educated into such a responsible frame of mind that they could at last be trusted to educate their own children? How do we explain the *increasing* momentum of state spending on education in the latter half of the twentieth century, a situation which is the very opposite to the one which Senior envisaged? Have important new arguments for state intervention in education appeared since Senior's time? Or has state education become a 'necessary' institution simply because it is one of those institutions to which we have become accustomed?

Such are the fundamental questions with which this book is concerned. There is no denying that this is an ambitious task and that these are enormous questions; to some of them there may be no final answer. But no apology is made for this enquiry. For it is a test of a mature and a free society that in each generation there are sufficient writers prepared to persist with awkward but searching questions and an equally sufficient number of patient individuals willing to consider them. Failure to undertake such discussion means the triumph of prejudice and an acceptance of institutions from mere habit or imitation rather than from any conscious and rational purpose.

The story of state education might well illustrate the way in which societies can easily deceive themselves about their own institutions because of an insufficient and inconstant scrutiny of the reasoning and evidence which is supposed to support them. Once such a state institution has been launched, howsoever adequate or inadequate its first justification, there follows the danger that the original political exertion will adopt a momentum of its own and grow beyond all proportion. For instance the employees and administrators of the new institution may become a vested interest of significant political influence. Furthermore, the institution may condition successive generations into accepting it simply by habitual dependence upon it. The institution then becomes so precious and ingrained that when an enquirer has the audacity to question it he is received with stunned astonishment as if he had questioned the necessity of motherhood or universal suffrage.

This book tries to take especial care to avoid the impatience of the observer who, finding one or two obvious weaknesses in the present system, rushes to the opposite dogma of believing that state intervention in education is at all times, in all forms and in all cases absolutely misconceived. What is attempted is not a theological dispute but an impartial enquiry into the reasoning and the facts of the case for state education today. Where parts of the reasoning are found to be weak or if some of the facts do not seem to square with theory, an attempt will be made to maintain an open-mindedness and a readiness to believe that the findings point only to a modification or limitation of the present form of state intervention and not its total abandonment.

What then is the reasoning put forward to support state, or government, education and what facts are necessary to test such reasoning? I shall examine first the pronouncements on this subject by political and economic theorists, leaving other arguments until later. Because much of the present rationale of state education has a long ancestry it will be necessary to pursue some arguments well back into the nineteenth century and to review what seem to have become outmoded disputes. This investigation is based mainly on the experiences of England and Wales, but, as explained below, this edition includes a special essay on the situation in nineteenth-century America (see Part V).

The Political Economy Approach

Political economists usually examine the case for state education in the context of two main principles. The first is that since the state exists to give protection, and since infants are in more need of protection than others, it has special paternalistic duties towards them. The first chapter endeavours to explore the full meaning and implications of this proposition, while Chapter 2 enquires how far the facts of the present day educational scene in England and Wales are consistent with the same 'protection of minors' principle. The second ground upon which political economists have traditionally tried to demonstrate a presumption in favour of state intervention in education is based on the so-called 'neighbourhood effects' argument. According to this view it is first observed that the behaviour of one individual usually is not confined to him but 'spills over' to affect other people in his environment. It is therefore claimed that his fellows cannot be entirely uninterested in the way in which he uses his life and freedom and that there may be a case for collective control in some cases. These 'spill-over effects' can take several forms, some of them positive, others negative. Chapter 3 demonstrates the oldest example of this type of reasoning as it has been and still is applied to education: the contention that the presence of ignorant or uneducated persons exposes the rest of society to a greater liability to the occurrence of crime and disorder. Present-day evidence relevant to this reasoning is investigated in this chapter. Chapters 4, 5 and 6 examine further applications of this kind of social benefit argument.

Chapter 7 assesses the importance of a more recent application of the 'neighbourhood effects' argument, the contention that education yields positive *economic* benefits which again are not confined to the educated but spill over to benefit society as a whole. After a look at the special contribution of the classical economists (Chapter 8) and the nineteenth-century arguments and evidence (Chapters 9, 10 and 11) there will follow in Chapter 12 a critical examination of the working of twentieth-century educational legislation in England. Part IV considers new fiscal devices to make education more flexible and more consistent with the criteria for state intervention examined in earlier parts of the book.

Finally, this Liberty Fund edition includes a new chapter in Part V, A Further Case Study of Public Intervention. This chapter is drawn from my earlier article, 'The Political Economy of Public School Legislation', that was originally published in the *Journal of Law and Economics* (October, 1967). It relates entirely to experience in nineteenth-century America. The original spelling and punctuation of this article have been retained. Readers in the United States may find it appropriate to read Part V immediately after Chapter 1.

Readers interested in Australia's experience with state education may also wish to consult my article, 'The Benthamites as Educational Engineers: The Reputation and the Record', *History of Political Economy*, Vol. 24, No. 3 (Fall 1992, pp. 595–622).

E. G. West

Carleton University
March, 1994

ACKNOWLEDGEMENTS

Many economists, historians, colleagues and students have, consciously or unconsciously, contributed to this book. Among my colleagues I would particularly like to thank Professor S. R. Dennison for reading earlier drafts of some of the chapters and for making helpful criticisms. I am very indebted to Mr Charles Hanson, who has pointed out several cases of incoherence or jargon in the earlier drafts. I am also grateful to Messrs. H. W. Richardson, D. E. Dalkin and J. M. Bass for their comments and suggestions. Professor J. Wiseman of York University has not only performed the service of reading through the script but has provided friendly assistance in the past. I have also had the benefit of discussion with Professor A. T. Peacock of York University. Among historians of education, I wish to thank Professor A. L. Beales of London University, Mr J. G. Tyson of the University of Newcastle upon Tyne, Mr H. Perkins of the University of Manchester, and Dr Carson I. A. Ritchie of the Woolwich Polytechnic. Mr Arthur Seldon of the Institute of Economic Affairs originally suggested this volume and without his help and encouragement, together with the cordial support of other members of his Institute, I feel sure it would never have materialised. Finally, a word of thanks to Mrs Ann Beeny for her patient and intelligent typing of the manuscript. Needless to say the responsibility for the arguments contained in this book remains entirely my own.

In preparing the material for the second edition I am grateful for valuable assistance from Michael Solly of the IEA.

I am also grateful to the University of Chicago for permission to reprint in this third edition 'The Political Economy of Public School Legislation', *Journal of Law and Economics* (October 1967), copyright 1967 by the University of Chicago, all rights reserved.

PART ONE

Protection of Infants Principle

CHAPTER ONE

State Protection of Minors in Theory

Whatever the true meaning of the term *laissez faire*, the most ardent of its nineteenth-century English supporters rarely argued that it should operate outside the boundaries of a proper legal framework. Within this framework they were prepared to make many exceptions to their general principle of freedom of contract and their special reservation for children was a prominent example of this attitude. However much they disliked over-interfering governments they believed that some element of governing was necessary. But what was the true duty of government? The answer of one of the classical economists, Nassau Senior, disciple of Bentham and friend of John Stuart Mill, was quite clear:

> I detest paternal despotisms which try to supply their subjects with the self-regarding virtues, to make men by law sober, or frugal, or orthodox. I hold that the main, almost sole, duty of Government is to give protection. Protection to all, to children as well as to adults, to those who cannot protect themselves as well as those who can.[1]

Senior went on to remind his readers that children were more defenceless than others. In view of this the state had extra pro-

1. *Suggestions on Popular Education*, John Murray, 1861, p. 6.

3

tective obligations towards them and in particular there was a strong presumption in favour of state intervention in education. This view, which seems to have been readily accepted by liberal economists ever since,[2] will now be examined in more detail in order to gather its precise implications.

Protection by Whom?

A moment's reflection will show that it is much easier to state the 'protection of minors' principle than to draw practical policy conclusions from it. If it is agreed that the state should be responsible for seeing that children are protected, the question arises: whom should it appoint to carry out this duty in practice? The first obvious point to clear up before deciding this issue is for the state to ascertain from its members how important a role they want the family to play. If they aim at giving the family a central place, then the question of protecting infants cannot be settled in isolation of this fact, for it establishes a presumption in favour of delegating the duty of child protection first and foremost to the parents and only withdrawing this arrangement when special circumstances require it. For these reasons the following remarks of John Stuart Mill, which seem to have had widespread influence on this subject, were too evasive and too legalistic:

> In this case [education] the foundation of the *laisser-faire* principle breaks down entirely. The person most interested is not the best judge of the matter, nor a competent judge at all. Insane persons are everywhere regarded as proper objects of the care of the state. In the case of children and young persons, it is common to

2. See, for instance, Professor Milton Friedman, *Capitalism and Freedom*, University of Chicago Press, 1962, p. 86.

say, that though they cannot judge for themselves, they have their parents or other relatives to judge for them. But this removes the question into a different category; making it no longer a question whether the government should interfere with individuals in the direction of their own conduct and interests, but whether it should leave absolutely in their power the conduct and interest of somebody else.[3]

Few would disagree with Mill's general sentiments. If we do not tolerate cruelty to animals still less should we allow the possibility of continued cruelty to children by granting *absolute* power over them to any single person. But Mill was mistaken in assuming that the common argument, that parents and relatives could judge for their children, was a claim for *absolute* power. What most people envisage is something in the nature of a *fiduciary* power to be removed in cases where abuse can be shown.

Whatever the true interpretation of his statement, Mill's anxiety to put this question into a different category did not make it any less important or less urgently in need of an answer. For the state is not a disembodied entity; it has to work through individuals to whom it prescribes certain powers. Now the function of supervising a child is such a personal and delicate matter that it is most important to visualise it in the form of a competition for influence between one individual, the parent, who by nature is closer to the child and therefore has better opportunity for gaining a comprehensive knowledge of his best interests, and another individual, appointed by the state, who has the advantage of some presumed expertise in protecting children. When the problem is expressed in this way the question of *absolute* power is beside the point. Certainly the difficulty is not one which can be solved easily by any universal or dogmatic ruling. Accordingly, the follow-

3. *Principles of Political Economy*, Ashley edition, Longmans, p. 957. This edition will be implied in all subsequent references to this work.

ing analysis is not intended to stake an unconditional claim for any of the parties concerned but is merely an attempt to examine the issues objectively. It will be followed in the next chapter by an assessment of prevailing English legislation in the light of the principles I hope to elucidate. In so far as I am critical of the ability of the 'protection' argument to justify universal state schooling, it must be emphasised that my criticism is not to the prejudice of the other arguments for this system; they will be examined in subsequent chapters.

Protection against What?

Before we can choose those individuals deemed to be best able to protect a child we have to solve the even more difficult task of defining the danger against which we are trying to protect it. Even state action against physical cruelty is not always simple to administer since the criterion is rarely a matter of unanimous agreement. But at least where physical injury has resulted in permanent damage to an individual, then the evidence is usually so obvious that the case for state protection against further assault is clear enough. In education, on the other hand, the argument is for protection not against physical injury but against ignorance. Here we have to search more deeply to see in what respect any faculties may be said to be injured, either in effect or in intention. When, for instance, the head of a poor family sees his children remaining ignorant of reading and writing, we cannot say that their faculties are injured in the same sense as in the case of physical brutality. The choice between food and education in these circumstances is not normally lightly made by anybody. If the state does decide to intervene in such cases, therefore, it cannot be on the grounds of the same sort of protection as that directed against physical aggression of any kind; the intervention called for will largely be to counteract not irresponsibility but poverty. This initial clarification seems necessary if we wish to avoid using the term 'protection' with its more usual connotation.

But there is a much more stubborn difficulty. When we now speak of protection against ignorance, we have to ask: ignorance of what? A person may be most ignorant of one thing but quite expert at another. Too hasty attempts to prescribe learning priorities can lead to results which not only endanger spontaneity and individuality but which can involve fundamental contradictions in any society which professes to encourage and support the ideal of liberty. Confusion on this subject often arises from a dogmatic insistence that the relevant ignorance is necessarily ignorance of what is taught in schools between statutorily prescribed ages. Schooling is only one instrument in the removal of ignorance; if other means are being used, the need for protection may well be superfluous. There are additional sources of learning in real life: the parent, the family, its friends, the church, books, television, radio, newspapers, correspondence courses, etc., 'on the job training', and personal experience. J. S. Mill himself can be quoted in this respect:

Even if the government could comprehend within itself, in each department, all the most eminent intellectual capacity and active talent of the nation, it would not be the less desirable that the conduct of a large portion of the affairs of the society should be left in the hands of the persons immediately interested in them. The business of life is an essential part of the practical education of a people; without which, book and school instruction, though most necessary and salutary, does not suffice to qualify them for conduct, and for the adaptation of means to ends. Instruction is only one of the desiderata of mental improvement; another, almost as indispensable, is a vigorous exercise of the active energies; labour, contrivance, judgment, self-control: and the natural stimulus to these is the difficulties of life.[4]

The best means by which individuals are likely to 'protect' themselves or their children from 'ignorance' should therefore be open to constant comparative appraisal. That a parent, for instance, wishes to take his child away from school at an early age does not necessarily signify that he is negligent. In so far as the school has become less efficient than other means of education, the parent himself may be acting from motives of protection and be making the same kind of shrewd comparative assessment that he makes before transferring his custom from one source of his child's food or clothing supply to another. Again, to assume that the education given in a school is always and under all circumstances to be preferred to alternative types of education is probably to assume also that all schools and home environments are homogeneous. This is by no means self-evident—especially in a changing society. It is interesting to recall that J. S. Mill himself was deliberately kept at home throughout his childhood by a father who was strenuously motivated by protective impulses. His father, James Mill, indeed kept his son away from school, 'lest the habit of work should be broken and a taste for idleness acquired'.[5] It is quite true that James Mill has been the subject of severe criticism from subsequent state educationists on the grounds that he was too forceful a task-master. The question is, however, whether a state school could have produced a 'better' John Stuart Mill. Such questions, of course, give rise to all sorts of speculations, but no apology is offered for asking them, since, as I hope to show, they lie at the root of the problem I am discussing.

4. *Ibid.*, p. 948.
5. John Stuart Mill, *Autobiography*, New York, Henry Holt, 1873, p. 36.

The Appropriate Scope and Form of Protection

The 'protection of minors' argument has in the past been used to support pressure not merely to educate a *minority* of neglected children but also to establish *universal* schooling whereby *every* child is provided for by the state. There are two major difficulties in the way of our accepting such reasoning, the first political and the second economic. On the political difficulty, it must first be observed that in order to justify a vast and comprehensive system comprising thousands of new state schools one must establish that such provision is needed to fill an obviously widespread deficiency and that the *majority* of parents and relatives are either negligent or ignorant. Now if this is the contention, it must imply either widespread schizophrenia or self-abnegation. For it envisages an electorate which virtually condemns most parents and relatives for being ignorant or negligent about their children when that same electorate consists to a large extent of the parents and relatives themselves. Otherwise the question immediately arises of why, if such ignorance and negligence is so serious, should we presume that it will not equally express itself at the ballot box and with equally 'unfortunate' results when the parents and relatives choose their representatives?

The extent of family responsibility can in part be checked by a survey among parents to ask their intentions if given hypothetical refunds of indirect and direct taxes in the form either of money vouchers spendable only on education in lieu of 'free' state education or of income tax allowances. The only statistical survey that has attempted to elicit answers to this question suggests that negligence would be far from typical.[6] Alternatively we can make a special historical investigation to check average par-

---

6. See *Choice in Welfare*, Part III, Institute of Economic Affairs, 1963. There are fuller references to this survey on pp. 263 and 278 below.

ental behaviour before the inception of state education, bearing in mind that such state intervention had to be supported by increased tax revenues which might otherwise have been spent voluntarily on education. In Chapter 10 I shall argue from historical evidence that nineteenth-century parental behaviour was much more responsible than is commonly supposed.

The second major difficulty in the way of accepting the 'protection' argument to justify a state school system is an economic one. Nowhere does it seem to have been shown why other forms of state intervention could not achieve the intended result of state protection more efficiently and with less cost than the present system of state schools (which amounts virtually to a system of *nationalised* schools). Much as J. S. Mill wanted the protection of children, even he did not in the end prescribe compulsory state schooling, nor even compulsory private schooling, but only compulsory *education*. Accordingly he held that the state should be interested not merely in the number of years of schooling but in checking the results of education whatever their sources, and he contended that an examination system was all that was necessary. If a young person failed to achieve a certain standard then extra education would be prescribed at the parents' expense. Another sanction which Mill also entertained was to make the right to vote conditional on some minimum degree of education.

Under Mill's scheme, if it were operating today, it is conceivable that some children would attempt to attain the necessary standards by much more dependence on television, parental instruction,[7] correspondence courses, evening classes, local librar-

7. In England and Wales there are 100,000 qualified women teachers at home compared with 160,000 teaching in schools. It is obvious that there are thousands of parents who are qualified, even in this formal sense, to teach in their own homes. Under Mill's system it is doubtful whether so much educational capital would be as underused as it is today. For since under his scheme the state would not have involved itself in the heavy taxation now needed to finance 'free'

ies, etc. These in turn would be measured against particular services offered by the private schools whose relative efficiency would be measured by parents and their children in terms of the size of their classes, for instance, or the qualifications of their staff and the personal attention they gave the children.[8] There are examples of this kind of minimum state intervention in other spheres.

Thus although the state insists on the acquisition of a minimum competence in driving before allowing persons to take their vehicles on the roads, it has so far found it unnecessary to prescribe the particular way in which persons should acquire the knowledge and skill, or to nationalise the driving schools and supply training 'free' by raising taxes on all. Again, protection against the supply of adulterated food to children (or to anybody else) is effected simply by a system of inspection, reinforced by regulations, breaches of which are punishable by law.

The case of food is interesting. Protection of a child against starvation or malnutrition is presumably just as important as protection against ignorance. It is difficult to envisage, however, that any government, in its anxiety to see that children have minimum standards of food and clothing, would pass laws for compulsory and universal eating, or that it should entertain measures which lead to increased taxes and rates in order to provide children's food 'free' at local authority kitchens or shops. It is still more difficult to imagine that most people would unquestion-

---

schools, average incomes after tax would be much higher. These would, for instance, enable many married teachers quietly to buy the help of auxiliaries in the form of domestic help and/or labour-saving devices to allow them time to teach their own 5- or 6-year-olds at home. Today it is just conceivable that the state could allow tax rebates for this purpose but the administrative and political obstacles are not trivial.

8. Bearing in mind that everybody would be more able to afford fee-paying schools to the extent that they would be asked to pay less indirect taxation (which nobody now escapes) than a state 'free' school system makes necessary.

ingly accept this system, especially where it had developed to the
stage that for 'administrative reasons' parents were allocated
those shops which happened to be nearest their homes; or that
any complaint or special desire to change their pre-selected
shops should be dealt with by special and quasi-judicial enquiry
after a formal appointment with the local 'Child Food Officer' or,
failing this, by pressure upon their respective representatives on
the local 'Child Food Committee' or upon their local M.P. Yet
strange as such hypothetical measures may appear when applied
to the provision of food and clothing, they are typical of English
state education as it has evolved by historical accident or administrative expediency.

Presumably it is recognised that the ability in a free market to
change one's food shop when it threatens to become, or has become, inefficient is an effective instrument whereby parents can
protect their children from inferior service in a prompt and effective manner. If this is so, then one should expect that the same
arguments of protection would in this respect point in the direction not of a free school system where it is normally difficult to
change one's 'supplier' but in the direction of fee-paying where it
is easier. In this sense one must question J. S. Mill's assertion that
in the case of education the principle of *laissez faire* breaks down
entirely. For if by *laissez faire* he meant (as he seems to have
meant) a fee-paying system, then our reasoning suggests on the
contrary that this is a technique which with some qualifications is
admirably suited to protection of all kinds and not least the 'protection of minors'. W. E. Forster endorsed this view in 1870.[9]

---

9. An alternative interpretation of J. S. Mill's position is that *laissez faire* broke
down because poor parents were unable to pay the fees. This would argue for
redistribution of income to enable them to pay (Forster's solution). But see E. G.
West, 'Private Versus Public Education' in A. W. Coats (ed.), *The Classical
Economists and Economic Policy*, Methuen, 1970.

So much for the analysis of the basic issues in the 'protection' thesis. We must tentatively conclude that if there is a logical case for a system in which schools are state, or government, owned and operated and schooling provided free, it does not follow from the protection principle. The question whether our present system rests, or should rest, on any other more important principles, e.g. the principle of 'equality of opportunity', will be examined later. But for the moment the discussion will proceed to a further test of the protection theory in the light of current English educational legislation.

CHAPTER TWO

State Protection of Minors in Practice: The English Education Act of 1944

Before 1944 children in England and Wales were protected by the provision of the Education Act of 1876 that parents should see that their offspring received some minimum education, specified as elementary instruction in reading, writing and arithmetic. Since this was a fairly unambiguous demand the local authorities' task of checking whether this duty was in fact being fulfilled was reasonably simple. Local authorities were also empowered to make and enforce by-laws for their area requiring the parents to see that their children between 5 and 14 years of age attended school. It was an acceptable excuse from these provisions, however, that a child could be shown to be receiving efficient instruction in the three Rs elsewhere than in school, including the home. When the 1944 Act superseded these provisions, the whole matter became much more complex. Section 36 of that Act states:

> It shall be the duty of the parent of every child of compulsory school age to cause him to receive efficient full-time education suitable to his age, ability and aptitude, either by regular attendance at school *or otherwise*. (My italics)

Accordingly, the duty of the local education authority is now to check not only whether an education is being given, but also whether it is 'efficient' and suitable to 'age, ability and aptitude', a formula which, as we shall see, has changed the whole situation since nobody is quite sure what it means.

One's first impression is that according to the precise letter of the law there is compulsory education, but not compulsory schooling, since the phrase in Section 36, 'or otherwise', conceives the possibility, for instance, of a child being educated at home by a parent or other relative or a private tutor. In other words current English legislation seems at first sight to be of the kind favoured by John Stuart Mill as described in the previous chapter. However, further investigation quickly removes this impression. Government responsibility for education has now become a very complicated affair and in particular local authorities see fit to assume much more control than mere testing by examinations in the three Rs. Protection against this kind of elementary ignorance, it seems, is no longer sufficient. The child has now presumably to be protected also against receiving an education which is *unsuitable* to his 'age, ability and aptitude', or is 'inefficient' or is only 'part-time'.

The reader will remember that according to our protection principles analysed in the first chapter we found that there was no universal criterion for determining the balance of power between parents and officials, but if the family was to be regarded as a specially important institution there was to be a presumption in favour of the former. However, it is evident that in England and Wales current legislation shows a bias in the opposite direction, for the weight of advantage now lies undoubtedly with the local authority and the Ministry. For instance, all local authorities are given the legal initiative in possible disputes. Thus Section 37 of the 1944 Act provides that, if it appears to a local authority that the parent is failing to perform his duty, it must serve upon him a notice requiring him to satisfy it, before the date specified in the notice, that the child is receiving efficient full-time education suitable to his age, ability and aptitude either by regular attendance at school 'or otherwise'. If the parent fails to satisfy the authority, it has the power to serve on him a school attendance order requiring him to cause the child to become a registered pupil at a school named in the order. Only in extraordinary circumstances and with the approval of the Minister may the child be educated at home. The circumstances envisaged mainly include those in which there is some disability of body or mind. Failure to comply with the requirements of a school attendance order is an offence.

In practice these arrangements favour the local authorities in two ways. First, there is no symmetrical arrangement which gives power to the parent to serve a similar order upon the local authority, when, in his opinion, the local authority itself is not fulfilling *its* duty, as laid down in Section 8 of the 1944 Act, of giving an efficient education suitable to the age, ability and aptitude of each child. It is true in theory that some sort of legal challenge could be produced, but the expenses involved make it out of the question for most individuals. Only one parent so far seems to have been determined enough to challenge the authorities on this point, but since it took the form of defying the school attendance order, it has cost her several summonses, fines and the threat of imprisonment; it is not likely that many parents will be prepared to go this far even though in this instance the action was eventually successful.[1]

The second way by which the local authorities enjoy an obvi-

1. *Baker v. The Norfolk Education Committee*, 1959. See also J. Baker, *Children in Chancery*, Hutchinson, 1964. This case is discussed in some detail on pp. 227–32 below.

ous advantage over the parent is connected with the fact that since they have the power to levy local rates for education and to spend them and centrally collected taxes on the provision of schooling, they are in a position almost to monopolise the bulk of our formal educational resources. This reduces, and for poorer families abolishes, all practical choice. Although the 1944 Education Act respects the parent by imposing on him the duty of seeing that his child is educated, in practice, and for most people, this means the 'duty' of doing what the local authority tells him to do. This can be seen even more clearly when one considers the special reference to parental wishes in Section 76 of the 1944 Act:

> In the exercise and performance of all powers and duties conferred and imposed on them by this Act the Minister and local education authorities shall have regard to the general principle that, so far as is compatible with the provision of efficient instruction and training and the avoidance of unreasonable public expenditure, pupils are to be educated in accordance with the wishes of their parents.

It will be observed that the duty to respect parental wishes is surrounded by important qualifications. With regard to the vague qualifying phrase 'shall have regard to', it would be difficult to show that a local authority in issuing a 'school attendance order' did not 'have regard to' the *general* principle in the clause. But since the principle is so widely drawn it would be difficult to select the weight given to any of the aspects of it or qualifications to it.

However, it seems likely that in many cases the parents' wishes will be overruled on the decision as to what is an 'efficient' education. And if there was a contest on this subject between a parent and a local authority one can hardly visualise the latter admitting that its own services are less efficient than those of the parent or of his private appointees. For this would be like giving to the National Coal Board the function of having the predominant voice in the choice of fuel for each home and expecting it to show no bias in favour of its own product, coal, compared with oil, gas and electricity. The significant point is that in such situations the predominant authority is allowed to be judge in its own cause.

The position of some schools which are outside the province of local authorities, but which are nevertheless officially acknowledged to be competent, is particularly interesting in this context. These are private schools which have the status of being recognised by the Minister as 'efficient'. It is open to any independent school, new or old, to apply for this recognition and success depends upon their being at least as well established in terms of staff and facilities as comparable state schools. The number of English and Welsh schools 'recognised as efficient' has been steadily growing in the past few years and in 1963 there were 1,550 of them containing about two-thirds (305,430) of all independent school pupils (485,458). How do these schools stand in relation to Section 76? Consider the situation where several parents having between them several children in an overcrowded state school want to transfer them to one of the recognised private schools but cannot do so because they are too short of income to 'pay twice'. Presumably there could be no official objection on the grounds of the efficiency of the new education; indeed the move would probably be beneficial all round. Assume that this move would save the authority's annual cost of, say, £50 per child. Then it could not usually be regarded as 'unreasonable public expenditure' if the authorities were, in deed or effect, to transfer this money to these parents on the assurance (which could easily be checked) that it was to be devoted to the payment of education at the recognised independent school. Such a proposition would seem completely to cover the two qualifications and the one instruction in the general principle of Section 76 which both the Minister and the local authorities are enjoined to respect. This principle, to repeat, states that

> . . . so far as is compatible with the *provision of efficient instruction* and training and the *avoidance of unreasonable public expenditure*, pupils are to be educated in accordance with the wishes of their parents.

(The two qualifications are in italics; the one instruction is the last part of the sentence.) It is common knowledge, however, that requests of this kind are invariably refused despite the fact that there are several direct and indirect administrative methods available for satisfying them in principle.

It seems, although there is no precisely expressed legal opinion on the point, that the only statutory duty on the local authority is 'to have regard to' the general principle of Section 76. Thus it is conceivable that a local authority could respond to the above request with the 'arms folded' reply that they had 'had regard to it' before they committed it to the waste paper basket! This kind of law, of course, provides no comfort to parents; the 'regard' which the local authority must bestow upon their wishes is of no use at all if it can be so perverse.[2]

2. There can be no doubt that many parents would settle for a grant representing less than the marginal costs of the state schooling of their children. Thus, in the example, some would accept £40, £30 or £20. This being so, the administrative 'regard' of Section 76 would be even more perverse since it follows that the authorities themselves are making unreasonable public expenditure by their refusal to rid themselves of a £50 expenditure by one of say £30. The only legal action that has so far involved Section 76 was that of *Watt v. Kesteven*, 1954–5. In this case the local authority did not have its own grammar schools. Instead it made arrangements with an independent school in its area and paid the fees for boys qualified to attend it. The plaintiff, however, wanted his two sons to go to

At this stage the ordinary person will be wondering what was the intention of Parliament in including Section 76 in the first place. Did it really want the parent to have any positive influence? If so, is the Section simply a case of bad legal drafting? If, on the other hand, Parliament really wanted the local authorities to have all the power, the two qualifications about 'efficiency' and no 'unreasonable public expenditure' are not needed by them as legal ways to block parental wishes; the testimony that they have 'had regard to' parental wishes was all that was required. The observer can only conclude that if Parliament's intention really was the second one, Section 76 was inserted simply as a piece of political smokescreening.

It is thus not surprising that Section 76, which was intended to give special respect to parental wishes, has in practice become a dead letter. Leaving aside for the moment questions concerning the fundamental liberty of the individual, one must now ask how serious is the result in practice. For presumably we need not be too anxious if we could be persuaded that the statutory 'education suitable to age, ability and aptitude' was a service which was in real life readily recognised and uniformly applied by the officials, headmasters and teachers whom local authorities think it is expedient to appoint on their behalf. Unfortunately, however, this is not so. For instance, the teaching profession in the recent past has shown far-reaching changes in its opinions on the most appropriate methods of teaching. The most conspicuous examples can be found in the striking changes in fashion in the use of

---

another independent school (recognised as efficient) since it was a Roman Catholic establishment. The request was refused despite the fact that the fees were lower in the latter school.

Apart from this example, Section 76 is now figuring prominently in the discussions among parents and teachers in Bristol, where several grammar schools are now under the threat of closure because of the city council's plans for a new 'comprehensive' school system. The parents are seeking legal advice.

theories of applied psychology. Again, today there are indubitably many areas of serious disagreement, sometimes among 'officially recognised' teachers themselves and sometimes between organised groups of teachers and their local education committee or between them and their education officers. Two outstanding current examples of this are the controversies over the suitability of comprehensive schools and the wisdom of segregating children in classes according to equal age or ability (a practice now known as 'streaming'). Although some educationists describe this situation as one of 'healthy variety', it must be a serious challenge to the simplicity of the 'age, ability and aptitude' wording of the 1944 Act. But nevertheless such terminology seems to be respected by local authorities in one situation, only to be waived the moment it becomes inconvenient in another. Thus when a parent wishes to contribute to the 'healthy variety' in *his* own way he is met with the old statutory formula that it is 'inefficient' or not 'suitable to age, ability and aptitude'. This objection seems to presume that the authorities themselves know clearly what it means, a presumption which is certainly not based on fact.[3]

But even when the parent does not wish to go so far, for instance, as to educate his child himself at home, one would have thought that his desire to choose *between state schools* was not only unobjectionable but probably often conducive to general progress. For in this case it cannot be argued that the education of his choice is *generally* inefficient since the schools in question are run by the local authorities themselves.[4] Nevertheless, in prac-

---

3. The general elusiveness of the 'age-ability-aptitude' formula is examined at length in Chapter 12.

4. The Department of Education has issued a *Manual of Guidance* to local authorities giving the most relevant considerations in deciding whether to allow a parent to change schools. Some of these considerations may have to be balanced

tice even here, a typical local authority can and usually does have the last word, making use where necessary of its reserve defence that a particular school is not suitable to age or aptitude. The commonest case is where a parent thinks a grammar school is more suitable to the age and aptitude of his child than a secondary modern school. But there are simply not 'enough' grammar school places available in many areas, and this is often the result of the refusal of some local councils to spend as much on education as others. This may be proved were the parent to move to another part of the country where it is quite possible that he would find a bigger proportion of children in grammar schools.[5] Indeed the conspicuous differences which prevail in the amounts that local authorities spend on education per head once more casts doubt upon the assumption of the 1944 Act that efficient and suitable education is a homogeneous and readily identifiable concept. Also the qualification to the general principle of Section 76 that the wishes of parents should be met so long as there is 'avoidance of unreasonable public expenditure' is not, it seems, very helpful since the local authorities themselves have not yet by any means reached a consensus on what is a 'reasonable expenditure'.

It seems that some local authorities may, in the eyes of many people, be guilty therefore of failing to reach a level of public expenditure which *can* be considered to be reasonable. In so far as this is maintained it follows that they are also failing to give efficient education suitable to 'age, ability and aptitude', so that the case for giving them supremacy over parents becomes even more obscure. In other words, if the funds now spent by the local

---

one with another. They include religious and medical matters, traffic dangers, and the special availability of such things as meal facilities.

5. For instance, 40 per cent of the secondary school population are in grammar schools in Merthyr Tydfil but only 8 per cent in Preston.

authorities were not in the first place taken away from the general public via taxes on such commodities as cigarettes, beer, cosmetics, sugar, television, petrol as well as income tax, it is possible that in many areas much more would be spent on the education of every child. To the extent that this is true there is a new need for the 'protection of minors' principle to come into operation, but in the opposite direction to that which is so often invoked. The relevant protection in this case is directed not against the negligence of parents but against the negligence of the local authority and its officials. The more that such official failure can be categorised the stronger the argument for changing the balance of power in favour of more direct parental responsibility.[6]

There is a further example of the frustration of parents' wishes freely to choose among the schools available in their area, and this time to an extent which seems to be even more serious. I refer now not to the desire to change the *category* of school as for instance in a change from a grammar to a secondary modern school, but to the parental desire to change schools *within a given category*. Consider the numerous instances of parents who wish to transfer their children from one state primary school to another. Here it cannot be objected that the type of education is unsuitable since 'primary education' is regarded as a service which is of common standard to all children. If the parent expresses his preference, for instance, on such educational grounds as that the school of his choice practices the system known as 'streaming' whereas the other does not, it cannot be objected

6. Even though it may be shown that much of the complicated government apparatus is superfluous or even negative in its attempt to protect children against *average* parents it does not follow that it is irrelevant for a minority of really negligent parents. An attempt to outline a more discriminating form of machinery to meet these cases will be reserved for Chapter 13.

that the parent is insufficiently informed to judge the efficiency of the two methods since the state experts themselves are seriously divided on this subject.

Nevertheless, local authority officials have succeeded in many areas in preventing even this type of transfer from taking place. Their reasons this time are so curious and so unconvincing that it is astonishing that they have been left unchallenged for so long. For they argue that if parents were allowed to select their child's primary school this would lead to one or two schools being patronised more than others with the result that the 'popular' schools would become 'overcrowded' relative to the less 'popular' ones. Thus according to Tyrrell Burgess,

> The main reason why a local authority might refuse a parent's request is that they have some 'zoning' plan for local schools. In many areas the provision of efficient instruction involves allocating 'catchment areas' to each school so as to avoid overcrowding in some and empty classrooms in others. *The Manual of Guidance* gives the authorities their cue when it says that it would not be compatible with the provision of efficient instruction and training if the school of the parent's choice were full.[7]

This 'zoning' system seems to be the gravest of all denials of parental wishes. For if they were taken seriously enough, the correct response would be to allow the popular school to use all possible improvisations and expedients to carry the increased load in the short-run and all possible assistance to expand in the long-run. By the same token, pressure would be applied to see that the less popular schools either shrank or took steps to bring their services up to the standards of the more popular ones.

7. *A Guide to English Schools*, Pelican, 1964. On p. 125 Mr Burgess outlines the elaborate procedure necessary for a parent who wishes his child to attend a school other than that for which he or she is 'zoned'.

Imagine the case of a retail shop which had become so relatively inefficient that customers were beginning to crowd into the premises of a rival establishment. To argue that the crowding was the inefficiency would be to confuse the 'symptom' with the 'disease'. To establish 'catchment areas' to prevent the 'crowding' would be to remove the very pressure which was working to put things right. Under such pressure the favoured shop would meet the 'crowding' with extemporary measures pending plans for extension, whilst the unfavoured shop would be spurred into copying the superior service of its rival. Staff who were frustrated by their treatment by unimaginative managers in the first shop would begin to find tempting vacancies occurring in the more successful and therefore 'crowded' second shop.

'Zoning', on the other hand, simply freezes the system and insulates the authorities from the necessity to improve educational provision in accordance with popular wishes. In other words it is a device which, intentionally or unintentionally, prevents the wishes of parents being properly respected and as such it seems to be thoroughly opposed to the spirit of Section 76 of the 1944 Education Act.

The kind of criticism made here, which has also emerged in many other parts of this chapter, is likely to encounter the reply that parents can express their wishes and complaints through the ordinary political machinery. They can, for instance, join parent/teacher associations; or as ordinary ratepayers with democratic rights they can lobby their local representative; or they can even try to get themselves elected to their local education committee. Again, Chief Education Officers are often anxious to answer this kind of criticism by protesting that their doors are always open to 'the public' for personal interviews. These arguments, however, are not satisfactory for three reasons. First, if the authors of the 1944 Act were acting on the assumption that parents, like other citizens, would merely 'take their place in the queue' within the ordinary political channels and would make their preferences known accordingly, it is difficult to explain why these legislators singled out parents for special attention in Section 76 for the privilege of having their wishes especially mentioned. Second, such officials as Chief Education Officers may feel they are amply doing their duty to 'the public' by their 'ever-open door' policy, but the hours in the day are limited and, even if an aggrieved parent succeeds in getting time off work and manages to fix an appointment with the Education Officer at a mutually convenient hour, it is doubtful whether such a meeting could cover all the relevant aspects. For there is usually not merely one problem but many, and they need more attention than a formal interview would allow. But even with more serious personal complaints, such as those referring to the efficiency of local headmasters or their staff, the questions are usually so embarrassing to local officials that they take refuge in some assumed professional ethic which they claim always prevents them from making 'invidious comment'. It is only too likely and natural that a Chief Education Officer conceives of his office primarily as an institution for quietly allowing the public to 'let off steam' rather than an agency for promoting real action according to the wishes of individual parents. Such officials should consider a hypothetical situation, like the one mentioned in the first chapter, where they themselves were provided with groceries 'free' but only at the shop nearest to them and any complaints to be handled by a 'Chief Grocery Officer' by previous appointment. They would then be in a better position to decide whether this arrangement gives sufficient consolation and to recognise more of its shortcomings.

Here we touch upon the technical disadvantages of the use of the political process to obtain given ends and in particular its failure to secure adequate *proportional* representation and the inevitable resort to highest common factor or majority rule solutions that necessarily ride roughshod over individuals and minorities.[8] To persuade parents to accept these serious disadvantages one must first equally persuade them that the present collectivised system of education via the ballot box is inevitable. If it can be shown that better techniques for securing wider political choice can be substituted, the argument for the present system of education faces an immediate challenge. These techniques, which have been only approximately indicated here, will be discussed in more detail towards the end of the book.

8. This is an important weakness; it is explained in more detail below. See especially pp. 219–20.

PART TWO

The Political Economists' Argument of the 'Neighbourhood Effects' of Education

CHAPTER THREE

The 'Neighbourhood Effects' Argument

Even in the absence of a justification for state intervention on the grounds of the protection principle, there remains another line of reasoning which is widely believed to give still stronger support for such intervention. This belongs to what is known as the 'neighbourhood effects' argument and a brief preliminary account of its present place in political economy is now required.[1]

Roughly speaking, the 'neighbourhood effect' argument stems from the common observation that 'no man is an island'. Many of his actions intentionally or unintentionally affect other people. Where these overspill effects are very pronounced, and do not show any signs of ever being organised or brought under control

1. For the application of the neighbourhood effects argument to education in England see the Robbins Committee Report, Vol. I, Ch. I and Appendix IV, Part III and the Crowther Report, Chapter 6. For further modern critical treatment of the general argument see J. M. Buchanan, 'Politics, Policy and the Pigovian Margins', *Economica*, February 1962, p. 28; R. H. Coase, 'The Problem of Social Cost', *The Journal of Law and Economics*, October 1960; Ralph Turvey, 'On Divergences between Social Cost and Private Cost', *Economica*, August 1963. C. K. Rowley in 'The Political Economy of British Education', *Scottish Journal of Political Economy*, Vol. XVI, 1969, pp. 152–76, applies Turvey's analysis directly to education. This chapter is confined to a simple verbal treatment of the subject because the book is intended for general readership.

by the market, one's normal reaction is to explore the possibility of government intervention. The most obvious instance of the resort to government is seen in the establishment of a state system of law and order to curb and to make socially accountable individual acts of aggression. Here, indeed, we have the basic *raison d'être* of the state in the first place. Beyond personally aggressive private actions, however, there are other particular 'neighbourhood effects' which are also identified and often listed in a descending order of seriousness or scope. Several of these are also commonly claimed to warrant state intervention. The most frequently quoted example in economics is the firm whose factory chimneys offend the neighbourhood with smoke and thereby cause people outside the factory to spend extra amounts on laundries, bronchitis cures, etc. Another alleged instance is the injury to 'local amenities' caused by the 'unfortunate' siting of a new house by a private speculative builder. Again there is the individual motorist who parks his car to the detriment of other road users. Campaigns to make socially accountable those responsible for road traffic and aircraft noises or exhaust fumes also belong to the same category of 'neighbourhood effects'. All of them are cited as cases where the costs taken into account by the individual in the market are unlikely to include some element of what are called *social* costs.

However, although most people seem to react to this situation by readily calling upon government to put these things right, they do not immediately see how complicated is their request. For one thing, if they examine more carefully the above examples of social costs they will see that they are not exclusively a consequence of private action. The noise from publicly-operated airways, buses and trains, for instance, has its ultimate sanction not in private action but in public legislation, that is, in government itself. Nationalised chimneys give off smoke no less than private ones. Public gasworks can spoil amenities while offensive smells can come from publicly operated sewage works.

A further complication is that social costs can be negative as well as positive; that is, some spillover effects may be unintentionally *beneficial* to the neighbourhood. Thus a farmer who drains his own land may improve that of the neighbouring farm, even though he cannot charge for benefits rendered. Still more complex are the many instances where both positive and negative social costs are produced by the same agent. An example of this is where a new industrial plant gives off smoke (detrimentally) but also reduces unemployment in the same neighbourhood (beneficially). Again the owner of the plant could be the central or local government as well as a private company.

It seems to have been widely believed at one time that the moment one had pointed out a privately originating 'neighbourhood effect', such as that of the smoke-laden atmosphere, actual intervention by the state was adequately justified. This, however, is not so. The identification of a 'neighbourhood effect' is only a *necessary* but not a *sufficient* condition for intervention. There are many serious offsetting considerations, the most important being that the task of measuring the chain reaction of costs and benefits is often insuperable. The administrative costs of intervention alone may be so high as to exceed the net benefits which such action sought to secure, even if they could be measured. Furthermore, it is likely that a particular mode of state intervention to meet a privately originating 'neighbourhood effect' may itself incur a second (i.e. publicly originating) 'neighbourhood effect' which has still more serious consequences than the first. For instance, a government wishes to meet a 'neighbourhood effect' of poverty within certain categories of people. If its mode of operation involved a scheme of National Assistance which was implemented too loosely, it could severely check the national output out of which the poverty is to be relieved, since not only could the assistance go to persons outside the intended category but also the necessary increase in taxation could have significant disincentive effects on effort and enterprise.

Suppose, again, that the government responds to the smoke pollution of a factory by placing a special local tax upon the offending firm. The resulting increase in relative costs of production may so discourage the expansion of the same firm as to encourage it to invest its surplus funds elsewhere. The result may be that the firm is now the cause of another 'neighbourhood effect', not smoke pollution this time but the more serious problem of unemployment.[2]

How then does the 'neighbourhood effect' analysis apply to education? Political economists usually have two particular instances in mind. The first is expressed in their contention that the *social* benefits of education are not confined to the 'educatee' but spread to society as a whole, most noticeably in the form of reduced crime and more 'social cohesion'. This can be expressed negatively: the private actions of an uneducated person may have unfortunate consequences for others in society. The general idea then seems to be that just as, for instance, the government can do something about black smoke (e.g. by taxation) it can do something about black conduct (e.g. by education). The second general example is the idea that education is an investment whose

2. Another aspect requiring deeper analysis: the larger the influx of new residents to the area the more harmful the effects of the smoke and the higher the tax necessary. But this increasing tax is itself an *increasing harm to the firm* so encouraging it to move or expand elsewhere. Since each new resident is not aware of the harm he is imposing on the firm and its employees, he also is causing an adverse neighbourhood effect but one which is not counteracted by government intervention but indeed has its origin in such intervention. This is the argument of R. H. Coase, 'The Problem of Social Cost', *The Journal of Law and Economics*, University of Chicago Law School, October 1960.

benefits also spill over to the *economic* advantage of society as a whole.

The Proposition That Education Reduces Crime

Here I shall confine my attention to the negative proposition that the state provision of education will successfully meet the 'neighbourhood effect' of crime. It will be helpful first to give a few quotations to illustrate the widespread influence of the idea both in the nineteenth century and today.

In 1847 T. S. Macaulay proclaimed in Parliament:

> I say that all are agreed that it is the sacred duty of every government to take effectual measures for securing the persons and property of the community; and that the government which neglects that duty is unfit for its situation. This being once admitted, I ask, can it be denied that the education of the common people is the most effectual means of protecting persons and property?[3]

In the previous year W. T. Thornton had typically expressed the prescription of the Utilitarians:

> No one now denies that proper schools for the lower orders of people ought to be founded and maintained at the cost of the state. The expense no doubt would be considerable, but it would scarcely be so great as that already incurred for prisons, hulks, and convict ships; and it is certainly better economy to spend money in training up people to conduct themselves properly, than in punishing them for their misdeeds.[4]

3. House of Commons, *Hansard*, 19 April 1847.
4. W. T. Thornton, *Over Population and Its Remedy*, London, Longman, Brown, Green and Longmans, 1846, p. 379.

Such Utilitarian calculation of the crime-reducing potentialities of formal education is still in evidence among responsible authorities today. Thus, referring to the 'neighbourhood effects' of education, the Robbins Report on Higher Education (1963) said:

> There are, of course, also important social and political benefits of education which accrue to the populace as a whole—a better informed electorate, more culturally alive neighbourhoods, a healthier and *less crime-prone population*, and so on. What is not always recognised is that these social and political consequences may in turn have significant economic effects—the efficiency with which goods are exchanged is obviously enhanced by general literacy, *to the extent that education reduces crime* (even if only by keeping children off the streets during the day) the country can shift resources that would have had to be used for the police function to other ends, and so on.[5] (My italics)

The Robbins Report makes this statement before freely admitting that the evidence is still not sufficient to make it anything more than an inspired hunch. The Crowther Report of 1959 and the Newsom Report of 1963, referring to the education of persons between 15 and 18 years (which include the most crime-prone ages), although much more hesitant on the matter, nevertheless, as I shall show in more detail below, favoured still more education in the current twentieth-century campaign against delinquency and crime.

In the light of the 'neighbourhood effect' argument examined at the beginning of this chapter, what can be made of its application to education? It is important to remember the complications; not only must the 'neighbourhood effect' be first identified

5. *Higher Education*, Cmnd. 2154, Appendix 4, Part III, para. 54.

in a meaningful way, but also the possible side-effects of the proposed government intervention itself should all be examined before such intervention is fully justified. How far then, first of all, has the particular 'neighbourhood effect' relationship between education and crime been reasonably established in practice? In other words, what evidence have we to show that the belief in state education as a general insurance against crime is anything more than dogma?

In answering such questions the early economists were inclined to rely upon crude statistics. Because the latter were presented as showing an inverse relationship between crime and education (usually measured by the degrees of schooling) the general inference was that ignorance (or the deprival of a schooling) was a major cause of crime. To the extent that poverty was connected with ignorance and undesirable habits, it too was thought to be an important contributory factor. In view of this kind of reasoning it would be intriguing to know the reaction of these early commentators to present-day statistical evidence. For this shows that crime has increased at the same time as state education has been growing. Certainly this does not deny that crime could have grown equally or even more in the absence of state education. But scientific objectivity demands that all things should be suspect, especially where there is a positive correlation. One can at least speculate, judging by their weakness for such crude statistical inferences on this subject, that the early economists would be tempted to point to the possibility that our *state* education, as distinct from their nineteenth-century *parochial* education, was a predisposing cause of crime!

Today indeed there is at least a growing scepticism about the potentialities of state education as a crime reducer. Thus *The Times Educational Supplement* in 1963 declared:

It is strange that as education spreads and poverty decreases, juvenile crime should steadily rise.[6]

Similarly, the idea that poverty is a major cause of crime is not so confidently held. Indeed some social scientists conclude from the evidence that the idea has no firm basis. Lady Wootton writes:

> . . . it is a conclusion which would, I think, have surprised our grandfathers. The converse was implicit—and sometimes explicit—in the thought of not so many generations ago; as it is implicit also in the thought of those who express disappointment that the coming of a 'welfare state', which they believe (though mistakenly) to have banished poverty, has not also greatly reduced the criminal statistics.[7]

The most energetic nineteenth-century advocates of state education would no doubt have been also perplexed by the fact that the same welfare state which has failed to reduce crime is one which also includes an extensive education system financed by public funds of unprecedented magnitude.

Today, of course, we would claim to be much more aware of the complexity of crime and its causes. Certainly much more sophisticated reasoning surrounds the subject and it has been established in particular that a proportion of convicted persons is suffering from mental disorders which, it is claimed, need psychiatric treatment. Many other possibly conducive factors are still being investigated and these include divorce, broken homes,

6. September 1963, p. 369. Mr William Singer, President of the Ulster Teachers' Union, told his annual conference on 21 April 1965: 'There is a growing body of opinion which believes that our educational system must bear its share of responsibility for many of the problems of behaviour, which show themselves in juvenile delinquency and vandalism.'

7. Barbara Wootton, *Social Science and Social Pathology*, Allen & Unwin, 1959, p. 80.

the persistence of crime in some families, poor church attendance, mothers' employment outside the home, health and type of employment. But it is interesting to observe that so far social scientists have not even yet reported any very clear correlation between education and crime. Thus in 1958 Lord Pakenham published the results of research into the causes of crime (financed by the Nuffield Foundation), which included the following observation:

> I do not think, however, that the distinguished experts, including the representatives of the National Union of Teachers who gave evidence before us, would claim that, up to the present, much progress has been made in connecting education and crime.[8]

Furthermore we are today more conscious of the limitations of the statistics of recorded crime. For instance, criminal statistics only register the action taken by the authorities against those offenders who are not clever enough to evade prosecution. Again, the law is enforced more efficiently in some areas than in others because there are differences in the strengths of local police forces. Similarly there are differences in the completeness with which crimes are reported.

Nevertheless, making generous allowance for these drawbacks, some of the statistics do seem to point strongly in certain directions. Clearly the evidence which was examined by the Crowther Committee could not easily be dismissed (see Table 1). Referring to the figures in Table 1, the Crowther Committee thought that it was important:

> . . . neither to overlook the exceedingly heavy increase in crimes associated with violence, sex and drunkenness, nor to exaggerate the total number of boys and young men affected. If one could

8. *Causes of Crime*, Weidenfeld and Nicolson, 1958.

TABLE 1

Convictions per 10,000 Civilian Males at Two Dates for Five Groups of Offences

Type of Offence	Males 14–16 (3 Age-Groups)		Males 17–20 (4 Age-Groups Less Forces)	
	1947	1956	1947	1956
Theft	165	174	181	260
Violence	3.7	9.2	12.8	40
Sexual	5.5	10.8	6.9	15.9
Drink	1.2	8	17.8	94
Disorder*	43	49	66	141

*Disorder—a miscellaneous group which includes riding a bicycle without lights and playing football in the street.

Source: Taken from a pamphlet published by the Christian Economic and Social Research Foundation, 1958. See Crowther Report, p. 40.

aggregate the five types of offence, the overall rate would still only be 5.5 per cent for the older age-group and 2.5 per cent for the younger.[9]

There was one aspect of juvenile delinquency, however, which the Crowther Committee found to be much more arresting. This was the fact that the last year of compulsory education was also the heaviest year for juvenile delinquency and that the tendency to crime during school years was reversed when a boy went to

9. The latest general information is contained in the 1963 Report of HM Chief Inspector of Constabulary (published in July 1964). It shows that about half the amount of indictable crime is being committed by young people under 21 and that crime is still increasing. Many minor crimes, including a large number believed to have been committed by children and adolescents, are remaining undetected.

work. Not only was this a long-standing phenomenon but also when in 1947 the school leaving age was raised from 14 to 15:

> . . . there was an immediate change over in the delinquency record of the 13 year-olds (who until then had been the most troublesome age-group) and the 14 year-olds, who took their place in 1948 and have held it consistently ever since.[10]

How should an economist treat such information within the general framework of the 'neighbourhood effect' analysis? It seems reasonable at least for him to conclude that the popular belief, as quoted for instance from the Robbins Report (see above, p. 36) that state education makes the public less crime prone, is unsupported by the available evidence. Beyond this he could argue, but with less certainty, that the evidence showed a *prima facie* relationship in the opposite direction, i.e. that state education involved *adverse* external effects and aggravated or even helped to cause the prevailing trend towards increased criminal behaviour. Certainly one could not object to the tentative conclusion that if any further official action was to take place it should first concentrate on a proper investigation of this question and that in the meantime there was to be a presumption against any further increases in the duration of compulsory schooling on this account.[11]

10. Crowther Report, para. 63.

11. In a lecture at the Central Hall, London, on 1 May 1970, to commemorate the centenary of state education, Sir Alec Clegg, Chief Education Officer of the West Riding, warned his audience about the trouble with the slower learners, 'mainly because we don't care about them and we don't know how to teach them'. He suspected that this trouble may become 'dangerously ugly' in some schools when the school-leaving age is raised. He pointed out that police in Washington had for some months been patrolling junior and senior high schools. In case anyone should think the same could not happen in England, 'let him bear in mind that crimes of violence amongst older adolescents have increased by just under 1,000 per cent in the last 18 years'. (*Daily Telegraph*, 2 May 1970.)

It therefore comes as a surprise to find the Crowther Report concluding that there was nothing in the current state of affairs

> . . . to make any thoughtful person doubt the value of being at school; indeed, the delinquency may arise, not because boys are at school, but because they are not at school enough.[12]

As is well known, the Report argued for the raising of the compulsory school-leaving age. In doing so it referred to the *beneficial* external effects on society of presumed increased economic growth (a proposition examined in Chapter 7), but at the same time it apparently refused to consider the possibility of any *adverse* external effects. Yet the Crowther policy of first raising the school-leaving age despite the evidence about delinquency and then trying to justify the measure after the event by offering hopes of future improvements in schooling seems to start at the wrong end. Indeed, such proposals seem to substitute dogma for reason and to betray the attitude that come what may the schools should not yield. In this attitude they probably reflect the limitations of state-sponsored committees which inevitably comprise many members and witnesses such as local education officers, state school headmasters, and the heads of teacher-training establishments who have a direct interest and belief in the expansion of state education itself. Such committees seem to welcome the rationality implicit in the 'neighbourhood effect' argument when it suits them, but are too ready to discard it the moment it becomes inconvenient.[13]

12. Crowther Report, *loc. cit.*
13. In January 1964 it was announced that the school-leaving age would be raised to 16 in 1970. The following month Lord Shawcross asked for increased support for the Rainer Foundation which gave special help to boys referred to it by probation officers, because *'On past experience it is reasonable to expect that the principle of raising of the school-leaving age will increase still further the problem of delinquency . . . '* (Letter to the *Daily Telegraph*, 20 February 1964.) But if the root

The Crowther Committee contended that delinquency among older pupils probably arose because a boy had more time on his hands to get into mischief when at school compared with when he was at work. Developing this argument, the Newsom Report[14] (on the education between the ages of 13 and 16 of pupils of average or below average ability) pointed out the difficulty of getting enough staff and resources to keep the boys occupied sufficiently. Accordingly this Report recommended that: 'The school programme in the final year ought to be deliberately outgoing— an initiation into the adult world of work and leisure'.[15] Again, undaunted by the evidence, the Report also recommended the raising of the school-leaving age. Once more the innocent observer must be allowed to question why, if the rate of delinquency declines when boys go out to work, should the commencement of this work be delayed still further *in favour of schemes for simulating work in school?* Why do we accept indiscriminately arguments about the need to protect young people from the 'uncertain pressures of adult life' as long as possible and neglect the possibility that the pressures of school life may be in some cases the crucial ones? Such thoughts are not so revolutionary when it is remembered that, in these days, going out to work does not necessarily mean the end of formal education, since technical colleges and day-release schemes are now typically provided for the young worker's continued instruction. Those who show an overweening concern about the welfare of school-leavers do not seem to have shown why their proposals for extra protection could not be implemented, for instance, by

of this adverse neighbourhood effect (increased delinquency) is government intervention (to raise the school-leaving age indiscriminately), why should we accept it so fatalistically and evade the real issue by resorting to new institutional palliatives?

14. *Half Our Future*, HMSO for the Ministry of Education, 1963.
15. *Ibid.*, p. 79.

schemes for appointing special supervisors, which would have the additional merit of being far less expensive than schooling. This is not of course to argue that all expenditure on further schooling is wrong. Where it is appropriate, and this may apply to most people, it is to be welcomed. But to apply a measure to all on the grounds that it is suitable to some is to sacrifice prudence to mere legislative expediency.

The reduction of crime is only one of many kinds of social benefit which society is supposed to expect from education. But it has been selected here for first attention because of its prominence in traditional reasoning and because it is a good illustration of the facility with which unchallenged and unverified theories can become assimilated in the folklore of educational debate. In addition to the errors of fact which are involved in it, such thinking also suffers through a lack of conceptual clarity. What do we mean when we say that *education* reduces crime? Are we thinking of education in the wide sense or do we mean only formal schooling? If the former, what *kind* of education have we in mind? If the latter, do we mean only *state* schooling or do we include non-state schooling? As we shall see in the next chapter, this kind of difficulty looms even larger when we look at other alleged social benefits from education, and in particular the idea that the external benefits of education consist of the attainment of more 'social cohesion'.

CHAPTER FOUR

Education to Make Democracy Work

In the explanation of 'neighbourhood effects' (in the last chapter), it was pointed out that they are sometimes expressed negatively, as with the smoking chimney, and sometimes positively, as with the farmer who drains his land and so benefits others. Whereas the discussion about the reduction of crime and delinquency by education has its parallel with the proposal to remove black smoke by taxation, the proposition that education promotes social cohesion is similar to the proposition about the positively beneficial behaviour of the farmer. Professor Milton Friedman discusses this aspect in the following terms:

> A stable and democratic society is impossible without a minimum degree of literacy and knowledge on the part of most citizens and without widespread acceptance of some common set of values. Education can contribute to both.[1]

Another American economist, Dr Burton A. Weisbrod, in a more ambitious and wide-ranging classification of the external effects of education, refers to the benefits of 'anything which increases welfare possibilities directly, such as development of

---

1. Milton Friedman, *Capitalism and Freedom,* University of Chicago Press, 1962, p. 86.

public spiritedness or social consciousness of one's neighbor'.[2] Similarly, Professor Jack Wiseman argues:

> Society as a group benefits from the existence of some minimum standard of education among its citizens, in the understanding of common values and acceptance of community obligation.[3]

Now in so far as such propositions point to the need for some active government policy, it has to be shown that substantial numbers of people would not acquire a necessary minimum of education themselves without the help of government agencies. Furthermore, in so far as the proposed government intervention is conceived in the form of our present 'nationalised' system of state schooling in preference to the mere provision of finance in the shape of subsidies to parents or to private schools, it has to be demonstrated not only that formal schooling is in all circumstances the best possible medium of education (better than, say, a mixture of television instruction, the use of public libraries, correspondence courses and parental tuition), but also that state schools are more efficient than subsidised private ones. This chapter will examine these contentions only in respect of the question of literacy and its usefulness in promoting political and economic communication. Those aspects of education which concern the more elusive 'neighbourhood effects' (e.g. social consciousness, common values, etc.) will be treated in the next two chapters.

Literacy as an Agent for Social Cohesion

We start from the obvious fact that literacy is of value not only to the individual possessing it but also to others who have dealings

2. *Journal of Political Economy*, October 1962, p. 107.
3. *The Economics of Education*, lecture given to British Association for the Advancement of Science, August 1958.

with him, whether it be a relative, an employer, a hire purchase institution, a chief constable, or an income tax assessor. As Weisbrod says:

> Without widespread literacy the significance of books, newspapers, and similar media for the transmission of information would dwindle; and it seems fair to say that the communication of information is of vital importance to the maintenance of competition and, indeed, to the existence of a market economy, as well as to the maintenance of political democracy.[4]

Such statements by themselves will seem almost trite to many people. Why go to this length in stating the fairly obvious? The reason is that those who are at pains to express them argue that the recipients of external benefits from some activity (for example, education) should, in Weisbrod's words 'be willing to subsidise the activity and, indeed, should seek to subsidise it'.[5] It is interesting, incidentally, to notice that Weisbrod, unlike some, does not argue in the first instance that the state should *provide* the education, but that it should simply subsidise it; that is, the state should support it financially, not nationalise it. Furthermore, Weisbrod's argument for subsidies by itself does not necessarily mean subsidies exclusively for schools. For education, to repeat, is a wider term than schooling. If people can, and wish to, become literate by other means, then any argument for subsidising should include the possibility of subsidies to a much wider number of agencies, such as television, correspondence courses, aids to parental tuition at home, etc., since, strictly in accordance with the arguments so far, a government is interested in the attainment of literacy, not the means of attaining it. Now according to a dictionary definition, literacy denotes the ability to read

4. *Op. cit.*, p. 119.
5. *Op. cit.*, p. 116.

and write; all this amounts to is a certain technical competence, and one which is almost as easy to test as is the ability to ride a bicycle. If such a test shows that most people will become literate through their own efforts and motives then the case for *universal* subsidies in this respect falls to the ground.

To what extent does nineteenth-century history indicate that English people, for instance, were in need of government help on this account? The evidence examined in Chapter 9 shows indeed that the majority of people in the first half of the nineteenth century did become literate (in the technical sense) largely by their own efforts. Moreover, if the government played any role at all in this sphere it was one of saboteur!

As long ago as the first few years of the nineteenth century it was a subject for government *complaint* that the ordinary people *had become literate*. For the government feared that too many people were developing the 'wrong' uses of literacy by belonging to secret 'corresponding societies' and by reading seditious pamphlets. In 1803, for example, T. R. Malthus echoed the government's fears by asserting the probability that: 'The circulation of Paine's *Rights of Man* . . . has done great mischief among the lower and middle classes of this country'.[6] Far from subsidising literacy, the early nineteenth-century English governments placed severe taxes on paper in order to discourage the exercise of the public's reading and writing abilities. Yet despite this obstacle, by the time government came round to subsidising on a tiny scale in the 1830s, between two-thirds and three-quarters of the people (according to one modern specialist—see p. 164) were already literate. Even then the subsidies were financed

6. T. R. Malthus, *Essay on Population*, Everyman's edition, Dent/Dutton, 1958, p. 190.

from a taxation system which burdened the poor more than the rich.[7]

Here then we have the paradox of a public managing to educate itself into literary competence from personal motives and private resources, despite the obstacle of an institution called government which eventually begins to claim most of the credit for the educational success. The notion held by many people that had it not been for the state they or at least most of their neighbours would never have become educated is a striking monument to the belief of the Victorian lawyer, Dicey, that people's opinions and convictions eventually become conditioned by the legislated institutions they make themselves.

But perhaps some people think that the majority of Victorians would have been too poor to afford education if the government had left them on their own. If so, this is an illusion which has obviously been encouraged by the increasing dependence of successive generations upon state education financed by taxes on themselves, taxes which so often fall inconspicuously on many goods and services, and which seem to have become accepted partly by habit and partly by absent-mindedness. When many people today think of taxation, they think of personal income tax

7. Moreover, the effects of the subsidies to schools were probably more than offset, in the early years at least, by the continuation of the 'taxes on knowledge', i.e. the enormous taxes on paper, newspapers and pamphlets which were not removed until the 1850s and 1860s. Here we have a good instance of the way in which government action itself (this time in the way it organised its taxation pattern) can result in socially adverse spillovers or neighbourhood effects (i.e. social costs). If it was seeking the *positive* neighbourhood effects of education it would have been more practical for the government first to have seen to the *negative* neighbourhood effects for which it was responsible; that is, it should have abolished the 'taxes on knowledge' before considering subsidising the pursuit of it. To subsidise and tax the same activity was illogical and costly.

which 'the other fellow' pays. Yet how many know that this tax accounts for less than half government revenue and that, for instance, the tax collected in 1962 on tobacco alone (a tax which is more significantly felt by the poorer) was £879 million, that is more than enough to have covered the 1962 current expenditure (£797 million) on education?

A new official British analysis of the value of welfare services compared with the amount of taxation paid by families has recently been published by the Central Statistical Office. Using a sample survey, government statisticians measured not only each family's cash benefits such as family allowances and pensions but also estimated the money value of state education and the National Health Service to each family. This valuation included the subsidies given in school meals, welfare foods and housing benefits. The tax contribution of the families measured not only income tax rates and national insurance contributions but also purchase tax, duties on drink, tobacco, motor vehicles, etc.—in other words the family contribution in terms of indirect taxation.

Table 2 shows the findings for families with two children. Table 2 implies that only a small minority of families make net gains. It must certainly be acknowledged, however, that these CSO studies have their limitations. Apart from statistical problems associated with the size and representativeness of the sample, the measures of benefits are incomplete since they omit such important items as defence, police administration and roads. Nevertheless the estimates of the amounts paid in tax by the very poorest are quite revealing (e.g. the family with original income of £629 in Table 2 pays nearly half its income in taxes). Since, in the absence of an earmarked system, nobody knows which tax pays for which government service, it cannot be demonstrated that even the

TABLE 2

Taxation and Welfare Benefits for Family
with Two Children, 1967

Original Income £ per Year	Value of Benefits Received	Amount Paid in Taxes	Net Gain (+) or Loss (−)
£	£	£	£
629	405	292	+112
738	354	282	+71
911	293	337	−46
1,106	247	372	−171
1,329	266	434	−167
1,597	309	523	−214
1,908	270	620	−351
2,316	282	772	−491
2,807	279	885	−606
4,061	304	1,541	−1,238

Source: 'The Incidence of Taxes and Social Benefits in 1967', *Economic Trends*, HMSO, February 1969.

poorest of families are not paying substantially for their 'free' education.[8]

Such information gives some idea of the extent to which most people could be 'richer' if the state did not feel itself obliged to provide social services like education 'free'. Even then it provides only a conservative picture; for if this two-way traffic of

8. The picture of net gains and losses is likely to alter if we measure the 'life-cycle' experience of the individual family rather than take (as in Table 2) a 'snapshot' view. For excellent discussions of all these budgetary redistribution questions see Alan R. Prest, 'The Budget and Interpersonal Distribution', *Proceedings of the Prague Congress of the International Institute of Public Finance*, Nos. 1–2, 1968. Also Alan Peacock and Robin Shannon, 'The Welfare State and the Redistribution of Income', *Westminster Bank Review*, August 1968.

payments and receipts was reduced there would be appreciable savings in administrative costs, not to mention the increased incentives to earn which would probably follow from reduced taxation. Later in this book I shall critically examine the implicit or explicit assumption that if money had always been left in the hands of families and had not been collected by the state to finance 'free' services, the heads of families would not have continued to spend it voluntarily on the education of their own children. Here I shall only refer in advance to the fact (substantiated in Chapter 9) that most families were already in the habit of paying directly for education (i.e. paying fees) when the state made its most serious intervention in 1870.

If it cannot be shown that most people would fail to become literate by their own efforts, Weisbrod's elaboration of all the possible beneficial external effects of literacy resolves itself into a largely academic exercise.[9] We might just as well spend our time listing the beneficial 'neighbourhood effects' of our habit of washing ourselves or attending football matches. Such analysis does not point to any significant policy at all beyond possible marginal provision in exceptional instances. No doubt the case of America has been somewhat different in so far as the problem was one of urgent need to encourage an immigrant population to speak a common language. Even so it is not clear that measures beyond a once-for-all effort by the government are called for.

At this stage of the argument, however, many people may reply that it is not merely *technical* literacy which is wanted but some category of literacy which is qualified by adjectives such as

9. In technical language Weisbrod may be dealing largely with what are known as 'Pareto irrelevant' externalities. See J. M. Buchanan and W. C. Stubblebine, 'Externality', *Economica*, November 1962; E. G. West, 'Resource Allocation and Growth in Early Nineteenth Century British Education', *Economic History Review*, Vol. 23, No. 1, April 1970.

'political literacy', 'economic literacy', 'cultural literacy'. The argument, in other words, now turns into the assertion that government intervention should be directed to the 'right' uses of literacy rather than to literacy itself. The idea of 'political literacy' will now be examined. The question of 'cultural literacy' will be discussed in the next chapter.

Political Literacy

It will be helpful to consider, first, that kind of literacy which people may have in mind when they associate it with policies for the maintenance or stability of democracy (see again the quotations of M. Friedman and B. A. Weisbrod on page 45 and pages 45–6 respectively). There seem to be two aspects; first, the task of acquainting the ordinary electorate with the rules and spirit of their constitution; second, the provision of avenues for political leadership.

Anxiety to see that the electorate is helped to become fully articulate in political matters, for instance, in the ability to read if not always to understand a party manifesto, to be able to lobby, to accept the need for some taxation, can be met in many ways. So long as healthy opposition to an existing government is allowed, one can always rely to some extent at least on the organised pressure of minority parties and groups such as trade unions, trade associations, etc., to educate in this sense. It does not at all follow that such knowledge is best obtained in state schools. It is also worth noting that state schools in practice give priority to subjects such as English literature, mathematics, science, geography, rather than to those such as British Constitution, economics, politics, civics, etc., which have more direct connection with political literacy. Indeed, state schools often deliberately avoid, and sometimes pride themselves on avoiding, subjects which have any connection with politics. Furthermore, many people would point to the dangers to political democracy of state education machinery which could easily become, as in Hitler's Germany and in some African countries today, an organ of propaganda to maintain a government in perpetual power.

The nineteenth-century economist and Utilitarian, James Mill, contended that a free press was all that was necessary for a healthy and stable democracy. Political education in a liberal society, he thought, could best come from widely dispersed groups airing their views in journals, books and newspapers. Mill believed that newspapers were fully accessible to most people as early as 1826 when he asserted that reading, writing and accounts were 'the acquirements now common to the lowest of people'.[10]

His son, John Stuart Mill, referring to the Lancashire cotton crisis of 1865, gave similar, if more guarded, praise:

> The instruction obtained from newspapers and political tracts may not be the most solid kind of instruction but it is an immense improvement upon none at all. What it does for a people has been admirably exemplified during the cotton crisis, in the case of the Lancashire spinners and weavers, who have acted with the consistent good sense and forbearance so justly applauded, simply because, being readers of newspapers, they understood the causes of the calamity which had befallen them, and knew that it was in no way imputable either to their employers or to the Government. It is not certain that their conduct would have been as rational and exemplary, if the distress had preceded the salutary measure of fiscal emancipation which gave existence to the penny press.[11]

Here again we may notice the testimony to widespread literacy in the technical sense of ability to read and write, long before the

10. *Westminster Review*, Vol. VI, October 1826, p. 270.
11. *Principles of Political Economy*, p. 757.

state made schooling compulsory and 'free'. We may also observe Mill's awareness (the last sentence in the quotation) of the serious obstacle that the taxes on paper had created in the recent past. It was the existence of such rapidly improving means of communication which no doubt influenced J. S. Mill in his decision to confine his policy proposals to a system of compulsory *education* as distinct from compulsory schooling. The enormous multiplication, improvement and cheapening of means of instructional media such as television, radio, paperback literature, weekly journals, correspondence courses, as well as newspapers in the century and more since the lifetime of the Mills would undoubtedly confirm their belief if they were called on to make the same judgement today. Altogether, therefore, it can be strongly argued that information about the simple rules and anatomy of politics and economics is more satisfactorily provided by a variety of sources than by a single system of state schools.

What of the second aspect of 'political' literacy, the notion that education can provide a suitable background favourable to the emergence of political leaders? Such arguments, it will be remembered, are now being considered within the economist's formal categories of 'neighbourhood effects', and are therefore put forward in the search for a case for government intervention. Thus Professor Friedman argues that education should be subsidised 'because other people benefit from the schooling of those of greater ability and interest, since this is a way of providing better social and political leadership'.[12] The first thing which strikes the observer of the British scene when he begins to test such a hypothesis at the time of writing (1964) is that political leadership, in the sense of electoral success, in 13 out of the 19 years since the end of the war has stemmed from Conservative

12. *Op. cit.*, p. 88.

government led by cabinets which, although responsible for a vast system of state schools, consisted almost entirely of members of Parliament who have not used them either for themselves or for their families. Similar comments would apply also to prominent members of the Labour Government formed in October 1964. One cannot ignore the possible interpretation of such evidence: that one's chances of becoming a political leader are higher if one is educated in the *non-subsidised* sector of education.[13]

The policy implications of such a situation are not quite clear. If we really do want to increase the quantity of political leaders then, from the evidence, there is a *prima facie* case for arguing that the state has been encouraging the wrong sort of schools. Some may put the argument a different way and protest that, since most present leaders do not represent them, or their families, or their class, the 'privileges' enjoyed by the students at independent schools should be shared by the rest of society. Some would contend that this should be done by still more public expenditure on the state schools so that they could compete more powerfully for the staff and facilities of independent schools. Others would argue openly for downright abolition of independent schools. Those who are not quite sure would apparently stand for a combination of all these policies under the vague title of 'integration'. But here the issue of education for political leadership merges with the argument of education for social equality. To many people it is not the most important matter that the un-

13. According to an analysis by the Advisory Centre for Education (ACE) 31 per cent of Labour MPs in the 1965 Labour government received secondary education in the *independent* schools sector (including direct grant schools). In an analysis of 341 children of MPs 39 per cent were at independent secondary schools (including direct grant schools). See *Where?*, Spring 1965. These figures compare with about 10 per cent of the total population which receives independent schooling.

subsidised but 'privileged' independent schools are more successful in producing political leaders; what is more important to them is that 'privilege' itself is wrong since it prevents equality of opportunity, a goal in its own right. Since this argument has little direct connection with political or economic literacy, it will be better to draw the present chapter to a close. The question of equality of opportunity looms so large in all educational discussion that it is treated as a separate case for state education in the next chapter.

CHAPTER FIVE

Equality of Opportunity

In everyday discussion on education the phrase 'equality of opportunity' crops up probably more than any other. Mindful no doubt of the popularity of such widespread usage, professional writers and government commissions are usually anxious to refer to it, especially if there is no pressing necessity for them to define it. But now that it is used by economists as another example of a 'neighbourhood effect' the time is overdue for them, at least, to make a critical assessment of the phrase. Weisbrod is probably the first economist to treat it thus:

> Equality of opportunity seems to be a frequently expressed social goal. Education plays a prominent role in discussions of this goal, since the financial and other obstacles to education confronted by some people are important barriers to its achievement. If equality of opportunity is a social goal, then education pays social returns over and above the private returns to the recipients of the education.[1]

Now we can all agree that the neighbourhood effect of removing black smoke from a local chimney is a 'return' which we could at least begin to measure. (This could be done, for instance, by noting the reduction in laundry bills.) But the 'return' from 'equality of opportunity' is surely something so intangible as to be inac-

---

1. Burton Weisbrod, "Education and Investment in Human Capital," *Journal of Political Economy* 70 (October Supplement), p. 119.

cessible even to the most ambitious of statisticians. Even as a proximate social goal it is not easy to say exactly what it means or to find in it consistent identity. In what follows, however, I shall try to clarify some of the major interpretations that people seem to put on the phrase, and how education is thought to be so closely associated with it. But one cannot begin an analysis without first warning the reader that despite the frequency with which is is put forward as a policy measure, 'equality of opportunity' is as elusive a philosophical idea as it is a practical target.

One way of starting the examination is to ask what people have in mind when they say that opportunities are *not* equal. In reply they would no doubt point to a number of economic and institutional barriers preventing some people from gaining access to occupations, professions or businesses. In feudal aristocracies, caste systems and in countries that practice *apartheid* these kinds of constitutional barriers to opportunity are obvious to all. Is there here any clear connection with education? Is education likely to be the best or most direct way of reaching equality of opportunity in these situations? One would hardly think so. Certainly if the education programme is to be sponsored by a ruling class whose position depends upon the maintenance of these barriers, we must be particularly sceptical of this as a 'solution'.

Suppose now that a revolution occurs and that eventually both caste systems and constitutional barriers are swept away. Will there be free opportunity at last? It is common to point at least to one remaining problem—the economic barrier. This has two aspects: first, the problem of private arrangements to erect obstacles against new entrants, whether they be sponsored by monopolistic manufacturers or by labour unions, i.e. barriers against private freedom to create wealth; second, the belief that once created and however created, wealth itself becomes a barrier to those who do not possess it.

The first of these aspects, the problem of monopolistic behaviour, is not usually included in debates about equality of opportunity. Yet such institutional restrictions may be more important than any lack of education for opportunity seekers. For instance, a monopoly labour union which forces a closed shop upon its employer and then rations the number of union cards available creates a much more obvious barrier to workers or to school-leavers outside the union than does any deficiency in education. As another example, a 16-year-old boy has no equality of opportunity at all with a boy of 15 years to enter certain trades if the rules of apprenticeship decree that he is too old. Moreover, we cannot always be sure that long programmes of works-based education (including, for example, day-release at a technical college) which await 15-year-old successful candidates for apprenticeships have not been designed with some view to discouraging the numbers in the trade in order to raise the earnings of those already in it. Where this is so, further technical education is not a key to equality of opportunity but one of the means of suppressing it.[2]

What of the second aspect of the idea of economic obstacles to opportunity, the proposition that wealth itself is a barrier and that in particular it blocks *educational* opportunity? Let us start with the common assertion that wealth creates privilege. While such a proposition is at least in one sense correct, what is immediately open to debate is its half-hidden suggestion that such privilege itself is necessarily an obstacle to others. Consider an example where this is obviously not so: assume that A and B are equally skilled and have similar jobs but that purely because of

2. The unavailability of apprenticeships as well as the failure to qualify for them because of age can also be a serious restriction on opportunity. The proportion of boys leaving British schools to enter apprenticeships fell from 37.9 per cent in 1961 to 33.5 per cent in 1963.

differences of taste A works 55 hours per week and B 45 hours. At flat rates of pay and in the absence of any other source of income or capital, in the purely monetary sense A is wealthier and therefore more privileged than B. He is privileged over B every time he buys food or anything else, that is to say, every time he enters the market. But because A now buys, say, two loaves of bread for every one that B buys can we say that A's consumption of a second loaf is unfair to B or is a barrier to his welfare? Surely not, for it is open to B to earn as much as A and so to be able to purchase it. Similarly B is privileged over A since he has more leisure; but B's leisure does not prevent A from having the same amount if he is prepared to pay the same price for it, i.e. give up the overtime money.

Suppose now that A works so hard and earns so much more as to put him in the ranks of what some people would call the 'middle class'. It may still be all right for him to buy extra loaves of bread, say some critics, but not extra education for his son. For even if there is no arbitrary privilege enjoyed over B who still has the opportunity to do the same, his son has no opportunity at all to change his father since he has been given to him by the lottery of providence.

It is for this basic reason that in the context of equality of opportunity the case of children is said to be different from that of the two adults A and B. What then should we do? We have somehow to devise, so the argument goes, some artificial government machinery to see to it that the children of the poor do not get such relatively unfavourable treatment compared with the others. We have to organise their lives in a similar way to organising a race in which each competitor starts level at the starting line. Logically this entails either that everybody starts on the line or that those with physical or mental handicaps are given shortened distances.

Such propositions bristle with difficulties and complications. To make for a clearer analysis it will be helpful first to put on one side the question whether children differ in *innate* ability. Accordingly it will be assumed first that all children are of equal *potential* ability, so that any apparent handicaps in the race are either due to differences of environment (which can be offset by more intensive schooling) or to differences in physical endowment (which can be offset both by intensive training and by mechanical aids of suitably varying degrees of elaboration). When this assumption is dropped later in the chapter it will be purely for reasons of exposition. The reader, having himself chosen which of these assumptions is more realistic, will then, it is hoped, be better able to see the full consequences of the particular position he wants to adopt.

Having made this assumption one is immediately confronted with problems both practical and philosophical. First, on the practical difficulties, how do we begin to measure the numerous and typical environmental handicaps which are supposed to hinder some children in the race? For instance, on what basis do we sort out those children who have not had the extra educational stimulus incidental to richer middle-class homes? More difficult still, how do we detect those homes, whatever their social class, which give better educational environments than others?[3] The quantity of empirical evidence needed to decide these matters will surely be enormous. Even then no two persons are likely to make the same judgement on it.

Next, on the philosophical difficulty, one has to try to assess the true status of 'equality of opportunity' as an ethical ideal. Is it demanded because it is a thing of justice, something that is an

3. In the previous example, although the son of A had a richer father, the son of B may have benefited educationally at home from the way in which his father spent the hours of leisure not available to A.

inalienable right of each child? Whatever the *validity* of the concept, the test of the *sincerity* and *consistency* of those who uphold it is whether they themselves are willing to make sacrifices in pushing the ideal to its logical conclusion. It is not impossible that some of those in the majority may only proclaim 'equality of opportunity' because they think that only others (a 'rich' minority) will have to make concessions. They may fail to see that to other people they themselves are rich. Since Chinese children, for instance, are poorer than their own and since they are not willing to send most of their own incomes to their relief, the concept of 'equality of opportunity' loses its absoluteness already, since it is constrained within geographical boundaries. Moreover, one would want to know the attitude of the majority in some school areas where there are minorities of people who are so substantially below the typical standard of living that the requisite compensation would require a significant contribution or sacrifice from the majority itself. For instance, within some school areas there may be groups of immigrant West Indians whose children have come from an illiterate plantation background. This will give them handicaps in the 'race' which are much bigger than those of ordinary working-class children in the same zone. In order to compensate for this (i.e. to bring them up to the starting line), following the equality of opportunity ideal, perhaps twice as much money should be spent on the education of a West Indian immigrant child as on the average one. The point is that it is not clear how far most ordinary people are prepared to accept the full logic of the ideal in these situations.

The same sort of problem applies to children who are so handicapped by such physical misfortunes, e.g. loss of limbs or sight, that it would need, say, 20 times as much money as the average to give them anything like equality of opportunity of winning the race. It is not convincing to reply that we shall give such children additional attention *when we can afford it*. Initial equality can *always* be afforded; it is simply a matter of dividing a given amount of scarce resources according to 'needs'. This division takes the form of a given set of ratios which can be applied to any national expenditure, however small it is. If, in the end, many of the proponents of 'equality of opportunity' do make reservations that some children (the physically normal, or the non-foreigners, or the majority) are 'more equal than others', then the concept loses much of its force as a philosophical ideal.

Consider next the conflict between equality of opportunity (however defined) and that of equality in the distribution of income. Where legal and juristic privileges have been largely removed, the desire of many people for equality of opportunity ultimately resolves itself into the desire for equality of wealth; for one of the most effective ways of removing those general educational 'privileges' of rich environments which give some children a better start in life is, according to them, to reduce the 'richness' as such. This policy is best argued openly in the context of a proposal for more progressive taxation to redistribute incomes still more. In terms of the previous illustration, for instance, it would mean that A's income after progressive tax would in the end not be so different from that of B despite the fact that A worked 55 hours and B 45 hours. The question now is of course whether A would continue to work so hard. If, in deciding this issue, we conclude that such extreme equality of income is impractical because it would abolish incentives (a belief shared today even by communist countries), then income differences have to be expected if only as a necessary expedient in an imperfect world.[4] In this case relative 'richness' or 'poor-

4. On this question C. A. R. Crosland, one-time Secretary of State for Education and Science, unambiguously declared his own opinion several years ago. 'We do not want complete equality of incomes, since extra responsibility and

ness' must be accepted as a daily fact of life, otherwise we shall be inconsistent. In this situation no educational purpose seems to be served by trying to pretend that income differences do not exist or by attempting to conceal this fact of inequality from children. And we are in danger of contradicting ourselves if, having allowed some people the freedom to earn more than others, we are at the same time striving for the day when most rich men's sons are forced to school with children of the not-so-rich according to some system of conscription.

Egalitarians often quote the work of their champion R. H. Tawney, especially since it is presented in particularly elegant prose. Tawney's analysis, however, contains many difficulties which his allegorical language seems only to obscure. Thus he condemns the popular meaning of 'equality of opportunity' as a 'graceful, but attenuated, figment. It recedes from the world of reality to that of perorations'. [5] Yet Tawney's own version of the concept does not get us much further:

> Rightly interpreted, it means, not only that what are commonly regarded as the prizes of life should be open to all, but that none should be subjected to arbitrary penalties . . . [6]

The trouble with this interpretation is to find anything which will at once qualify as a 'prize' for a successful individual but which will not be regarded as an arbitrary penalty of 'inequality' by less successful or hardworking neighbours. Writers such as Tawney who *admit* the practical need for 'prizes' do not seem

---

exceptional talent require and deserve a different reward.' *The Future of Socialism*, Jonathan Cape, 1956, p. 217.

5. *Equality*, Allen and Unwin, second edition, 1931, p. 139.

6. *Ibid.*, p. 147. Tawney deals with equality of opportunity in 18 pages in which he uses about 20 metaphors which refer among other things to donkeys, carrots, tadpoles, lightning conductors, ladders, thrones, breakwaters, reefs and chasms.

prepared to face their full consequences. If A works twice as hard as B and receives at least twice as much money, or if A saves more than B out of equal labour income, we can hardly inform A that he is forbidden to spend his extra earnings on the education of his son. For it is possible that the real incentive to work harder or save more may have been the desire to give his son a good education; the extra money earned would only be a measure of his power to do so. If people protest, as Tawney does, that the really objectionable riches are those which are self-perpetuating and do not arise from contributions to production but come rather from inheritance, monopoly or gambling, then such argument points to the need for a change in the law to provide inheritance taxes, monopoly legislation and gambling taxes respectively. Objections to *artificially* contrived wealth certainly do not amount to a case for a nationalised system of state schools. In so far as egalitarians suggest that such wealth is inherently more typical of our society than extra wealth from productive contributions (which include saving and investment) they reveal not only a lack of confidence in the competence of legal reform, taxation reform and legislative measures to promote competition but also a reserved belief that what they call the 'necessary prizes' of their own system amount to nothing more than 'an attenuated figment'.

Many who agree that inequality of income and wealth is inevitable may offer yet another solution: the proposal to place legal prohibition on all private expenditure on education, that is to allow rich people to buy extra bread, for instance, but not extra education. This of course involves fundamental problems connected with liberty, and some people may regard liberty as an important social goal which competes with equality of opportunity itself. But in any case it is very doubtful whether the compulsory desegregation which is implied could be a practical proposition, at least in Britain or in any country where there is no 'iron curtain'. For the moment it was attempted, many people would respond by sending their children abroad to be educated or even by emigrating themselves.[7]

It is probable that among many of the most ardent advocates of equality of educational opportunity today are those who not only desire full equality of incomes, so making superfluous the words 'riches' and 'prizes' as descriptive and relative terms meaningful to individuals within their own country, but who also entertain the still more extreme notion of *equality of consumption*. According to this view it is not enough even that A and B are compelled to earn equal incomes; it may still be distasteful to the egalitarian that A can buy more education because he elects to consume, say, less beer than B. Such egalitarians will not rest until all are coerced into spending their incomes in equal amounts among equal groups of goods and services. In terms of the race analogy, all contestants must not only start at the same point but must reach the finishing line simultaneously and then drink equal quantities of wine from the winners' cup. It is not likely, however, that most people ultimately want such rigid conformity and uniformity.

Of course since we have so far assumed equality of *potential* ability it would follow that, if it was ever possible that we could arrange entirely equal environments, all participants in the race

7. On this point too, C. A. R. Crosland is equally forthright: ' . . . a flat proscription is undesirable on libertarian grounds. Once incomes have been distributed as the government of the day thinks fit, it is generally right, save in war-time or post-war periods of national crisis, that citizens should be left free to spend them as they wish . . . And the interference with private liberty would be intolerable; the closing of all independent schools would naturally encourage a strong demand both for private tutors and places in schools abroad; and the resulting inequalities would compel the extension of the ban to these facilities also.' *Op. cit.*, p. 262.

would in fact finish together.[8] Whether we pursued an ideal of 'equality of opportunity' or 'equality of consumption' the desired result would be the same; so any differences between the ideals strived for would not matter. But even if it was possible to reach this stage some people who initially argued for 'equality of opportunity' may object that things had gone too far. They may explain that the true purpose of their ideal was that it would allow society to seek maximum prosperity. Even if there still remained at some point a 'pool of ability' which was even yet untapped, because of the most severe environmental handicaps, they may now argue that the costs of removing these handicaps, i.e. breaking through to 'the pool', may be much higher than the extra revenue to be expected by concentrating resources on that ability which had already been tapped. It is obvious that for those who argue thus their own conception of 'equality of opportunity' is not an end but only a means to another end, viz. maximum economic prosperity. As such, of course, equality of opportunity loses all status as an ideal in its own right even if any clear meaning is still attached to it.

So far the discussion has been conducted on the assumption that all children are of equal potential ability. The moment we drop this we are accepting that some children are, for instance, naturally dull and others are naturally bright. Suppose that we can counteract all the subtle environmental handicaps by some additional and intensive education for the naturally dull children sufficient to get them up to the starting line of the race. Suppose also that beyond this we can even prevent some parents spending extra amounts on their children merely by virtue of their being richer than others. It is quite obvious that it is impossible now

---

8. The situation is more complex if we grant differences in personality, e.g. that some are more lazy than others.

for all competitors to finish together. In other words where there is inequality of potential (ability) there is bound to be inequality of result. If we insist that there shall be equality of result it follows that we penalise ability.

It is abundantly clear that in real life, where they do see inequality of result, many people too hastily jump to the conclusion that there has been inequality of opportunity. The more that this confusion takes hold, the more we shall substitute 'equality' (or 'uniformity') for 'equality of opportunity' and the further we shall be away from the initial ideal. Any single person cannot of course say that it is wrong for others *consciously* to prefer 'equality' to 'equality of opportunity'; these are value judgements which concern them alone. All he can do is to show them where the reality and the ideal cannot meet in real life. Because in education the phrase equality of opportunity is protested at every stage, i.e. at every age intake, it is important that we ascertain that we are not simply wanting to stop every race just after it starts (e.g. at the age of 11 or 12) and then to move up the starting line to begin another race (say at the age of 12 or 13) simply because we do not like the way the first one was shaping.[9]

Some readers may better grasp the full nature of the distinction between equality and equality of opportunity by looking at the following satirical passage:

> While the proposals for the abolition of grammar schools and nationalisation of the public schools are on the right lines, they offer only a partial solution to the problem of ensuring educational equality. Unfortunately, even when all schools are identical, containing classes of identical size taught by identical teachers to identical syllabuses—there will still be children who, through he-

9. Of course the analogy with the race track does not entirely fit. There is no *one* prize in the educational stakes. Every participant wins but some win more valuable prizes than others.

redity or environment, will learn more quickly and pass examinations more easily: in short, exceed their fellows.

This state of affairs would be intolerable in any truly egalitarian society. Therefore, while the present method of assessing educational attainment by examinations, intelligence tests and teacher observation should be retained, the method of following up these results should be reversed. The anti-social child who persistently shines in class should be discharged from school by his 14th birthday at the latest. Exceptionally gifted children, indeed, or outright geniuses, should be 'scummed off' at an earlier age still, and denied any education at all. Under this scheme, average pupils might expect to receive some kind of higher education, perhaps up to sixth-form level. But university education would be reserved for the least educatable. Only the dimmest of all would go to Oxford or Cambridge.

Some reactionary obscurantists will object that the scheme would lead to economic and social disaster. Such people are incorrigible. They seem to have absolutely no idea of what education is about.[10]

It is arguable that even this writer has not gone far enough for some egalitarians. Different lengths of *formal* schooling appropriate to needs will not be enough since there remains the additional *informal* education requirement called 'mixing'. Thus it would be incorrect to remove from school exceptionally gifted children earlier than others. Such children should be made to stay but not to do anything. Otherwise the two types of children would not receive the proper chance of learning to live together.

Can the Government Ensure Equality of Opportunity?

Such then are some of the major avenues of discussion along which it seems the concept of equality of opportunity is likely to

10. Peter Simple, *Daily Telegraph*, 15 January 1965.

take us. I do not wish to select any one of them as being 'right' or 'wrong'; it is for the reader to choose the one closest to his own preconceptions. What the author can do, however, is to illustrate the probable consequences of entrusting a government with the task of implementing a policy of 'equality of opportunity', *however* defined.

It is obvious that the need to call in a government to secure something that people are not already securing by their own private endeavours implies a need for some sort of legal restraint or coercion. Thus, where it is felt necessary to prevent rich parents from buying extra education, particularly strong administrators will be needed to enforce the new system. The first consequence to notice is that these officials will be in unique positions of influence. The new situation, in other words, is one of inequality of political power, a form of inequality that is repulsive to most democrats and certainly makes a poor exchange with inequality of income. The danger is that the desire of some parents to exert themselves to do the best for their children will now express itself, not in the form of extra work to earn money for private education, but in personal manoeuvres to court special favours from those, such as state education officers, who are increasingly flattered by the strategic positions of influence in which they find themselves.

To a considerable extent some administrators in Britain already enjoy such arbitrary power today. I showed in Chapter 2 how the English Education Act of 1944 was already worded in favour of local authorities, giving them the legal initiative in possible disputes with parents. It is a tricky business for any parent to try to get his child out of an inferior school and into a superior one even in his own district. Thus even the Director of the Advisory Centre for Education counsels parents to be polite and courteous when dealing with state headmasters and to try to be particularly diplomatic when negotiating with the Education Officer:

> It is useless to bluster or threaten the Education office. Its position is formidable, for although it is doubtful if the zoning system would be upheld in the courts, the local authority can always make the excuse that the school is in any case full.
>
> It may be worthwhile to try to persuade the Education officer to make an exception by a skillfully and reasonably argued case. He might accept objections to a co-educational, or a single-sex school, to corporal punishment, or traffic hazards. It is just possible that a parent could put up a persuasive case on the grounds of streaming (though a personal or professional dislike of a particular teacher is unlikely to succeed).[11]

English people do not usually have to be coaxed to be polite in their ordinary dealings with everyday suppliers of goods or services such as the grocer, the butcher or the newsagent anxious for their custom. Perhaps more significant for egalitarians may be the reflection that the special talent required for diplomacy, political negotiation and juridical expertise is distributed unequally among parents. In this sense inequality of opportunity for some children will probably now stem from their misfortune, not this time in having parents who are poorer, but in having parents who are politically weak. It follows that whatever one's definition of equality of opportunity, the state's attempt to secure it, at least from English experience, involves not only this sort of failure but also the strong probability that these things will be made worse than before.

Even if parents were equally gifted with the political powers of negotiating with local officials, inequality of the opportunity for

11. *Sunday Times Supplement*, 10 November 1963, p. 11.

children to mix would still exist because of the geographical distribution of different social and income groups. Working-class people tend to live in working-class districts so ensuring that the local primary school usually takes predominantly working-class children. In a sample investigation of primary schools in 1962 published by the National Union of Teachers the following observation, which refers to infant schools, confirms this point. In answering the question 'How would you describe (socially) the people who live in your catchment area?' three-quarters of head teachers said they were either entirely or mainly working class.[12] The rationing of school places on a geographical basis is, as the 'zoning' system implies, the most obvious and easiest criterion which presents itself to local administrators. Yet such methods are likely to secure much less social mobility than would probably occur without a system of nationalised schools.[13] Emotional references to 'education apartheid' or 'caste division' which are attributed to the persistence of a mixed system of public and private education are quite out of perspective if an adequate solution is not first offered for these present contradictions in our state system—a system which, while it is supposed to be able to put such things right, seems, indeed, to provide the most potent source of inequality.

12. *The State of Our Schools*, 1963, p. 32.
13. Comprehensive schools so far do not seem to have solved this crucial difficulty and is it difficult to see how they can. Indeed in some cases they may have made things worse. One comprehensive school teacher (letter to *The Times*, 21 January 1965) asserts: 'the concept of the comprehensive school as a "community school" serving its neighbourhood condemns some schools in London to an intake of exclusively working-class pupils, and the consequently low standards of academic achievement and discipline soon brand such schools in the eyes of the public and the teaching profession as inferior to the schools in more favoured areas. There is already a hierarchy among the London comprehensive schools resembling that of grammar and modern schools.'

Comparison with the Market

If, given an acceptable distribution of income, people accept the services of the free market in the provision of goods and services, it must be presumed that they prefer this system to others as the best available instrument for fulfilling their personal goals in the fullest way that their incomes will allow. That I can shop around for food for my family means that I have equality of opportunity with my neighbour with each pound that I spend, especially if my neighbour and I exchange useful information about the daily offerings of the market in our everyday conversation. In this sense equality of opportunity as a *social* goal is directly proportionate with equality of opportunity as a *personal* goal. Moreover, that I obtain the best available food for my children means automatically that the social goal of protecting children is pursued simultaneously. Why, given the same income inequalities, the pursuit of the social goal of 'equality of opportunity' in education by the use of the market should be impracticable is never made clear. Certainly many people at this stage of the discussion refer to pronounced market imperfections in education. Nevertheless, evidence to show that the market is particularly imperfect in education is only a *necessary* but not a *sufficient* ground for state intervention to provide the education. What has also to be shown is that the shortcomings of the state system will not be even worse.

In fact there is no reliable evidence to show that if a market were re-established over the *whole* or most part of education it would seriously suffer from inefficiency and monopolistic tendencies. The behaviour of the few existing independent schools is no sure guide because, first, they are such a small part of education supply; second, many of them exist in a world of the 'unnatural' business uncertainty that goes with constant rumours of 'nationalisation'; and third, others are excluded from the pressures of free market competitors to the extent that they are protected by endowment finance. And even if there were dangers of market imperfections it is not clear why reliance cannot be placed on the same sort of restrictive practices legislation that is used to maintain competition in other business fields.[14]

There is indeed much to be said in favour of the market even if only in terms of a choice between evils. Consider a low-income family, living in a poor district, which has the ambition of possessing a new car. It can, by resolutely cutting down on its other expenses, accumulate enough savings to buy the same car as can the resident of a high-income district. The family does not have to move to the better district to achieve its aim. But if the poor family has so much confidence in a child that it is anxious to secure for it the best education, its power to help by similar saving and economy is usually limited to using savings in the provision, say, of a few more books, records, or a continental tour, unless it is fortunate enough to obtain a scholarship to one of the few private schools. The point is that the family is hardly likely to be able to afford to move to the 'better' neighbourhood in addition to all its other exertions.[15] This is especially so where the family occupies a rent-controlled or a council house, a privilege

14. Sometimes the free market is objected to on the grounds that it is unthinkable to treat education as a commodity to be bought and sold—like soap. The confusion here is in the judgement of the vehicle by the things it carries. One might just as well object to the provision of schools by municipal organisation on the grounds that it is unthinkable to treat education as something that can be put on the rates—like refuse disposal. The market in fact is used for all kinds of professional services including medicine, insurance and law. While these services share, with soap, the same type of exchange mechanism, all similarities end at that point.

15. Cf. Milton Friedman, *op. cit.*, p. 92. Exceptional people, however, have been known to rent a room in a favourable school area and then return when the child has been taken on the roll of the local school.

which only the most extreme circumstances would encourage it to give up. For these reasons it is difficult not to conclude that a free market in education, like a free market in new cars, is likely to provide more avenues of social and economic mobility than the present system.

In educational discussion the case for the market is often briefly dismissed on the grounds that it enables the rich to make the fullest strategic disposition of their wealth and so act to the educational detriment of the children of the not-so-rich. There seems to be a serious need to examine most of the assumptions behind this kind of argument. For the findings of this chapter raise the question of whether it should not be reversed; of whether, in fact, the free market is not an ally rather than an enemy of the egalitarian. Certainly the contraction of the state out of education, *without reducing taxes and leaving the distribution of income as it is*, would worsen the relative educational position of the poor compared with the rich minority who habitually use the private sector of education. But it seems that the popular argument has confused the market as such with the significance of the conditions (italicised in the previous sentence) in which it is presumed to operate. But if it can be shown that the present 'free' state education given to the average family is paid for out of taxes levied on the same average family it is difficult to see how a government, which was withdrawing from the provision of education, could justifiably refuse to reduce the family's tax contribution and thereby increase its net income. And if by progressive income tax adjustments the rich are precluded from such increases in net income it is difficult to see why the average family, being now better poised to exploit the advantages of market freedom, will not enjoy an *improved* position *vis-à-vis* the rich. Conversely, for the state to use part of the average family's gross income to do the educational spending for it is, on present evidence, to reduce its choice socially, geographically and qualitatively. And this is a situation which puts it at a greater disadvantage compared with a rich family and thus makes for *more* inequality.[16]

It remains to be seen, of course, whether new administrative devices will one day appear which eventually allow the state system to compete with the choice ranges available outside it. Some writers, such as Mr C. A. R. Crosland, who accept the necessity for a given degree of income inequality because of the need for practical incentives and believe that independent schools should not and cannot be abolished, still think that the state system can eventually remove its traditional disadvantages by bringing state education up to and beyond the qualities of the private sector. Since, however, proposals for doing this inevitably involve the necessity of increasing expenditure on state schools such writers must be questioned on where the extra money is to come from. If, for instance, it is the higher incomes which are intended to provide the extra finance this would seem to conflict at some point with Mr Crosland's accepted limit to the redistribution of incomes because of the need for incentives. If it is the middle or lower incomes which are to finance the improvements in state schools then, in so far as 'rich' children are attracted into them

16. The restriction of choice stems not only from the practice of keeping children within their immediate neighbourhood zones. Choices are also unequal between local government areas, i.e. counties and county boroughs. For instance Dr J. W. B. Douglas, director of the Medical Research Council, says that if the existing grammar school places were fairly distributed throughout the country in proportion to the measured ability of the children, the chances of getting a place, 18 per cent, would be equal for Welsh children and those in the South of England. 'In fact, 29 per cent of Welsh children go to grammar schools as compared with only 13 per cent of children in the South' (*The Home and the School*, MacGibbon and Kee, 1964). Thus the southern children have inequality imposed upon them not only because their families' educational 'expenditure' is trapped within the state system but also because they get less return for it than the Welsh.

(which is one of the objectives), this will in effect mean a redistribution of income in favour of the rich: the opposite of the usual egalitarian programme.

Even those egalitarians who insist on stamping out all vestige of pecuniary privilege need to consider most carefully which are the best techniques available. The solution to which they usually resort, the abolition of the independent schools, is not *inevitably* best fitted for their purpose. Since, as has been shown, the present state system is one which itself creates inequality (because of zoning, etc.), further reflection may prompt egalitarians to consider whether the state schools are the best ones to be abolished. A policy, not of state schools for all, but of independent schools for all, is just as appropriate in principle so long as arrangements are made to confine parents to spending uniform amounts on each child.[17] One way of doing this would be for the state to allocate vouchers of equal value for each child (or graded according to scholarship merit if desired) and to decree that no addition from private funds was to be allowed. For the egalitarian this must be considered to be far preferable to the present system whereby local authorities are allowed to spend significantly different amounts per child in different areas. Whilst it might be objected that the requirement of preventing some parents from spending extra amounts from their own resources would be difficult to police, the same is true of the alternative requirement to ban private schools and tutors. Finally, and this could be the deciding point, the market system has a supply side advantage denied to the nationalised system: free competition. If it is capable of at least matching the present state system in equality of opportunity, a private system with competition would see to it that all

---

17. Subject to a system of inspection to ensure against some minority of irresponsible parents choosing bad schools.

children were not only reasonably equally served, but more efficiently served as well.

The Fleming Proposals

Mr Crosland, who would tolerate some independent schools within a mixed system, argues for a full adoption of the policy outlined by the 1944 Fleming Committee by which the state progressively buys places at independent schools until all of their students are financed by state bursaries.[18] Although he makes it clear that such financial aid to families is to be made according to a graduated income scale, the net effect on income distribution is unknown in the absence of any indication as the source of the revenue necessary for such progressive state expenditure increases. But at least, to those who favour a break away from the present 'Hobson's choice' system, of zoned neighbourhood state schools, the Fleming proposals, constituting as they do a special type of voucher system, will be regarded in principle as some step in the right direction.

Those who dislike segregation according to ability (especially those who speak with alarm about the rise of meritocracies) will, however, object to Crosland's method of allocating these particular state vouchers according to a system of competitive entry. They may protest that since the middle classes already have a habit of getting their children to win the most scholarships, to provide them with any further opportunities will be a regressive, not an egalitarian, step. The fact is that the Fleming proposals, so long as they are applied to a mixed system of state and independent schools, will only make for a different polarisation or pattern of inequality, not its abolition. For those who are offered, on

18. *Op. cit.*, p. 263.

whatever basis, state bursaries to go to independent schools outside the state system will have potential choices and privileges
over those who remain involuntarily locked in the state system.
Such proposals will always fall short of a scheme which distrib-
utes bursaries or vouchers or reduces taxes for the wider educational choice of *all* children. The case for *universal* vouchers will
be examined in detail in Chapter 13.

'Integration' with the State System

Present-day government references to education point to a policy
that, ostensibly, lies somewhere between the Fleming solution
and complete abolition of independent schools. This policy is one
of 'full integration' of independent schools into the state system.
Such schools will be placed under an 'educational' trust which will
comprise largely present headmasters and governors but which, it
is hoped, will yield to pressure from the government so that it will
not have to fall back too often on compulsory powers.

An unofficial Labour committee, 'The Public Schools Committee', whose general thinking seems to be in line with that of
the government, published on 5 May 1965 further policy proposals. The composition of the 'public' schools, and, by implication,
the independent schools is to include a wide cross-section of the
population and school places are to be granted on the basis of
need instead of parental income. The 'broad function' of each
school (the criteria for selection and, where necessary, the appointment of governors) is to be settled by the Minister or a
body responsible to him. In other words, independence is to be
forfeited. The committee will not be content with 'token reform': it believes that no change short of 'complete integration'
could eliminate the 'privilege' with which the independent
schools are now associated.

It is difficult so far to assess the full implication of these proposals since they are expressed in ambiguous terminology. But the committee's special use of the word 'privilege' demonstrates an inexorable faith that the state system is something which is free of such 'blemishes'. As we have seen, many state pupils have substantial privilege over others by the chance 'virtue' of their geographical location. Indeed because independent schools are spread most unevenly over the country, the new policy of integration will mean that state scholars who happen to live in areas which are thick with independent schools will enjoy a new privilege. For the 'privileged' areas will now offer more potential choices because of the greater availability in their district of the newly 'integrated' independent schools side by side with the state schools. Thus government actions to integrate in order to end inequality and 'privilege' will amount largely to a quixotic display of good deeds; for in the end there will not be quality but another twist in the pattern of inequality.

In the proposal to select students 'according to need instead of parental income', there is a reluctance to define 'need'. Those who have in the past ventured to be more specific have found to their surprise that they are strongly opposed by persons whom hitherto they regarded as allies. Thus Mr Crosland, Secretary of State for Education, felt obliged to tell a Labour Party conference on 6 March 1965 that he himself rejected what he called the 'nihilist' school of thought:

> ... those pessimists who would convert all (independent) schools into Borstals or mental institutions.

One must assume that the 'nihilists' are strongly opposed to Mr Crosland's criterion of 'need', which presumably is one which will be operated according to competitive entry, on the grounds that it will militate against a representative school intake and encourage meritocracy. Thus the second selection criterion proposed by the Public Schools Committee, 'a wide cross-section of the population', is likely to face severe conflict from the desire to select according to 'need', the first criterion. And in view of the wide composition of the committee it is probable that such conflict will be quite severe when the day comes for it to get beyond the present comforting, but nevertheless kaleidoscopic, terminology.[19]

Meanwhile one must question not only whether the pursuit of equality of opportunity is really a disguised wish for flat uniformity but whether equality, however interpreted, is such an absolute that the pursuit of other values like liberty, family life and efficiency should be completely subordinated to it. *The Times*, commenting on the report of the Public Schools Committee, expressed the belief that those who are anxious 'to do something about the public schools' really want to use education as a means of social engineering:

> They appear to look forward to an homogenized society in which the influence on a child's future of family, kinship and social ties is reduced to a minimum, and in which the determining and allocating functions, hitherto performed by these agencies pass instead to the processing plant of a uniform system of education. Instinct informs those who are attracted by this vision of society that the progress that may be expected towards it from going over to a fully comprehensive secondary school system will be checked unless the direct grant and independent schools are cracked and scrambled in the same dish. Instinct should likewise inform those whom that vision does not attract that the inde-

19. The 24 sponsors of the committee included Miss Margaret Miles, headmistress of Mayfield Comprehensive Girls School, Putney; A. J. Ayer, Professor of Logic at Oxford (educated at Eaton), and Mr Ted Hill, President of the Boilermakers' Union.

pendence of these schools, the variety they offer, the pace they set, the values they embody, and the standards they have achieved are now more than ever worth developing.[20]

The discussion on equality of opportunity can now be concluded where it started, in the context of 'neighbourhood effects'. Even if there are no difficulties of definition, to treat 'the social goal' of equality of opportunity as a neighbourhood effect which can inevitably be fostered by state education is unwarranted and unproven since it overlooks the probability that such a cure makes things worse than before. On this, let Dicey have the last word:

> It has been well noted that deficient, or rather non-existent, as was any system of national education, 'there is probably no period in English history at which a greater number of poor men have risen to distinction', than at the end of the eighteenth and in the earlier part of the nineteenth century.[21]

20. *Times* Leader, 6 May 1965.
21. Dicey, *Law and Public Opinion in England*, Macmillan, 1952 edition, p. 113. Dicey was quoting Leslie Stephen, *English Utilitarianism*, i, pp. III, 112.

CHAPTER SIX

Education and the Quest for 'Common Values'

The economists quoted at the beginning of Chapter 4 (pp. 45 and 46) referred to the beneficial neighbourhood effects from education which stemmed not only from literacy but also from what they describe as the communication of 'common values'. In this chapter I shall examine state education provision in England in the light of this objective alone.

What Kind of State?

It is patent that any attempt to examine success in achieving this kind of social goal must start with an explicit statement about the kind of political structure within which we are operating, otherwise much of the discussion will be at cross purposes. What are thought to be desirable 'common values' in a collectivist or totalitarian state are not likely to be identical with those believed to be appropriate to an open or democratic society. On the whole, it seems that there are two major philosophic bases from which we must choose. The first involves an organic concept of the state, in which all individuals are regarded as component parts of a larger entity called 'The State'. The second view regards the individual as the basic structural unit, while the state is seen as a collectivity of individuals with no separate ends of its own.

Now there is no 'scientific' way of choosing from these two philosophical structures; moreover it is probable that many people have not thought about the problem long enough either to see it in these terms or to make up their own minds on it. But it seems at least incumbent on the author at this point to declare his own preference so that there can be no doubt about the general frame of reference in which the rest of this chapter is set. Accordingly then let me state that I find it difficult to accept any political philosophy in which the individual is not the primary philosophic entity. It follows therefore that I reject the first of the above concepts, the organic theory of the state, and that the rest of this chapter will only be of interest to those who have not definitely made up their minds to the contrary. But since intuitively one feels that very many people are in fact disposed to the individualistic view, there is a conviction that what follows will be much more than a mere academic exercise.

As I see it, the kind of political structure appropriate to the individualist philosophy is a democracy which upholds the liberty of the individual and respects each separate individual as much as his neighbour. Under these circumstances the idea of 'common values' is only meaningful if it refers to values which are acknowledged by every member or minority in society. In so far as education is supposed to be a useful vehicle for transmitting these values it can be only that kind of education which represents the diffused wishes of the whole populace. Certainly this function of education is not a matter for 'experts'. This is an issue which must be decided by every member of society since he, or she, alone is the ultimate author of the 'common values' with which we are concerned and which education is supposed to be able to promulgate. In practice, of course, we can expect that some individuals will naturally be more strenuous than others in their desire to keep alive particular ethical or cultural standards or modes of life. Religious and philosophical groups, for instance, being especially sensitive to the need for social and other values, are natural and spontaneous educators within society long before most governments exert themselves in these respects.

That there will be a wide variety of cultural, moral and religious expression is a consequence to be expected from a free, individualistic society. Indeed the final test of any democratic constitution is whether it provides the proper background to enable individuals to find fulfilment in these fundamental purposes of life. A democratic political organisation should certainly facilitate and not swamp such endeavour; its representatives should not, for instance, be hasty to intervene at every sign of apparent clash between people of seemingly different convictions. Furthermore, the true individualist and libertarian, knowing that he happens to be in a majority on a particular issue, should not take every opportunity to resort to the political process simply to try to make a minority conform to his views; for this would demonstrate that kind of liberty which grants the freedom to others only to do or say what the majority happen to do or say. Where beliefs and convictions are extremely diversified in real life, the only 'value' which can ultimately be regarded as 'common' to all is *tolerance*; and the best way to nurture it is to give people the fullest opportunity of exercising it; for no purpose will be served by trying to disguise the fact that differences do exist.

It follows then that a government in a democratic society has to tread warily before intervening. In particular a government is faced with an imperative obligation to distinguish between education to assist in the *communication* of values, and education which results in the *imposition* of its own values.[1] To show how easily governments overstep the mark in favour of a particular ideology, it is common to point to the examples of indoctrination in Hitler's Germany, or to the educational 'brainwashing' of Stalin's Russia. What is not so commonly recognised, however, is that many other, more ostensibly democratic governments, in their haste to erect 'national systems of education', have also been guilty, not so much of imposing their own values, as of standing in the way of those common to minority groups.

State Intervention Reduces Private Provision

It is well known, for instance, that religious and philosophical groups were predominant in education long before the English government intervened to make a 'national system' in the nineteenth century. To take a random illustration, consider the distribution of the 170 schools in Manchester in 1869 on the eve of the celebrated Education Act of 1870 (Table 3). In the subsequent century many of these voluntary schools either disappeared or were considerably weakened following the establishment of the undenominational state schools. Through the mechanism of taxation the state is able to make its own position almost unassailable whenever it wishes to invade an area of private provision. For one thing tax revenues necessary to finance the new government establishments dry up the source of funds that would otherwise have been used in the private sector. For another, by charging fees which are lower than those of private establishments it can compete them out of existence, just as a

1. This phraseology is borrowed from Professors A. T. Peacock and J. Wiseman, *Education for Democrats*, Hobart Paper 25, Institute of Economic Affairs, 1964, p. 24.

TABLE 3

Distribution of Denominational Schools in Manchester, 1869

Number of Schools Connected with

Protestant Dissenting Bodies

	Church of England or National School	British and Foreign School	Wesleyan	Presby-terian	Other	Roman Catholic	Jews	No Religious Body	No Returns
Asylums	1	—	—	—	—	—	—	5	—
Day Schools	56	6	6	4	8	17	1	56	10

Source: Table 12, *House of Commons Return on Schools for Poorer Classes in Birmingham, Leeds, Liverpool and Manchester,* 2 March 1870.

monopolist, in seeking market aggrandisement, can use 'fighting' companies to sell below cost and kill competitors in one area after another. In this way it will be demonstrated in Chapter 10 how the state in the nineteenth century was not so much the *creator* of new schools (the popular image) as a powerful *take-over bidder* of other schools, making use of its practically over-whelming resources.[2]

In terms of our 'neighbourhood effect' analysis, it will be re-membered that it was education, not necessarily *state* education, which was presumed to be useful in the communication of 'common values'. It seems quite consistent with this analysis for such bodies as the church, and other organisations which to a large extent have been virtually driven out of business in educa-tion, to argue, if they see fit, that the new state-provided schools are less successful than the previous ones in this particular task.

2. For an eyewitness impression of the fate of Manchester Schools only seven years after the 1870 Act, see Chapter 10, Appendix.

Here, of course, we reach back to the warnings and prophecies which were made in the heat of the great nineteenth-century education controversy. Now the very severity of this old religious dispute seems to make the seemingly clinical treatment of education by twentieth-century economists look rather innocent. The 'neighbourhood effect' approach certainly seems at this juncture to appear naïve and inadequate. Perhaps this is because one so often associates such emphasis on 'neighbourhood benefits' with those who seem in haste to show that the private sector has 'failed', and who have for a long time closed their minds to, or forgotten, the old moral controversies because of an intuitive belief in some ideal political government which can one day settle such friction once and for all. There is no doubt that this kind of thinking has strongly contributed to the circumstances that have finally caused English legislators to try to put moral development under government tutelage. The Education Act of 1944 now provides:

> It shall be the duty of the local education authority for every area to contribute towards the spiritual, moral and physical development of the community.

Morality 'on the Rates'

How far is this kind of intervention really compatible with the kind of liberal society outlined earlier? Indeed how far can we argue more formally that this kind of state intervention involves such detrimental 'neighbourhood effects' itself that the net result is one of social *deterioration*? Such questions are not easy to answer; this is a matter for honest dispute and one must try to avoid dogmatism in reviewing the evidence and in trying to find out what people really want. Perhaps the best way through this complex terrain is to start by examining the evidence contained in contemporary official reports, bearing in mind that they are usually the work of people who are engaged in and sympathising with state-provided education. Whilst the rest of this chapter will concern itself mainly with the examples of religion and morality, much of the argument will be equally relevant to freedom of expression by racial and cultural minorities.

The Newsom Report of 1963 explains that most local authorities have so far interpreted their statutory obligations (under the 1944 Act) so as to include instruction in religion, and in practice the agreed syllabus provides for instruction in the Christian religion. But since not all teachers and not all parents are Christians, and since indeed some people are openly opposed to religious instruction, many schools are faced with a perplexing problem. Some schools face it by allowing pupils to be 'excused' the 'scripture lesson'. Others content themselves by settling for fairly 'safe' courses in 'moral instruction':

> Some schools still reduce religious instruction to simple Bible reading with as little comment as possible—a sure way of losing the attention of most boys and girls. Some turn it into ancient history with as big or as little claim on the attention of the average adolescent as any other period remote in time.[3]

Ordinary state school teachers too often lack conviction when giving scripture lessons, and young people are the first to detect this:

> Boys and girls are the first to demand that teachers should know what they are talking about. What does this mean in religious instruction? What at least one apprentice wanted may be inferred from a discussion recorded during a day-release period in a steel

3. *Half Our Future, op. cit.*, para. 166, p. 55.

works. 'You said about teachers in school; did they explain, you know, after-life and that to you, you know? They're in no position to explain it because they perhaps know as little as you do about it. You see a minister knows what he's talking about, I don't think a teacher does. At least he does perhaps about maths, but not about religion, because he's the same as us, unless he's a right and religious man . . . '[4]

The Newsom Report therefore includes a cautionary proposal that the Church should now be a specially invited guest inside state schools:

Appropriate provision for professional training would help schools to make more effective use of ordained ministers of religion who for some time past have been recruited as specialist teachers. . . . Questions will not be asked if the pupils feel they do not know their teacher; they cannot be properly answered unless the teacher can get behind the fumbling words to the real problem that puzzles the pupil.[5]

It looks then as if the present situation is wide open for those who wish to assert that if, in the first place, the state had not driven such a wedge between church and school, less would be heard of this sort of problem. Such persons would, no doubt, argue that whatever the faults of the nineteenth-century church-run schools, it could hardly be said that their moral and religious instruction suffered from being impersonal! They would contend that had there been less state intervention, the growth that was already well under way in the private sector of education in the nineteenth century would have led to far healthier results. The alienation of the church, they would argue, would not have occurred in the first place, for although modern scientific sub-

4. *Ibid.*, para. 168.
5. *Ibid.*, para. 170.

jects would still have found their way into education, school chapels or chaplains would still have their place in the typical educational environment. Science and religion would have expanded as partners and not been put into such different worlds.

Those 'non-religious' scientists who may interject that the decline of church influence has been not such a bad thing after all must ask themselves again whether their idea of liberty is really the same as that which has been made explicit in this chapter, or whether it is merely the liberty to think and teach only what *they* think and teach. But even on their own scientific grounds it seems they will nowadays be forced to consider the widespread opinion of psychologists and social scientists that religion 'works' in the sense that people who 'have it' seem to be more adjusted to their own personal problems in life.

According to the structure of our ideal democratic state, to repeat, human values can have meaning only if they are the spontaneous and vigorous expression of individuals. It appears obvious that the best way for such values to become clarified and strengthened is through direct contact between the persons who uphold them. After nearly a century of experience it is clearer than ever that attempts to cause values to be communicated through the political process are fraught with serious difficulties inherent in that process itself. For whereas common human values depend for their sustenance on a variety of expression that embraces all individuals and minorities, the political machine, which is preoccupied with 'getting things done', has to resort to the steam roller of majority ruling, a device which results in unsatisfactory compromises. These in turn give rise either to severe and continual friction (as in France) or else to the ultimate acquiescence of minorities (as in England). In both countries it is evident that the cause of 'social cohesion' may well be hindered rather than assisted.

The 1870 'Religious Difficulty'—A Creation of Politics

The failure to find a really adequate solution to the so-called 'religious difficulty' at the time of W. E. Forster's 1870 Education Bill was undoubtedly the main political error to which present English perplexities can be traced. A main purpose of the Bill was to set up School Boards to seek speedier ways of filling the 'gaps' in the private provision of schooling.[6] Hitherto governments had been relying upon subsidies to private and voluntary schools. Since this method was now thought to be too slow in stimulating supply, a new and revolutionary principle, in the form of collectivist or nationalised 'Board' Schools, was introduced. Immediately the question arose whether, and in what form, religious teaching was to be undertaken in these politically created establishments. The debates in Parliament concerned themselves with four possible methods: first, an Act of Parliament to enforce the teaching of one religion in all schools; second, an Act of Parliament to exclude religion altogether from schools; third, the granting of discretion about religious teaching to the government of the day; fourth, the granting of discretion to the new local boards.

The first method was condemned by the Victorians as illiberal. This plan of enforcing one particular kind of religious instruction, it was said, would result in oppressive uniformity. It would ignore or cut down all local varieties wherein lay the strength of English social and religious life. Had not the Schools' Inquiry Commission of 1868 just observed:

> . . . the one good thing that results from the present unsystematic state of education in this country is great variety of type. The one thing in which we have an advantage over Prussia, for in-

6. In Chapter 10 it is argued that the size of these gaps was exaggerated because of statistical errors.

stance, is that our schools are not moulded into the sort of mechanical uniformity which is, perhaps, the chief defect in the Prussian system.[7]

The second method, the enactment that religion should be excluded altogether from Board Schools, provoked a controversy which vividly illustrates the deficiency inherent in the process of collective political provision of education. The supporters of this method contended that if schools, which were supported by local rates, were to be sectarian, then minorities would be compelled to pay for the kind of religious teaching that was favoured by a majority. Forster retorted that he could not introduce a Bill to enact that the Bible was not to be taught in schools because this would have *encountered great opposition*. Thus revealing himself as a victim of the inflexible machinery of politics, a machinery which works by the counting of votes and the tyranny of majority wishes, Forster went on to make the anguished complaint that to forbid Bible teaching in school would be to get rid of the *religious* difficulty by replacing it by an *irreligious* difficulty. He was therefore forced to choose the solution which would give the politician the least trouble, the one which would offend only the minority, not the majority:

> The religious difficulty is a great difficulty, I admit; but if we were in our educational zeal to exclude this book [the Bible] by Act of Parliament the irreligious difficulty we should thereby create would be far greater. By retaining its use in schools some individuals may object to pay the school rate on account of the particular religion supposed to be favoured at the schools; but were we to say that the *majority* were not to have their children taught the

7. Nineteenth Century Parliamentary Papers: Schools Inquiry Commission, 1868, Vol. I, p. 477.

Bible even if they desired it, we should have the school rates objected to, not by *individuals*, but by large *multitudes*.[8] (My italics)

The leader of the 'non-sectarians', Mr. Dixon, the member for Birmingham, who argued that 'in schools aided by rates the teaching ought to be unsectarian and even secular . . . ' explained that unsectarian teaching was a 'teaching which excluded all Christian dogmas and tenets, but not Christian precepts; while secular education excluded all Christian dogmas, tenets, and precepts . . . ' An unsectarian programme, Dixon contended, would be likely to secure 'more Christian harmony'. Lord Robert Montagu responded that this kind of harmony would be the harmony 'in a congregation of the dead . . . ' It was impossible, he maintained, to meet Dixon's request to inculcate 'the neutral subjects on which we are all agreed' and that 'which belongs to our common Christianity'. No one, objected Montagu, could 'conceive a substantial truth—an objective reality which was common to all opinions about it'.

The 'non-sectarians' had further argued that religion was the main responsibility of the church and that worship should therefore be practised outside school hours and especially on Sunday. Montagu replied that religion did not belong to one day or to one time more than another. If the neutralised 'common Christianity' proposed for the schools could successfully explain common tenets, why was it not proposed to have it taught on Sundays as well as weekdays? Again, to object to religious teaching because it caused strife was beside the point, thought Montagu. Strife was a healthy consequence of free expression; it arose when people stood up for their opinions:

8. Debate in Parliament on the Elementary Education Bill, 1870. A verbatim report prepared by the National Education Union, 1870, p. 47.

Certain religious education, even with strife, seemed better than the exclusion of religion from the schools in order that there might be that peace which reigns in the Shades of Hades. All these arguments about strife and about dogmas, were shallow, and did not go below the superficial appearance of things. Every proposition which asserted a general truth, and therefore every proposition which could influence a man's character or determine his conduct, must necessarily be dogmatic. It must be so, because it must exclude the general contrary proposition and all the particular contradictory propositions. Religious platitudes, on the other hand, and lukewarm-water moralities, could not stir up strife, for they were not worthy of dissent, and must be spued out of the mouth. The exacerbated antagonisms of religious tenets were far preferable to the lukewarm notions of a common Christianity.[9]

The third method of treating the religious difficulty, whereby the government of the day was to have discretion in all cases, was already in operation. Governments had been allocating subsidies to schools from central government revenue (as distinct from local rates) for many years before 1870. Those local people who subscribed to establish a school had to write to the Privy Council, stating their intention of building a school and that a certain type of religious instruction was to be given. The Privy Council would reply by sending a draft deed of management which determined, in accordance with the proposal of the subscribers, the management and the type of religious teaching of the school. In this way the government determined, through the Privy Council, the kind of school suitable to the specific population for whom it was intended. It thus appears that in a sense Anglicans, for instance, had been subsidising Catholics and *vice versa* for a long time since, as general taxpayers, both contributed to the central

9. *Ibid.*, pp. 64, 65.

revenue out of which the subsidies came. This particular method of cross-subsidisation, however, does not seem to have aroused much conflict between the religious groups. It was only when taxation included the principle of lost rating which came with the Board School, that matters came to a head. Once adopted this system was of course expected to increase substantially the magnitude of cross-subsidisation.

But the appropriateness and efficiency of this third method[10] was contested on the grounds that it was too slow; according to the member for Stroud, this system 'had not yet covered the country with schools'. What was wanted was a method which could hasten the existing rate of progress. Board schools had to be hustled into existence to meet the supply emergency.[11] They could not wait to make appropriate religious groupings each in separate negotiation with the Privy Council. The religious difficulty therefore remained.

The fourth method of dealing with the problem was proposed by the 1870 Bill. Local boards were to be given the duty of determining the religious instruction in all the schools within their district; or of deciding whether religious instruction should be given at all. Boards were to be elected in the towns by the Town Council and in the country by the Vestries. Forster announced that parents were to pay fees except in cases of extreme poverty:

> We also empower the school board to give free tickets to parents who they think really cannot afford to pay for the education of their children; and we take care that those free tickets shall have no stigma of pauperism attached to them. We do not give up the school fees, and indeed we keep to the present proportions—

10. This method was in principle equivalent to the 'direct grant' system which applies to a few independent schools today.

11. This particular argument was crucial and so Chapter 10 is wholly devoted to a retrospective test of its validity.

namely, of about one-third raised from the parents, one-third out of the public taxes, and one-third out of local funds. Where the local funds are not raised by voluntary subscriptions the rates will come into action.[12]

Again Robert Montagu objected. He expressed his lack of confidence in the kind of people who were currently being appointed by a system of double election; the ratepayers, for instance, were to elect the Town Council which in turn was to elect the Board. This, he said, would make for still more remote control, and he probably had in mind the difficulty that people do not vote for a Town Council on just one issue, education; they vote for other services too, and therefore make inevitable all the disadvantages of a 'package deal'. Montagu's crucial objection, however, was that a bare majority on a School Board could impose its religious preference on a large minority. He pointed to the example of Liverpool. The 'low residuum' for whom the Board Schools were to provide consisted largely of an immigrant Irish population which was Roman Catholic. Was it in accordance with liberal principles, asked Montagu, that such poor children, mostly children of Roman Catholic parents, should be dealt with as the School Boards might choose?

> They might establish a Church school, or a school for secular education—which was even more distasteful to Roman Catholics—but they certainly would never build a purely Roman Catholic School.[13]

The debate continued in the Commons for six months. The final outcome favoured the fourth method but with a compro-

12. *Ibid.*, p. 13.
13. *Ibid.*, p. 70.

mise which restricted the alternatives open to the School Board without removing from them their authority over religious teaching. There was introduced into the Act a clause, which still remains law, stating that 'no religious catechism or religious formulary distinctive of any denomination' is to be taught in any Board School.[14] Moreover Section 7 (1) provided a 'Conscience Clause' which gave the parent the right to see that his child was removed from religious instruction classes within the school. But although this clause has been claimed as a great triumph of political commonsense, the most skilful politician could not claim that it was anything more than a second-best solution. A minority which was told that they need not make use of religious teaching paid for with their own money could not possibly regard the Conscience Clause as adequate compensation. If, for instance, the minority comprised one fifth of the electorate, the majority might try to excuse itself with the thought that the solution was at least 80 per cent correct. But to any individual within the minority it was 100 per cent incorrect. This example illustrates most clearly the main weakness of collective provision. In the 1870 debate Vernon Harcourt exposed the problem in the following terms:

> It is like saying to the minority: 'We have made you pay for a dinner consisting of materials which you cannot consume, but if you wish it we will be so gracious and liberal as to allow you not to eat it!'

14. This is known as the Cowper-Temple clause. Disraeli warned that a religion without formularies was, in fact, a new religion, and that in leaving its exposition to the teachers we were creating a new sacerdotal class. 'Mr Gladstone and Mr Forster both admitted that logically the view of the opposition was unassailable: but as a practical question they saw no solution possible which did not carry the concession as far as they proposed.'—H. Craik, *The State in Its Relation to Education*, Macmillan, 1896.

This pungent comment originally referred to the problem facing those minorities who in 1870 lived in the 'gap' areas. Today, it applies to the whole parental population, since those who dislike the menu provided by our monopolistic and 'zoned' state schools are certainly 'free' to buy alternative education, but on the understanding that their tax contributions to the state system will not be refunded.

The 1870 Act—A Pyrrhic Victory

With the individualist premise stated at the beginning of this chapter, and a thorough application of the economist's 'neighbourhood effect' analysis (or social cost/benefit analysis), what overall assessment of the 1870 Act can now be made? The first general point to make (explained in more detail in Chapter 10) is that this same piece of legislation which set out to fill certain 'gaps' has itself created other 'gaps' of a more subtle but no less important nature. In other words it is clear that the original state intervention to reduce certain presumed social costs (or adverse neighbourhood effects) has precipitated serious social costs itself, which are uniquely associated with the process of legislation.

To get a clear view of the precise nature of the social costs arising from the 1870 legislation itself, it must first be observed that the Board Schools which originated in that Act subsequently became the prototypes of the state schools which now really do 'cover the country'; they provided, in fact, an accidental instrument for the state take-over of existing schools and the nationalisation at birth of subsequent ones. This process will be explained in much more detail in Chapter 10, but for the moment the following quotation will serve to give the general picture:

. . . the Board Schools tended to be better equipped, larger, and more efficient, and the voluntary schools found the strain of competing with institutions aided by the rates heavier and heavier.[15]

The main point here is that, by keeping potential competitors away and driving others out of existence, the local authorities have seen to it that the synthetic structure of religious education prescribed originally for a few Board Schools has been so diffused that it is now a typical part of English education. In so far as this structure leads to inefficient teaching of religion, as the 1963 Newsom Report indicates, and in so far as it is connected with a prevailing moral 'drift' this is a social cost which has its origin in the early legislation and one which spread very rapidly over the country. Thus by 1900 the Board Schools had so widened the 'gaps' for themselves that they already contained 54 per cent of the total elementary school population, the education of which was therefore placed increasingly under all the moral and religious disadvantages referred to in this chapter. It is interesting that in 1964 a British Home Secretary, calling on the community as a whole to try to solve the growing wave of delinquency, wistfully observed that in Victorian times religion and moral precepts were still powerful as deterrents to wrongdoing. He complained that for those who had lost belief and respect nothing firm had been put in their place. 'Feet are on shifting sands'.[16] Those who share his views should presumably consider the extent to which the evolution of our education system has contributed to this general malaise. To put the argument in different terms: economists postulate that education is an avenue for the

15. H. C. Barnard, *A Short History of English Education*, University of London Press, 1949, p. 196.
16. Home Office, *Report on the Work of the Children's Department 1961–63*, HMSO, March 1964.

communication of our heritage of common values and as such it provides social benefits. The present analysis indicates that *one particular form of education* (state schooling) has resulted in the emasculation of some of these values so that it is more appropriate to treat this 'contribution' not as a social benefit but as a social cost.

A second and more specific judgement that can be made of the 1870 Act relates to the four methods of solving the 'religious difficulty' which Forster examined. It seems clear that these methods did not exhaust the possibilities available. Other methods would have suggested themselves had he concentrated his attention more on the causes of the alleged 'gaps'. According to the reports, it was not so much that *some* parents did not want to school their children as their lack of money to do so which was the chief obstacle. On Forster's own figures, which he quoted during the first reading of the 1870 Bill, *most* parents voluntarily paid fees, and these covered one-third of the current cost of education (these fees contributed £420,000 in 1869). This seems to be a remarkable tribute to average Victorian parental responsibility when we remember that wages were much lower than they are today and that children could make an important contribution to family income, especially at times of unemployment and sickness. Consider especially parents who were poor largely because they had large families to keep. Most of them, according to the 1870 debate, withdrew their children from school quite early not because they were negligent but because their net incomes were obviously too low for them to continue with the school fees. In other words the basic trouble was poverty, not negligence.

Forster's solution of 'school boards' was, in this respect, only meeting the problem at one remove. To create a new political institution, the school board, to cater for an existing institution, the poor family, could only be justified if there were no technical means available for meeting the poverty of the latter more directly. Forster did not demonstrate adequately that this was so. Indeed, in his own provision that in cases of extreme poverty 'free tickets' were to be given to poor children to enter Board Schools, he came close to another solution which was worthy of much greater attention. For if 'free tickets' could be given to poor families for Board Schools, why not for *any* school? The administrative procedure of refunding and inspecting the schools that received these tickets would have been far cheaper and less complicated than his Board School method.[17] Furthermore, the 'gaps' were to be found typically in the poorest localities; since the Board Schools were partly financed by rates on these localities, a form of taxation which is particularly regressive (i.e. takes a larger proportion of income from the poor and puts a particularly heavy burden on large families), the problem of poverty was unnecessarily exacerbated. Indeed the inevitable levy of local rates was one explanation of the subsequent phenomena of parents transferring their children from voluntary schools to the new Board Schools. A system of 'free tickets' for the poor financed by the existing Privy Council central fund for education would have avoided this situation. Moreover, because the 'free tickets' would not have been 'tied' to a particular school, the religious difficulty would have been largely overcome. Such tickets in the hands of the Liverpool Irish, for instance, would have naturally given rise to a demand for Catholic schooling in their area and the problem would have quietly settled itself.

17. The 1870 Act (Section 25) did in fact allow the school board to pay school fees at any non-Board Schools if they thought fit. But this power does not seem to have been intended as the main instrument of the legislation and in practice it was not widely used. School boards with their own schools disliked paying for people to go to rival establishments.

Moreover it would have largely avoided the social injustice, which has since grown, of forcing minorities to 'pay twice' if they wish to secure their real preference. Finally, at the prevailing rate of natural expansion of schooling and bearing in mind the continuing expansion of the national income in the nineteenth century, the problem of the 'gaps' could have been expected to diminish anyway.[18]

As it was, Forster presented Parliament with a false dilemma. His decision was partly due no doubt to a fashionable and almost doctrinaire late nineteenth-century belief in the effectiveness of local or municipal government, a belief which seems to have no deeper foundation than the observation that other countries had more of it than his own country. It was, he thought, a disgrace that England was 'behind almost every other civilised country, whether in America or on the Continent of Europe, in respect of rural "municipal" organisation'. The clamour for compulsion in education also stemmed from the fact that England was about the only country in Europe without it. In neither case could a

18. One indication (many others will be given in Chapter 10) of the pace at which schools were in fact 'covering the country' may be given here. It consists of information about existing schools collected in the nineteenth century by the enumerators of the 1851 population census:

1851 Census (School Appendix)

Dates at Which Existing Schools Were Established

	Before 1801	1801 to 181	1811 to 1821	1821 to 1831	1831 to 1841	1841 to 1851	Date not specified
*	487	443	1,087	2,217	4,432	16,760	3,999
†	2,876	599	1,120	1,265	3,035	5,454	1,062

*Private, i.e. entirely profit-making.
†Public, i.e. supported in any degree for non-profit objectives.

twentieth-century rational critic claim that such argument followed the strictest path of logic.

This chapter has been devoted to the subject of 'common values'. It will end with quotations which have a more direct bearing on what Burton Weisbrod calls the need for 'public
spiritedness or social consciousness of one's neighbour', a need
he associates with education. That the English state education
system is not yet entirely successful in this respect seems to be
yet another view of the Newsom Report:

> Boys and girls growing up in a welfare state, for instance, ought to
> know how the social services are paid for and how they operate
> locally. They ought also to realise the continuing need for sensi-
> ble self-help and for voluntary assistance to those unable to help
> themselves. If the school is one which engages in community ser-
> vice projects, these ideas will not be unfamiliar. But we note, for
> example, that a church organisation which has held conferences
> for some 2,000 school leavers records 'We have yet to meet any
> suggestion that any of their own money should be used for chari-
> table or humanitarian or religious purposes, on a budgeted
> basis.'[19]

It is indeed ironic that old-fashioned phrases like 'voluntary assistance' and 'self-help' are coming back into the language a century after Gladstone warned:

> It appears to me clear that the day you sanction compulsory rating
> for the purpose of education you sign the death-warrant of volun-
> tary exertions. . . . If this be the true tendency of the system
> which my noble friend seeks to introduce, are we preparing to
> undergo the risk of extinguishing *that vast amount of voluntary
> effort which now exists throughout the country?* Aid it you may;

19. *Half Our Future, op. cit.*, para. 212.

strengthen, and invigorate, and enlarge it you may; you have done so to an extraordinary degree; you have every encouragement to persevere in the same course; but always recollect that you depend upon influences of which you get the benefit, but which are not at your command—influences which you may, perchance, in an unhappy day, extinguish, but which you can never create.[20] (My italics)

20. Education Debate, House of Commons, 1856. Details of the 'vast amount of voluntary effort', as also of the way in which much of it was subsequently extinguished as Gladstone feared, are given in Chapter 10.

CHAPTER SEVEN

Education and Economic Growth

There is another widely postulated 'neighbourhood benefit' from education which remains to be considered. This can be summed up in the proposition that education is an investment which increases the real income of all taxpayers regardless of the degree to which the 'free' education service is used by any one of them for his own direct purposes.

Before looking at this idea in this chapter it will be necessary to meet the objections of those who protest that it debases education to test it for its material rewards. Education, it is urged, is noble, sublime, an end in itself. The first point to be made in reply to this sort of objection is that an activity which costs annually over £2,000 million and which claimed over twice as much public expenditure in 1969 as in 1961 can hardly expect to get away with no economic scrutiny at all. The second point to observe is that among those who plead that education is to be above mere monetary consideration the teachers' organisations are most prominent. These of course are also interested in the collective negotiation of salaries which figure so largely in the swelling expenditures mentioned above, so they can hardly be described as being the most disinterested bodies to pass judgement.

More important is the question of how to settle priorities when so many other services are also being described by their protagonists as being 'an essential' or 'a necessity' for which we must not count the cost. For instance, similar absolute claims are made for public health expenditures—'We cannot afford not to have it', 'Health is Wealth', 'Health is invaluable, it is a must'. The unhappy and inescapable fact is, of course, that within a tax budget, an extra million pounds spent on hospitals is often, by necessity, a million pounds less for schools and *vice versa*. The onus is upon those who say that such expenditures are 'different' to show how they would settle these struggles between the 'absolutes'. The moment they attempt to do so, however, they too are in the world of economic assessment.

Apart from this, even if people do take part in educational activities from motives which exclude financial consideration, no harm is done by those who wish to make systematic note of the economic consequences or by-products of these activities. The Robbins Committee certainly did not think that education was 'contaminated' by economic assessment. Indeed they gave economic productivity a conspicuous place among the primary objectives of education:

> We deceive ourselves if we claim that more than a small fraction of students in institutions of higher education would be where they are if there were no significance for their future careers in what they hear and read; and it is a mistake to suppose that there is anything discreditable in this. Certainly this was not the attitude of the past: the ancient universities of Europe were founded to promote the training of the clergy, doctors and lawyers; and though at times there may have been many who attended for the pursuit of pure knowledge or of pleasure, they must surely have been a minority. And it must be recognised that in our own times, progress—and particularly the maintenance of a competitive position depends to a much greater extent than ever before on skills demanding special training.[1]

1. *Higher Education, op. cit.*, para. 25.

Similarly the Crowther Report recognised the same sort of point:

> More recently, however, the emphasis has come back to education as an investment. There are perhaps two special reasons for this. The first is the new doctrine (how new few people now remember) that the nation can control its own economic development. And secondly, there is the new emphasis placed upon the belief that the prosperity, and even the safety, of the nation depend on 'keeping up in the economic race'.[2]

Now that it is becoming thus fashionable to speak of the economic aspects of education we are faced with another phenomenon. Many of those with personal stakes in education, once outraged by the suggestion that it could be treated like an industry, are now likely to be more outraged if people 'can't see' that it is the 'most important' industry we have. In this way one dogma replaces another as a result of partisan anxiety to rationalise growing public expenditure on education under all circumstances. It is imperative, therefore, that we exercise particular caution before proceeding with this analysis; indeed most economists themselves having a vested interest in education must be aware that their professional integrity is here especially vulnerable.

The Need for Definition

How can we make a sober assessment of the economic worth of education and how far is it the proper business of the state to

2. See also *Conditions Favourable to Faster Growth*, HMSO for the National Economic Development Council, 1963, p. 1. This document, which urges more government expenditure on education, admits that there is no easy way of quantifying the 'rate of return' and that the methods so far used are debatable. It seems that the whole notion of education for growth can still claim no more precision than an ordinary hunch.

provide it once this kind of investment is shown to be desirable? The first essential is to insist on a proper definition of terms used in discussion since there is probably no other field where semantic snares are so numerous. Consider, for instance, the following argument: improvement in knowledge is the major source of economic growth; education is the major avenue of knowledge; therefore society will benefit by more public expenditure on education.

Although one could quarrel even with certain aspects of the first part of this syllogism (knowledge = growth), let it be accepted for the moment. The interesting question is what to make of the term 'education' in the second proposition, the 'education' which is supposed to be the major avenue of knowledge? Apparently it can only be located by noting every gateway, channel, road or line of communication in ideas, every source of inspiration and every medium of discovery. In fact the word 'education' does not do full justice to the idea involved and it groans under the weight of so many connotations. But notice the semantics of the second and third propositions. The concluding statement implies only that narrower and more popular notion of education which is the formal institutional activity (mainly schooling) to which public expenditure has been directed. This is like saying: 'Industry creates wealth, therefore let there be more public expenditure on industry', when we mean more expenditure, say, on nationalised electricity, railway, coal industries to the neglect of the non-nationalised sector among which of course are to be found the less obvious and less politically organised 'money-spinners' ranging from cosmetics to stereos and from exports of antiques to 'pop' singers. Professor Fritz Machlup's classification of the economically useful knowledge that is produced through education is a useful precautionary guide. We should distinguish, he says, (1) education in the home; (2) education in school;

(3) training on the job; (4) instruction in church; (5) training in the armed forces; (6) education through television; (7) self-education; and (8) learning from experience.[3]

Such classification is necessary because it draws attention to the opportunities foregone (opportunity costs) if we direct our scarce resources only towards one category, e.g. the public sector (no. 2). Furthermore, even within the categories most favoured by the public expenditure (schools and universities), not every subject or combination of subjects has the same *economic* significance, and therefore even proposals to spend more on *formal* education for economic growth are unhelpful unless priorities, for example, between Greek and engineering, are assessed as carefully as possible. Yet, in spite of this elementary economic axiom, in Britain there has been hardly any attempt to measure the differential effectiveness of education according to the categories mentioned. Only too often it seems we are expected to accept the quiet assumption that formal schooling can be equated with 'education'. Yet it is no more satisfactory intuitively to assert that because formal schooling (including college and university activity) is the biggest kind of education, it therefore requires the monopoly of our attention, than it is to claim that since coal is at present our biggest source of fuel supply we should neglect the use of oil or nuclear energy. Intuition in any case is not a substitute for measurement. Systematic investigation often yields information which confounds our fondest beliefs. The American economist, Professor George J. Stigler, who measured the kind of education which leads to increases in income-earning power of the individual, concluded that in 1940 as much as *two-thirds* of it was acquired not in colleges or schools but by experience and instruction within the factory or office.

3. *The Production and Distribution of Knowledge*, Princeton, 1962, p. 51.

It is to be expected that in a dynamic economy existing knowledge will suffer much obsolescence. For instance, those who have been well-schooled in a municipal college of commerce on double-entry book-keeping may have to be 'schooled' all over again most probably on the premises of their employers who use mechanised accounts. The more out-of-date the teaching in our formal educational institutions the more resources we can expect to be devoted to such on-the-job training. But the more firms have to resort to their own training the more we should suspect that formal education has become too insular and protected. Although it may be in the interests of those employed in formal teaching to avoid recommending interference from outside, some such pressure is necessary if we want any effective check on the efficiency of the allocation of our scarce educational resources.

> It is the nature of teachers to recommend that which they know best themselves. To recommend anything else is to impose on themselves the trouble of going to school again. . . . Besides there is nothing in the occupation of a teacher which tends to give that large acquaintance with men and things which enables a man to discover what are the wants of society in respect of instruction, and how those wants may be supplied. Nor has the state any peculiar means of forming a right conclusion on this subject.[4]

Educational Inbreeding

It has now become part of our accepted political technology that when a government requires advice on education it resorts first and foremost to 'those in education'. The organised teaching profession is an obvious choice since politicians like to negotiate

4. A witness to the 1868 Schools Enquiry.

with identifiable flesh and blood persons; whereas the 'untidy' and heterogeneous categories in Professor Machlup's classification do not lend themselves so conveniently to such direct political representation. The Robbins Report was typical of most other official documents in that it was mainly the work of persons engaged in formal educational institutions who were appointed by a Minister with a department composed mainly of individuals with a similar background. The Minister, wanting counsel on education, confined the Robbins terms of reference to a review of 'the pattern of *full-time* higher education in Great Britain and in the light of *national needs and resources* . . .' (My italics) However, this method of imposing upon the representatives of one part of a large industry the duty of assessing the 'needs' of the whole of it seems to invite all the disadvantages of sectional inbreeding. It is not surprising then that state educationists applauded the Robbins proposal to increase aggregate public expenditure on full-time higher education (i.e. colleges and universities) from £206 million to about £742 million annually by 1980 without too much attention to internal priorities and none at all to the external opportunity-costs of alternative types of education foregone.

More Discriminating Methods of Assessment

Several economists have recently been attempting to find a systematic method of correlating formal education with economic prosperity in order to find appropriate government targets.

The Income Differential Approach

This approach is to be found in the work of the Americans G. Becker and T. Schultz. It consists of contrasting the lifetime earnings of more 'educated' persons with others who are less 'educated'. The positive difference is expressed as a net return to education and is then related to the costs involved. In this way it has been shown that, at least in the recent past, an American with full college education has earned much more than other Americans. Typical estimates of returns to such higher education at different periods have varied between 8 per cent and 14 per cent in the USA, but so far no such calculations have been made for the United Kingdom.

Before governments can confidently plan on the basis of cost/benefit studies, several problems demand serious consideration. First, there is the question of costs. Conceptually the costs of a person's education are taken to be the opportunity costs, that is the full value of the hours sacrificed to education, and this in turn can theoretically be estimated from the monetary valuation of all the benefits he could have enjoyed had he not spent the time on education. One alternative use of his time could be leisure. But it is difficult enough to place a money value on the leisure of any one person let alone having to face the problem of aggregation so as to include all those who are being considered for education. Another alternative use of time is remunerative employment. Again a wealth of information is needed to put a realistic money value on the alternatives postulated.

Next on the matter of benefits. First of all it is difficult to assess the non-financial benefits enjoyed during education. And even the financial benefits are uncertain. Can we conclude that the returns now being enjoyed by one person from education given in the 1930s are an entirely true measure of the returns to be expected from a similar period of education given to another person in the 1960s?

Again the first person's higher income may be partly attributable to superior intelligence or ambition so that it is difficult to separate the independent contribution of education. Economists try to allow for this difference but their methods are so far somewhat arbitrary. Second, high rates of earnings may persist in certain sectors, not directly because of wider investment in the education appropriate to such occupations, but because of the specially strong monopoly power in these sectors. In these cases, and there are many of them, the high differential earnings do not call primarily for more education but for remedial policy measures to remove the market imperfection. For instance, Professor Friedman's argument that the relatively high earnings enjoyed by American doctors can be partly attributed to the American Medical Association's success in limiting new entrants to the profession points first to the need for breaking down such artificial barriers. In so far as stiffer and stiffer examinations are used as a means of keeping down the annual rates of entry, the associated increases in education cannot claim credit for economic growth; indeed such increases are evidence of obstacles to growth and a relative waste of resources.

To insist, for instance, that an individual who is training to be an accountant should besides accountancy learn two foreign languages as well as the differential calculus may be commendable to educationists and profitable to a professional association of accountants, but it is not necessarily the most rational allocation of scarce resources from a consumer's or taxpayer's point of view. To take another example, once the right to determine standards of teaching is virtually granted to professional teaching bodies the taxpayers cannot be entirely sure that the raising of entry requirements for the teaching profession springs from genuine 'educational' considerations rather than from sectional interest. In England the teaching organisations have recently insisted on the substitution of a three-year for a two-year training course at a time which coincides with an awkward student population bulge and teacher shortage. Such a move at one stroke checks the annual supply of education personnel and increases the demand, so increasing the supply 'price' of teachers. Their supply will be reduced because of the initial reduction of the numbers of more experienced teachers leaving training college, whereas demand as a whole will be increased since more experienced teachers will be required to staff the expanding training colleges.

Since we cannot be confident that professional restrictions and political lobbying play an unimportant role in determining relative incomes, 'social returns' to education based on statistics of income differentials can be seriously misleading. For if the incomes of certain occupations are deliberately and continually rigged by their organised leaders using monopolistic practices, they will persistently maintain their income differential. This being so, to say that education into such an occupation yields a return to an individual and to society of, say, 20 per cent, is misleading. First, even to an individual the investment will only pay off if he passes the necessary examinations and succeeds in fulfilling other requirements to make himself a member of the privileged group. Second, even if he does so, society will not be better off. For it could have obtained his services at lower cost had it concentrated its attention on weakening the monopoly power of the professional group. This would mean making entry less difficult, so increasing the number of willing recruits and reducing the costs of an otherwise too ambitious training programme.

It has been pointed out by Messrs T. Balogh and P. P. Streeten that if those who depend on the income differential approach for calculating returns to education were to apply it to many underdeveloped countries they would discover even higher rates of return than at home:

All this would show, however, is that pay scales in the civil service, in universities and in the professions are still governed by the traditional standards of a feudal or colonial aristocracy and by natural or artificial restrictions. It would provide no clue as to how public money ought to be distributed between 'investment' in 'physical capital' and in people . . . This approach . . . not only appeals to the snobbery and self-esteem of the educated, appearing to provide an economic justification of existing income differentials, but also buttresses vested interests.[5]

Similarly H. G. Shaffer has argued[6] that because in America there is a higher return to white than to non-white labour the implication of a policy that regards education as a desirable investment is that expenditure should be marginally switched from one group to the other. The general point is that we must be on guard against applying hastily the results of the cost/benefit studies of statisticians who draw upon data set in an environment assumed to be 'given'. Clearly it is important that prior attention should be given to the constitutional deformities that already exist in that environment, since otherwise these evils are in danger of being aggravated.

Where such monopoly practices are absent there is more to be said for the income differential measure of education investment. For in the ordinary competitive case an increase in the price of a service may indeed be the result of genuine increase in the demand for it. Moreover if this price differential sticks over a long period we can suspect that demand has been constantly increasing. A *marginal* increase in the supply of per-

5. 'The Coefficient of Ignorance', *Bulletin* of the Oxford University Institute of Economics and Statistics, vol. 25, 1963.

6. 'Investment in Human Capital: Comment', *American Economic Review*, December 1961.

sons educating themselves for this occupation is then a correct and welcome response. But even here one has to be careful. For how big is marginal? The more entrants there are the more the income differential will be removed and the less the investment will be worth. It pays therefore to go carefully, investing a bit at a time. To have indiscriminate educational campaigns and surges is the wrong policy and simply to proclaim that education 'as a whole' pays is mere sloganising. It is just as unhelpful to assert that industry 'as a whole' is profitable. Even though recent estimates put a return to American higher education at 12 per cent at the outside, it may still be possible to get 30 per cent from investment in a gold mine. The logic of those who neglect the marginal approach and who insist on looking at things as 'wholes' would presumably result in the absurdity of their recommending withdrawing all expenditure on education and spending it on gold mining!

The Manpower-Needs Approach
In view of all these difficulties in picking the educational winner from an investment point of view, the important question is: who *should* bear the responsibility of making the crucial decisions? One way would be to leave it to individuals after returning to them the taxes which are normally used for state education expenditure and to assist them with both information and a suitable market for educational loans. In lieu of this, however, and for reasons that are sometimes called 'institutional' (which often seems to mean that because we have already given ourselves one set of institutions in the past we have become so conditioned to them by some sort of self-hypnotic process that we are petrified against change), some kind of manpower planning by central authority is often presented as a 'necessary' function of government. Accordingly employers are asked by government officials

how many specially qualified persons they will need at a given future period and ratios of trained manpower to total employment are projected into the future bearing in mind 'likely shifts' in the importance of different industries.

It would take a very bold person indeed to claim that such central forecasts have so far been of substantial advantage. It is one thing for employers to say that they will 'need' so many qualified employees in the future; it is quite another thing that they should be willing to pay the costs of 'buying' them when the time comes. Usually the 'recipe' for the production of goods and services is not inexorably rigid. Whereas in the field of chemistry it is known that H_2O produces water, and that the addition of $1H$ will not increase output, such assymetrical increase of the 'ingredients' *is* possible in the production of many industrial products where H is, say, skilled and O is unskilled labour, or where H is capital and O is labour. Even if the 'recipes' were rigid (like H_2O) there is, in a dynamic economy, continual invention of new products and processes bringing with it a constantly changing permutation of optimum resource use. This means not only that the demands for different factors of production (such as specially educated labour) shift in relative intensity but also that the product in question may be subject to an increase or a decrease in demand. For all these reasons, yesterday's manpower plan can look hopelessly out of date today. As an example of the way in which forecasts can go awry, consider the estimate of the Ridley Committee on fuel and power in 1951 (Table 4) acting on what it thought to be the 'best estimate of the pattern and scale of consumption' for ten years' ahead, and compare it with the actual out-turn.[7]

7. Taken from Ralph Harris, 'Economic Forecasting: Projections or Targets?', *Statist*, 24 January 1964, p. 241.

TABLE 4

Changes in Fuel Consumption, 1951–61

	Ridley Estimate (per cent)	Actual Change in Consumption (per cent)
Coal	− 4	− 28
Coke	+41	− 1
Gas	+27	− 4
Electricity	+38	+ 84
Oil fuels	+82	+250
Total in coal equivalent tons	+16	+ 9

Another hazardous element in forecasting is the uncertain future behaviour of import and export price ratios (the terms of trade). Many forecasts have been exploded, for instance, because they were made at a time when their authors were obsessed with the belief that the dollar would always be a hard currency, a belief which has subsequently been disproved by events.

The fear is sometimes expressed that if, in the absence of central manpower planning, individuals were left to their own discretion as to which occupation to train for (as in the first solution on p. 118) there would be chaos. If there is at present a shortage of design engineers, it is argued, their inevitably high salary would attract enormous numbers to train for that occupation. When they were trained there would then be a sudden glut which would depress the salary, or prevent it rising as fast as others, or cause unemployment. The most appropriate reply to this fear is to ask whether a system of manpower planning will not make things even worse. Governments which are fond of such 'lumpy' decisions as 5-year plans and 'recruitment campaigns' often do not like the embarrassment of having to change their courses of action once set in motion. This being so, they may well over-supply a given type of scientist, for instance, through their rigid adherence to their plans in the face of changing and unforeseen circumstances. The 'see-saw' effect on salaries or employment may then be worse confounded. Thus the present (1965) shortage of doctors in Britain has been blamed on the 1957 Willink Committee's recommendations. This committee, fearing a surplus of doctors, recommended a 10 per cent reduction in the intake of medical students. This reduction lasted until 1961 with the result that hospitals and GP services are now receiving too few recruits and will do so until 1966.

It has been appealing and prestige-winning for political parties to vie with one another on the number of scientists they will or can 'produce'. This phenomenon has been especially marked since the belated and apparently frightening discovery of the impressive number of scientists being produced in post-war Stalinist Russia. But any assessment of the effectiveness of the subsequent British manpower planning schemes must take into account that the British 1961 Census of Population showed that out of a total of about 260,000 scientists and technologists 50,000 were in jobs that did not make full and direct use of their qualifications.[8] Where career choices are made collectively in surges, any errors that ensue will be large and dramatic compared with a situation of dispersed and discrete decision-making by the individuals concerned, aided by the best information and advice they can get, bearing in mind that they will lose personally by wrong

8. The governments of many underdeveloped countries seem to be so overawed with the word 'education' that their plans for educational investments often misfire in a much more conspicuous way. Thus W. Malenbaum has discovered that unemployment in India varied directly with the degree of higher education. Quoted by T. Balogh and P. P. Streeten, *op. cit.*, from *Pacific Affairs*, June 1957.

calculation. Scientists are a heterogeneous body of people and governments probably stand to lose less in terms of votes from their errors of planning than if they were a politically organised and articulate group. On the other hand, in so far as particular groups of scientists or other professionals *are* thus organised, the danger is that governments, in order to avoid the embarrassment of events, may seek the powers to 'make' their own predictions come true. This can be done, for instance, by tactically yielding to the demands for subsidies and taxes, all in the aid of threatened pressure groups of highly trained specialists who complain that they were originally encouraged to make irrevocable career choices by an earlier government, in line with its previous planning estimates.

From the viewpoint of growth, whatever the relative failings of dispersed private decision-making in education compared with a centrally administered system, there is one outstanding drawback which relates exclusively to the latter. In a mixed economy like ours in which a large proportion of the national income is taxed, any further encroachment by the government will aggravate the already appreciable disincentive effects of taxation, since revenues from taxes will have to go up still more to finance more education. Some observers (including the Robbins Committee) do argue, of course, that extra tax revenues will come from the higher national productivity to which extra education is supposed to contribute. One would have more confidence in this argument, first, if it was made clearer what the intended connection between economic growth and education was supposed to be, second, if politicians were not already preempting the anticipated fruits of economic growth for other objects such as housing and pensions, and third, if the share of the government sector was stable and not already on the increase as it is at present. In any case, even if the revenues for extra education did succeed in coming via *existing* taxes on extra growth, this does not meet the reply that such growth might be still larger if tax rates were *lower* and incentives therefore higher.

The External Economies Argument Again
Even if the direct returns from education measured on the income differential method are less than the investment return from machine tools or gold mines, it is often argued that education should still have priority since it causes many more spillover (neighbourhood) effects which are beneficial to the economy as a whole. The reader may like to look again at page 33 above (Chapter 3) where this theoretical notion was explained in detail. These favourable neighbourhood effects, or external economies as they are sometimes called, are supposed to help economic growth, either by wide 'social' benefits or by spectacular community advantages arising from certain occupations. Take first the social benefits expected from education: the argument is that in so far as education abolishes ignorance and promotes order, it reduces the amount of money necessary, say, for a police force; resources for further economic growth will be released if the expenditure on the latter was greater than on the former. Such apparently is one of the main examples from the social benefits thesis and, as will be shown when the writings of the classical economists are examined, it has enjoyed a very long history. After the empirical survey in Chapter 3 where no evidence could be found that the present system of education led to reduction in crime, one must for the moment take leave to doubt this part of the proposition. In any case the argument seems to assume that if the government did not spend on education but returned the money to ordinary people (e.g. through reduced

taxes) they would not buy in the long run at least the same quantity of education privately. There is no evidence the author knows of that supports this assumption.[9]

The other application of the 'neighbourhood effects' thesis is the argument of special occupation benefits. If I understand it correctly, some occupations are supposed to have what may be called 'halo effects', which are of special significance for economic progress. Thus it is argued that a system of higher education which, for instance, produces doctors may leave 'society' better off in a sense which does not ordinarily apply. If the government did not do anything it is true there would still be doctors, but there would not be *enough* of them. In other words, the present-day doctor (to use him as a hypothesis) who has already been trained with taxpayers' money, may proceed to do them the special favour of subsequently refraining from charging sufficient fees to represent the *full* benefits of services rendered. The taxes are thus worthwhile because of these extra benefits which take the form, e.g. of a healthier working force, happier families, etc. The reader must judge for himself how substantial such 'halo' effects are. For my part I have not so far found any satisfactory evidence to show that professional salaries or fees are in fact so low that they do not already take account of *all* the benefits they render us.

Normally, if a service is useful it will usually command a price in the market sufficient to call it forth, whether it be engineering or window-cleaning. If the demand for any service has increased and its price likewise, the prospect of a high income differential

9. In underdeveloped countries where manpower and central planning are closely linked, mistakes which result, as we have seen, in increased unemployment often lead also to increased disorder. Thus Balogh and Streeten (*op. cit.*) point out that 'An unemployed or unemployable intelligentsia can be a source of revolutionary rather than economic activity, and young people brought up to despise manual work can reinforce the resistances to development.'

spread over a future lifetime will be an incentive to more young people to invest in the appropriate training and more will offer themselves until the increased supply sufficiently dampens their price advantage. It is true that sometimes this mechanism will be blunted because of the inability of intelligent but poor candidates to find the money to invest themselves; higher incomes will then persist. But in this situation we must not jump to the conclusion that those already in the particularly favoured occupation, e.g. scarce doctors, are extra-special mortals with halos producing special 'neighbourhood effects'. It means in all probability that existing doctors are enjoying higher than average earnings (or, if you like, that sudden external economies have been swiftly 'internalised' or appropriated by them in higher earnings). More doctors are 'needed' only in the sense that some potential recruits are finding entry difficult because of technical deficiencies in the capital market.

Such shortcomings are understandable when it is remembered that in the investment in human beings, who in a free society are not mortgageable, it is difficult to give the lender adequate security against default. But the consistent answer to this problem is not to provide education free. A more appropriate solution would be to make individuals bear their own costs of educational investment but to make capital available on terms equivalent to those for physical capital; in other words to institute a loan system, a proposition to which I return in Chapter 12. In this way we avoid paying for a service a second time via extra taxation except in so far as government involves itself in individual administrative expenses.

The External Effects of New Knowledge

How far is the educational process related to *advances* of knowledge as distinct from the *diffusion* of existing knowledge? And if we discover a clear relationship how do we know how much money should be spent on education for this reason? Consider the following statement:

> . . . because new ideas are not used up by being understood, and because the results of basic research are rapidly disseminated free of charge (over the entire world in many cases), the economic contribution of basic research will not be fully reflected in the relative earnings of the producers of this new knowledge.[10]

Granted that such assertions are true, how can we draw unambiguous policy conclusions from them? Education and basic research are not costless; what we want to know is how much of our scarce resources we should devote to them. It is arguable at one extreme, for instance, that if the results of basic research in country A can be spread free of charge to B and C then it would be more economic, in the absence of any special reason such as that of strategy or prestige, for B and C to do no research at all, but simply sit tight and wait. This is the policy from which Japan is popularly believed to have benefited in the past. But if we do decide to invest in knowledge-producing activity ourselves, we must be on guard once more against the semantic traps in interpreting the word 'education'. Educationists, having a special interest in increased expenditure on formal 'institutionalised' education, are tempted at this point to look for any advance in knowledge and to call it 'education'. It is in this way that many people find themselves thinking that the desire for economic progress is interchangeable with the desire for formal education. This of course is naïve. 'Education' is a heterogeneous term and formal education includes such things as athletics and beauty culture which may not be thought to have much bearing on advances in economic knowledge. But, more important, advances

10. Robbins Report, Appendix IV, Part III, p. 86.

in knowledge occur also outside formal educational institutions. Research is done in firms as well as universities and people differ on the 'correct' proportion of basic research to applied research.

The Robbins Committee conceded that alternative investments in coal or electricity (other welfare services like health were not mentioned) also yield beneficial external effects, but they claimed intuitively that the externalities connected with 'education' are far more important. Even so, since their terms of reference bound them to that kind of 'education' which was institutionalised and full-time, their conclusion can have only limited meaning. For presumably there are external effects connected with all the other categories of education, as well as from privately-sponsored research organisations. The Committee did not demonstrate that the external benefits from formal education always exceed those from non-formal education. However, this must be known before we can decide upon the best allocation of expenditure and the best total of taxation required. The Robbins Committee attempts (para. 626) to make the process of invention and the capacity for leadership look as though they are largely university- or college-inspired. However in reality invention is a sporadic phenomenon and occurs in such unexpected quarters that it is ingenuous to picture it exclusively in the form of an army of Ph.D.s in white coats solemnly advancing.[11] Similarly the recognition that business leaders cannot be produced simply by education seems now to be endorsed even by the University Grants Commission's unenthusiastic attitude to the adoption of management studies in universities.

11. Mr Paul Chambers, chairman of ICI, delivering the Chuter Ede lecture in London in 1964 before an audience invited by the NUT, castigated by implication the Robbins argument in these words: 'Life at a university with its intellectual and inconclusive discussions at the postgraduate level is, on the whole, a bad training for the real world and only men of very strong character surmount this handicap.'

A good illustration of what seems to be a combination of special pleading and semantic confusion in the Robbins Report occurs in a remarkable passage on page 205. Education, it claims:

> . . . creates the milieu in which the day-to-day calculus of the price system has to operate. The difference as regards economic potential, between a tribe of savages and a civilised community depends much more on education than on material equipment. If a series of nuclear explosions were to wipe out the material equipment of the world but the educated citizens survived, it need not be long before former standards were reconstituted; but if it destroyed the educated citizens, even though it left the buildings and machines intact, a period longer than the Dark Ages might elapse before the former position was restored.[12]

Such hypothetical situations are surely beside the point. We are not seeking policy for a society of savages but for our present society. We already have both material equipment and a stock of educated personnel. What we have to decide is the degree of marginal increase in one or the other. The argument in the quotation of 'look where you would be if it wasn't for me' is made by every occupational group in turn. In the setting of the supposed bomb catastrophe, the reader must presumably judge for himself on the relative recuperative abilities of a Ph.D. compared, say, with a bricklayer or a farmer. Without such workers society would never recover at all. But perhaps the quotation includes in its reference the education possessed by the bricklayer and the farmer and most other workers. If so it is difficult to see the moral of the story. If on the other hand the 'educated citizens' are confined to those educated within universities and other institutes of full-time higher education, one must ask not only whether the rest of the world populace is so dispensable that the

12. *Ibid.*, para. 625.

'educated citizens' can so quickly recover without them, but also in what special directions these special citizens are supposed to be educated. Or do they include *all* types of scholars, the arts as well as the science men, in full-time institutes?

For the larger part of recorded history most of those who have been engaged in 'higher learning' in such establishments, especially those dominated by Platonic Greek culture, have regarded material things with contempt; preoccupation with applied science, for instance, has been viewed as a deviation from the true calling of pure science. It seems only recently, when discussion about economic growth has become more fashionable, that many academics seem to have warmed to it and now want to make it their own, claiming most of the credit in the process. Nevertheless, even today many of the representatives of our higher education system are still scornful of ordinary commerce; profit-seeking and enterprise are frequently represented by them as anti-social or distasteful. The Robbins Committee's assertion that formal education is favourable to that 'milieu in which the day-to-day calculus of the price system has to operate' has, in this respect, a very hollow sound indeed.[13]

Having made such ambitious but intuitive claims for formal education in the context of economic growth, the Robbins Committee confesses that it is not possible 'to demonstrate this exactly by recourse to detailed statistics'. In the end therefore one of its main cases for a recommended increase in annual public expenditure on formal higher education from £206 million to about £742 million by 1980 rests on the inspired hunch of aca-

13. For a discussion of the way that education breeds a restrictive and resentful attitude to economic growth and market competition see G. J. Stigler, *The Intellectual and the Market Place*, Occasional Paper I, IEA, 1963; Joseph A. Schumpeter, *Capitalism and Democracy*, Allen and Unwin, 4th edition, 1950, pp. 152 ff.

demics supported by a seemingly desperate final appeal to the work of their colleagues, the historians:

> But, on a broad view of history, which is surely more to the point in this connection, the evidence is very strong. The communities that have paid most attention to higher studies have in general been the most obviously progressive in respect of income and wealth.[14]

Such sweeping claims are again too imprecise for policy purposes even if they are correct. What is meant by 'higher studies'? State formal education? Non-state formal education? Informal education? Private research? In particular one would like to know how the Robbins Committee would allocate the credit for the most striking of all English industrial advances in the late eighteenth century which occurred despite the complete indifference of English universities and the entire absence of state education.[15]

The Correlation and Residual Approaches[16]

The Robbins Committee's appeal to history belongs more formally to what educational economists call the correlation and the residual approach. Attempts have been made, for instance, to correlate education with the differences in gross national products between countries and within a given country over time.

14. *Ibid.*, para. 626, p. 206.

15. Scottish universities were an exception. According to Adam Smith they were unique in being about the only higher educational institutions in Europe which were not run in complete defiance of market principles, i.e. they operated under the discipline of payment by results.

16. For a lucid and critical assessment of these and other methods of measuring the relationship between education and growth, see the paper contributed by Professor W. G. Bowen in Appendix IV of the Robbins report. This was a contribution which should have engaged the attention of the Committee more than it seems to have done.

But those attempts have also encountered serious problems. It is difficult enough to make figures of gross national products between countries comparable in the first place. But even if countries A and B devote 3 per cent and 5 per cent of equal national outputs respectively to education it could still be possible for A to have the same real 'educational output' since it could be using its resources more efficiently. Furthermore a high educational expenditure correlated with a high GNP may be an effect rather than a cause of prosperity in the same way that a millionaire's Cadillac is evidence not of the means of making his fortune but of his enjoyment in the consumption of it. That is to say education may be a consumption rather than an investment good.

The 'residual approach' is more modest. In effect it says 'look, capital has increased by 10 per cent and labour has increased by 10 per cent but national output has increased by 30 per cent. If labour and capital cannot therefore claim all the credit, what can?' More formally, this approach starts with the given data of a total increase in output over a given period and then tries to impute it to specific 'inputs'. Where the increase in output is larger than the increases in capital and labour, there must be an unknown factor at work. Shall we call this mysterious residual influence education? This would be going too far, although, as suggested above, many academics seem anxious now to 'throw a net' over all of it and claim it entirely as their own prize fish. Other important influences are also probably at work, and these include improvement in the quality of capital assets, better monopoly legislation, possibly a lower level of taxation, the economies of large scale, improvements in industrial relations and in the health of employees, and a fall in the price of imports relative to exports. And even when we get to education we have to remember once again all the varieties of nonformal education, from the accumulation of experience and on-the-job training to trade journals and management conferences, that can also claim legitimate kingdoms in the empire of 'education'.

The Appeal to History

In view of the Robbins Committee's emphasis on making an appeal to history to see whether education 'pays' it will be fitting to conclude this chapter with such an investigation, albeit brief. There is one episode in English history which more than any other seems to have impressed historians in respect to the importance of the contribution of formal education to economic growth. There is a widely held impression that from about 1867 technical progress was more sluggish in Britain than in America and Germany. In particular the efficiency of the British iron and steel plants was thought to compare unfavourably with those of Germany. Such a situation has called, obviously, for some explanation. Historians have been impressed with the diagnosis which was popular with the Victorians themselves and which received much publicity from the efforts of Lyon Playfair, one of the English jurors at the Paris Exhibition of 1867. It was he who drew parliamentary attention to the fact that at this exhibition the Germans and other continentals had run away with most of the industrial prizes, a result markedly different from the 1851 Great Exhibition when Britain had apparently been supreme in these respects. Playfair, a professor of chemistry, expressed his firm conviction that it was the efficient German state schools with their scientific curricula which were largely responsible for Germany's improved position. By comparison, he thought, Britain was manifestly negligent in adapting itself to the complex needs of a new scientific age. As a conspicuous example of this deficiency, Playfair cited the case of a building erected at Glasgow with iron girders imported from Belgium. These girders, he explained, were cheaper because the Belgians had applied chemical analysis to the limestone and ore used in pig-iron production. Playfair's kind of testimony had perceptible influence on Parliament, and state support for higher technological and scientific education soon followed and coincided with the general intervention in education which was already gathering force after 1870.

Despite its long-standing influence with historians, Playfair's diagnosis was, in retrospect, unsatisfactory. Recent study reveals that English industry was not in fact as hampered by lack of scientific skills at this time as was once believed.[17] The relative decline in economic progress was more attributable to long-term changes in market opportunities which were in turn partly due to England's early start in industrialisation. Apart from this, innovation suffered from defective institutions which were the responsibility not of entrepreneurs but of the state. Thus subsequent investigation showed that it was *the patent laws* which accounted for the use of Belgian girders in Glasgow to which Playfair referred.[18] The Belgian chemical process was common knowledge among English entrepreneurs but they were prevented from using it because although the patent was in the hands of only one English producer the law did not compel a patentee to exploit his patent.

As for scientific advances in steel, it was an Englishman, not a German, whose invention was of most consequence. Sidney Gilchrist Thomas, who discovered how to make steel out of phosphoric ore in 1875, was an English police court clerk and had conducted his experiments in the backyard of a small suburban house. As a matter of fact this invention redounded to the advantage not of the English but of the Germans for it created a gigantic German steel industry which would not have been possible

17. See H. J. Habakkuk, *American and British Technology in the Nineteenth Century*, Cambridge University Press, 1962, p. 216.

18. See the Royal Commission on Scientific Instruction 1868.

without it. The Germans were able to use the invention not because they were more fore-sighted or had impressive state schools but simply because the invention enabled them at last to exploit their own ores, which were phosphoric.

This episode well illustrates the need for scepticism in 'education' policy which has been argued throughout this chapter. For it clearly shows, first, how one country can reap the benefits of an advance in scientific knowledge without having to pay for and organise it domestically. Secondly, it is a good instance of the earlier generalisation that invention is a sporadic and unexpected phenomenon. The familiar modern observation that we are now living in a complex scientific and industrial era is frequently made with the half-hidden suggestion that today, in contrast say to the early nineteenth century, we cannot possibly continue without central guidance and responsibility. But the inventions of every age look complex and revolutionary to their contemporaries and make individuals feel helpless with astonishment. Gilchrist Thomas's invention, however, was not only complex, it was 'scientific' in the modern sense, i.e. the application of a scientific discipline (chemistry) to industrial processes. Yet he was the product neither of formal state nor full-time higher education, nor even of a government research department. His invention was developed by ordinary firms before company taxation was increased to help pay for new and centrally directed services that successive governments have felt themselves obliged to finance. Finally, this story shows how easy it is for historians to jump to the conclusion that the most important hidden residual influence accounting for an increase or decrease of economic progress is an increase or decrease of formal education. The more obvious 'residual' in this instance was the restrictiveness of the patent law, and government action was logically and more urgently needed in the form of an intervention to remove this obstacle before going any further.

PART THREE

Theoretical and Empirical Antecedents

CHAPTER EIGHT

The Classical Economists on Education[1]

The classical economists are typically associated in the popular mind with the early nineteenth-century doctrine of *laissez faire*. Nevertheless, as has been frequently observed by historians of education, sometimes quizzically but always with happy approval, these same writers were of all people among the most forceful advocates and pioneers of state education. It seems too, that with the present feverish emphasis on the idea of education for economic growth, reference to the 'respectable ancestry' of these early writers is enjoying something of a revival. It is interesting for instance that Lord Robbins, writing as a professional economist some years ago, was anxious to settle the libel once for all that the classical economists objected to the principle of state intervention to provide for social services and to protect needy minorities, and he mentioned education as a typical case in point.[2]

In view of all this, an objective analysis of the precise nature of

---

1. This chapter first appeared as an article in the *British Journal of Educational Studies,* May 1964, and is reproduced by courtesy of the Editor.

2. See his work, *The Theory of Economic Policy,* 1952. The Robbins Report on *Higher Education* gives favourable mention to the classical economists, p. 204. See also John Vaizey, *The Economics of Education,* Faber, 1962, Chapter I.

the educational contribution of these writers seems overdue. It is necessary to add that such an investigation should be particularly careful to avoid the common and all too hasty tendency to take from out of his particular setting any nineteenth-century writer who spoke up for education and to present him as one of many characters who played an integral part in an unfolding plot of history, a plot which reached its triumphant climax in the 1944 Education Act. One purpose of this chapter is to question the appropriateness of this treatment as it is frequently applied to the classical economists. This will arise from an examination of the special form of their arguments and from uncovering serious conflicts of opinion on matters of policy, some of which lay beneath the surface of their main writings.

As a generalisation it is fair to say that nearly all the economists looked upon education from a utilitarian point of view. Certainly it was Bentham who put this view in its most rigid and mechanical form, a characteristic which in education was later reproduced more in his disciple, Edwin Chadwick, than in James Mill. But all the economists were strikingly united in one aspect at least of what can be called *negative* utilitarianism, that is, in the idea that education could reduce crime and disorder. Adam Smith himself, the doyen of the classical economists, competed even with Jeremy Bentham for first place in persuasiveness and vigour on this matter. Referring to the education of the inferior ranks of the people, Smith asserted:

> The state however derives no inconsiderable advantage from their instruction. The more they are instructed, the less liable they are to the delusions of enthusiasm and supposition, which among ignorant nations, frequently occasion the most dreadful disorders.[3]

3. *An Inquiry into the Nature and Causes of the Wealth of Nations*, ed. R. H. Campbell and A. S. Skinner, Indianapolis, Liberty Fund, 1982, p. 788. Subsequent references are to this edition and will be referred to as *W.N.*

Such views were by no means original. They had been expressed, for instance, although with less urgency, both by his own tutor Francis Hutcheson and by the seventeenth-century economist, William Petty. But there seems to be no doubt that Smith's attitude to them was considerably sharpened by the influence of the French physiocrats whom he visited on his continental tour in 1768. Whereas Petty and Hutcheson relied upon a religious education, the French writers were now urging scientific instruction. Turgot, for example, typified the current excitement of his confreres on this subject in the following memorandum addressed to his king:

> I venture to affirm that if this program [universal state education] be adopted, your subjects will have changed out of all recognition within a mere decade, and their intelligence, good behaviour, and enlightened zeal in your service and their country's will place them far above all other modern nations. For by that time children now ten years old will have grown up into young men trained to do their duty by the State; patriotic and law-abiding, not from fear but on rational grounds, understanding and respecting justice, and prompt to help their fellow citizens in time of need.[4]

In the hands of the English Utilitarians such thinking became sharpened into cold calculations of social profit and loss. Bentham estimated that government funds spent on education would probably be more than offset by the reduction of expenditure on prisons, and that therefore state investment on education was socially profitable. This reasoning became common currency in the hands of such influential Parliamentarians as Henry Brougham, J. A. Roebuck and T. S. Macaulay. But several of the

4. Quoted in Alexis de Tocqueville, *The Old Regime and the French Revolution*, Part III, Chapter III. For an account of Smith's meetings with the Physiocrats in Paris, see I. Cumming, *Helvetius*, 1955.

political economists also developed the argument to the same extent. Miss Martineau, the populariser of the classical economists, seems to have faithfully represented many of her peers when she wrote:

> Nor can I see that political economy objects to the general rating for educational purposes. As a mere police-tax this rating would be a very cheap affair. It would cost us much less than we now pay for juvenile depravity.[5]

It is interesting that it was the Scottish members of the classical economists who appear to have been the most insistent in associating popular education with law and order. An observation they were continually fond of making was that the Scots were more law-abiding than others and that this was a consequence of their better education. Adam Smith having made the suggestion, his fellow Scottish economists, James Mill, J. R. McCulloch and Thomas Chalmers, were quick to pursue it. Addressing the opponents of education James Mill said:

> It is not necessary that they should compare a Turkish and a British population. Let them only reflect upon the state of the Irish as compared with the English population; then compare the population of Scotland with that of England.[6]

T. R. Malthus seems to have been content to accept this opinion from his associates. He observed that

> The quiet and peaceful habits of the instructed Scotch peasant, compared with the turbulent disposition of the ignorant Irishman, ought not to be without effect upon every impartial reasoner.[7]

5. Quoted in Herbert Spencer, *Social Statics and Man Versus the State,* 1884.
6. *Edinburgh Review,* Article IX, 1813.
7. *Essay on Population,* 7th edition, Chapter IX, 1826.

Whitbread, who was avowedly influenced by Malthus, was one of the first to quote crude statistics in Parliament in support of such arguments. In the debate of his 'Bill for establishing a Plan for the Education of the Poor' in 1807, he said:

> Search the Newgate calendar. The great majority of the executed in London every year were Irish; the next in order were English, and the last Scots. This was in exact proportion with their respective systems of education among the lower orders.[8]

Such triumphant reference to elementary statistics continued for half a century.[9] Apart from the general weaknesses in such simple statistical inferences it is difficult to see how Whitbread's particular argument could support a proposal for state legislation on education, since Ireland was covered by legislative enactments for the compulsory provision of schools similar to those in Scotland.[10]

James Mill quoted figures to show that there were 11 times as many criminals in England as in Scotland in proportion to their respective populations.

> We desire our opponents to tell us in what respect the circumstances of the English population have not been favourable than those of the Scottish except in the article of schooling alone.[11]

8. *Hansard*, IX, cols. 539–50.

9. See, for instance, the more elaborate tables in Dr J. Kay, *The Social Conditions and Education of the People in England and France*, Longman Brown, 1850.

10. 'An Act for the Erection of Free Schools' in 1570 had ordered the provision of free schools in every diocese. The equivalent legislation in Scotland was initiated in 1615. Bad administration hindered the implementation of the statutes in Ireland as compared with Scotland, but after a succession of parliamentary commissions the system was strengthened by annual education grants from the English Parliament to Irish voluntary education from 1816 onwards, that is 17 years before the first parliamentary grant to English education.

11. *Edinburgh Review*, Article IX, 1813.

There were several possible answers to this question, but one to which most of the economists themselves would have strongly subscribed is contained in the fact that Scotland did not have the English Poor Law.[12] All the classical economists, and not the least James Mill, were persuaded of the demoralising effect of this legislation; and therefore it was not appropriate for them to neglect it in this particular context. Indeed, in an earlier article James Mill had advised that the reform of the Poor Law was far more urgent in England than the provision of education.

Mill also partly answered himself later in his same article when he declared that schooling was rapidly growing in England. By 1826 he was convinced that literacy was typical among 'the lowest people'.[13] England had almost caught up with Scotland in school provision in 1835 without any compulsory provision.[14]

With regard to the general proposition that education reduces crime, the twentieth-century observer, with the benefit of hindsight, is much more sceptical.[15] For one thing, even at the level of the classical economists' own statistical method of evidence, the growth of education in the subsequent one-and-half centuries has not been associated with a noticeable decline of delinquency; more and more modern authorities are pointing with bewilderment to the reverse. William Cobbett seems to have been quite alone in this observation in his own day. Cobbett opposed Roebuck's Bill on Education in 1833 on the ground that crime in England was even then increasing at the same time as education was

12. The Scottish poor-relief system was based on the Acts of 1503 and 1579. Its outstanding feature was that no legal recognition was given to the right of able-bodied poor to support. Vagrancy and mendicity were therefore more prominent in Scotland.

13. *Westminster Review*, VI, October 1826.

14. See Brougham's speech in the Lords, 21 May 1835.

15. See Chapter 3 of this text.

spreading. 'If so, what reason was there to tax the people for the increase of education?'[16]

Apart from these difficulties, however, it is not at all clear that the very definitions of 'crime' that were used in the nineteenth century were always quite the same as those implied or accepted today. The Benthamites clearly separated 'crime' from 'sin'. Ethics were reduced by them to a science. In their view action which was 'bad' arose simply from ignorance of the best way of pursuing happiness. At this stage their philosophy was subtly transformed from *negative* to *positive* Utilitarianism, a much more elusive and metaphysical area of thought. For the Utilitarianism, education programmes were aimed solely at removing a very special kind of ignorance. Their precise objective was to remove the ignorance of what they, the Utilitarians, thought to be the best happiness-seeking instruments. People, as J. Roebuck insisted in Parliament, could not be happy by themselves; they had to be taught how to be happy. Nobody could be truly liberated into a state of happiness unless his mind had previously been manipulated by Utilitarians. Only after state instruction would it be logical for the government to resort to punishment. Otherwise pleasure would be minimised and pain (crime) would be maximised. The narrowness of this view was no doubt best revealed in William Godwin's uncompromising attack upon it:

> It is not easy to say whether the remark, 'that government cannot justly punish offenders, unless it have previously informed them what is virtue and what is offence', be entitled to a separate answer. It is to be hoped that mankind will never have to learn so important a lesson through so corrupt a channel. Government

16. *Hansard*, 1833, Vol. XX. Cobbett continued: 'It was nothing but an attempt to force education—it was French—it was a Doctrinaire plan, and he should always be opposed to it.'

may reasonably and equitably presume that men who live in society know that enormous crimes are injurious to the public weal, without its being necessary to announce them as such, by laws to be proclaimed by heralds, or expounded by curates. . . . All real crimes are capable of being discerned without the teaching of law. All supposed crimes, not capable of being so discerned, are truly and unalterably innocent.[17]

Nevertheless, most of the classical economists ventured beyond the mere 'police argument' for education and shared some of the more paternalistic or *positive* Utilitarian thinking. Their reasoning at this level, however, was not always internally or externally consistent. The Malthusians, for instance, wanted to use state schools to instruct the people about the consequences of early marriages and large families, in the hope that the rate of population increase would be kept in check. Adam Smith, however, thought that an increasing population was normally a sign of increasing prosperity, and so could not have subscribed to this argument. For his part, Smith, too, had his own special and paternalistic prescriptions for happiness, prescriptions which derived from his individual system of philosophy and sociology, and which he also wished to administer through the semi-authoritarian instrument of state-assisted schools. Smith's argument was that the most serious contemporary cause of unhappiness was associated with the growing factory system and its division of labour. State education, he contended, was required mainly as an antidote to this new environment. This case is put forward in Book V of *The Wealth of Nations*, where he examined the several duties of government:

In the progress of the division of labour, the employment of the far greater part of those who live by labour, that is, of the great

17. *Enquiry concerning Political Justice and its influence on Mortals and Happiness,* London, 1796.

body of the people comes to be confined to a few very simple operations, frequently to one or two. But the understandings of the greater part of men are necessarily formed by their employments. The man whose life is spent in performing a few simple operations, of which the effects are perhaps always the same, or very nearly the same, has no occasion to exert his understanding or to exercise his invention in finding out expedients for removing difficulties which never occur. He naturally loses, therefore, the habit of such exertion and generally becomes as stupid and ignorant as it is possible for a human creature to become. The torpor of his mind renders him not only incapable of relishing or bearing a part in any rational conversation, but of conceiving any generous, noble or tender sentiment, and consequently of forming any just judgement concerning many even of the ordinary duties of private life . . . [18]

His dexterity at his own particular trade seems, in this manner, to be acquired at the expense of his intellectual, social and martial virtues. But in every improved and civilized society this is the state into which the labouring poor, that is, the great body of the people, must necessarily fall, unless government takes some pains to prevent it.[19]

This passage has often been referred to by historians of education, and they are naturally more interested in this particular part of *The Wealth of Nations* than in others. To economists, however, who are just as interested in many other sections of the work and especially in Book I, the extract above comes as a strange surprise. For all the many other references to the division of labour elsewhere in the work are made with abundant enthusiasm and optimism. Indeed a careful comparison with certain phrases in Book I reveals an obvious inconsistency of treatment of this sub-

18. *W.N.*, pp. 781–2.
19. *W.N.*, p. 782.

ject. The very first sentence of the opening chapter of the book
sets the major theme, subsequently developed:

> The *greatest* improvement in the productive powers of labour,
> and the greater part of the skill, dexterity and judgement with
> which it is any where directed, or applied, seem to have been the
> effects of the division of labour.[20] (My italics)

Later he claims:

> Men are much more likely to discover easier and readier methods
> of attaining any object, when the whole attention of their minds
> is directed towards that single object, than when it is dissipated
> among a great variety of things. But in consequence of the divi-
> sion of labour, the whole of every man's attention comes natu-
> rally to be directed towards some one very simple object.[21]

In the light of these conflicting views the quotation with which
educationists are more familiar, and which seems disposed towards state education, can hardly be accepted as completely representative or as a final judgement on the matter.

It is sometimes suggested that the classical economists were
anxious to press arguments for state education based on presumed direct consequences for economic growth. This claim is
not easy to substantiate. The reduction of crime and promotion
of 'happiness' was easily their most overriding consideration.
Anxiety for economic accumulation is indeed strongly dispar-
aged in certain remarks of Adam Smith in the context of education, remarks which are very reminiscent of modern references
to the 'affluent society'. In the Glasgow Lectures he argued that
education was needed not to promote economic growth but to
counter its undesirable consequences. The division of labour

20. *W.N.*, p. 13.
21. *W.N.*, p. 20.

principle alone could be relied upon to foster sufficient production of goods and services and to open up job opportunities for old and young. It was because a boy could get a job easily that he

> . . . begins to find that his father is obliged to him, and therefore throws off his authority. When he is grown up he has no ideas with which he can amuse himself. When he is away from work he must therefore betake himself to drunkenness and riot. Accordingly we find that in the commercial parts of England, the tradesmen are for the most part in this despicable condition; their work through half the week is sufficient to maintain them and through want of education they have no amusement for the other but riot and debauchery. So it may justly be said that the people who clothe the world are in rags themselves.[22]

Criticisms based on Smith's dislike of 'mutual emulation' displayed by relatively opulent workers is to be found in *The Wealth of Nations*.[23] Again in his preceding book, *The Theory of Moral Sentiments,* he presented the case of the man who 'devoted himself for ever to the pursuit of wealth and greatness' who ' . . . in the last dregs of life, his body washed with toil and disease . . . begins at last to find that wealth and greatness are mere trinkets of frivolous utility. . . . '[24] It is true that Smith advocated the modernisation of school curricula to include such subjects as geometry and mechanics in order that the potential factory worker should be better acquainted with his environment. But the primary purpose does not seem to have been the pursuit of more productivity or inventiveness for materialistic purposes. Such

22. Adam Smith, *Lectures on Jurisprudence* LJ(B), ed. R. L. Meek, D. D. Raphael and P. G. Stein, Indianapolis, Liberty Fund, 1982, p. 540. See E. G. West, 'Adam Smith's Two Views on the Division of Labour', *Economica*, February 1964.

23. See *W.N.*, p. 99.

24. *The Theory of Moral Sentiments,* ed. D. D. Raphael and A. L. Macfie, Indianapolis, Liberty Fund, 1984, p. 181.

proposals should be read in reference to his philosophy and sociology, which contended that some basic knowledge of certain elements of a worker's surroundings would probably give rise to more reflection, which would probably develop into speculative and absorbing thought. This in turn would produce a state of mind desirable in itself, and would ward off the mental boredom which so often encouraged restlessness, mischief and crime.

The later economist, J. R. McCulloch, was certainly exceptional in relating education to economic growth in statements which do have a twentieth-century ring about them. In attempting to explain the superior economic development of Britain over other countries which enjoyed similar *natural* advantages, McCulloch pointed to their relative failure to apply intelligence. They would not improve until 'the sun of science had shone upon them'. 'I do not know that it would be going too far to affirm that knowledge is really productive of all wealth in civilisation.'[25]

But even here it is important to notice that such statements separate their author from those who were campaigning for a system of mainly government-supplied education. For McCulloch argued that the economic superiority of Britain over Prussia and France was precisely due to the relative failure of their education, and it was in these very countries that *centrally administered* school systems did exist. Britain, on the contrary, relied on a privately supplied education which McCulloch thought in 1825 to be 'now so generally diffused'.

Above all aspects of education this is one which clearly separates all the classical economists from those who have shaped our system as it now stands in Britain. While the early economists argued for *some* state education, they conceived it in very quali-

25. *A Discourse, delivered at the Opening of the City of London Literary and Scientific Institution*, 30 May 1825.

fied terms indeed. If one was asked to select the most conspicuous of the main features which distinguish them from current practice, it would be their insistence that fees should not be abolished and should always cover a substantial part of the cost of education. Their main reason for this requirement has either been subsequently forgotten or carefully avoided by interested parties. Fee paying, according to most of the economists, was the one instrument with which parents could keep desirable competition alive between teachers and schools. Adam Smith's proposal for state provision for the education of the poor was limited to state subsidies to school *buildings*. He went to great lengths to insist that the teachers' salaries were to be derived largely from parental fees. It was the absence of such a principle in the case of endowed schools which caused him to write about them in his most condemnatory manner:

> The endowments of schools and colleges have necessarily diminished more or less the necessity of application in the teachers. Their subsistence, so far as it arises from their salaries, is evidently derived from a fund altogether independent of their success and reputation in their particular professions.[26]

He spoke from personal experience on this matter. His years at Oxford University gave him a most unfavourable opinion of protected university teaching.

> In the University of Oxford, the greater part of the public professors have, for these many years, given up altogether even the pretence of teaching.[27]

Often the authority in this case was one step beyond the body which managed the endowment, 'as in the governor of the prov-

26. *W.N.*, p. 760.
27. *W.N.*, p. 761.

ince; or, perhaps, in some minister of state'. But all such remote
control could do was to force the teacher to attend his pupils a
certain number of hours or to give a certain number of lectures
per week. The rest was left to the teacher's private diligence,
upon which Smith from his own experience did not seem to have
placed much value.

Adam Smith's own experience as a university teacher led him
to favour a fee-paying system. His own salary at Glasgow may
have been about £70 with a house, and his fees near £100.[28] He
thought that this arrangement ensured at least some efficiency,
since such a variable element of a teacher's reward was sensitive
to the quality of the services rendered. Consequently, the higher
the proportion of the total reward made up in fees the more the
security against pedagogic inertia. The heavily endowed institutions, on the contrary, were usually not in the interest of the
students but for the ease of the masters. The most monotonous
and uninspiring teaching, for instance, was protected against the
normal sanction of derision.[29]

> This discipline of the college, at the same time, may enable him to
> force all his pupils to the most regular attendance upon this sham-
> lecture, and to maintain the most decent and respectful behaviour
> during the whole time of the performance.[30]

Adam Smith contended that in such a situation it was not surprising that no innovations were made in the curriculum, and
that dead languages prevailed while new sciences were neglected. The worst examples were the universities. These, ac-

28. Rae, *Life of Adam Smith*, 1895, p. 48.
29. Lecturers often used to read from a book and sometimes in a foreign
language.
30. *W.N.*, p. 763.

cording to Smith, had become sanctuaries of 'exploded systems' and 'obsolete prejudices'.

But although endowments thus blunted the ordinary forces of a free market in education, examples could be found where market forces were allowed to operate without such major restrictions and therefore with much better results. Those parts of education where there were no endowments were, according to Smith,

> . . . generally the best taught. When a young man goes to a fencing or a dancing school, he does not indeed always learn to fence or dance very well; but he seldom fails of learning to fence or dance.[31]

Complete failure presumably could only occur at public (i.e. endowed) institutions:

> The three most essential parts of literary education, to read, write and account, it still continues to be *more common to acquire in private than in public schools*; and it very seldom happens that any body fails of acquiring them to the degree in which it is necessary to acquire them.[32] (My italics)

Most of the later economists upheld Adam Smith's principle. Thus Malthus argued that if each child had to pay a fixed sum, 'the school master would then have a stronger interest to increase the number of his pupils . . .'[33] Similarly, McCulloch thought that the maintenance of the fee system would

> . . . secure the constant attendance of a person who shall be able to instruct the young, and who shall have the strongest interest to

31. *W.N.*, p. 764.
32. *W.N.*, p. 764.
33. Malthus, Letter to Whitbread, 1807.

perfect himself in his business, and to attract the greatest number
of scholars to his school.[34]

Otherwise, if the schoolmaster derived much of his income from
his fixed salary, he would not have the same interest to exert
himself,

> . . . and like all other functionaries, placed in similar situations,
> he would learn to neglect his business, and to consider it as a
> drudgery only to be avoided.[35]

The most hesitant of the economists to accept this principle
was John Stuart Mill. According to Mill, education was one of
those exceptional cases in which the *laissez faire* principle broke
down because of the lack of adequate judgement on the part of
the purchaser:

> Is the buyer always qualified to judge of the commodity? If not,
> the presumption in favour of the competition of the market does
> not apply to this case.[36]

Medicine was an obvious example of this sort of market failure. Even if the patient could be relied upon to purchase some
minimum amount at his own expense and from his own free will,
we were not bound to admit 'that the patient will select the *right*
medicine without assistance'.[37] (My italics) Similarly with education: 'The uncultivated cannot be competent judges of cultiva-
tion.'[38] Long experience was necessary to appreciate education,

34. Note XXI, McCulloch edition of *The Wealth of Nations*, 1828.

35. *Ibid.* James Mill also shared such reasoning—see *Edinburgh Review*,
Article IX, 1813.

36. J. S. Mill, *Principles of Political Economy*, p. 953. For the full contrast
between Smith and Mill see E. G. West, 'Private versus Public Education: A
Classical Economic Dispute', in *Journal of Political Economy*, October 1964.

37. *Ibid.*, p. 954.

38. *Ibid.*, p. 953.

and therefore the market could not adequately provide for it. Pecuniary speculation could not wait: 'It must succeed rapidly or not at all.'[39] Among the classical economists, only Nassau Senior seems to have come out on the side of J. S. Mill in this serious difference of opinion. Senior, too, did not trust the average good sense of the parents, and for similar reasons. The fact was that neither Senior nor Mill liked the type of school that the free market was providing by the middle of the nineteenth century. This was undoubtedly due to their opinion that these schools were inferior to the large-scale models which the Poor Law institutions were dutifully producing to the order of their Benthamite supervisors. With regard to the existing provision of education, although Mill failed to quote the evidence, he believed that

> . . . even in quantity it is [1848] and is likely to remain, altogether insufficient, while in quality, though with some slight tendency to improvement, it is never good except by some rare accident, and generally so bad as to be little more than nominal.[40]

This quotation stands in striking contrast to the belief of Adam Smith (quoted above) that private schools were superior in efficiency to those publicly provided. Whereas J. S. Mill thought that the competitive market principle broke down in education because the customer was not a competent judge of his interests, Adam Smith (and his later follower, Robert Lowe) argued that the competitive market principle had not been allowed to operate properly in the first place owing to the hindrance of endowment. Smith quoted extensively from the literature of ancient Greece to show how well the free market worked in the

39. *Ibid.,* p. 954. Pushed to its extreme, this argument would preclude the possibility of *any* entirely new product gaining a threshold.

40. *Ibid.,* p. 956.

absence of such obstacles.[41] He would probably have agreed with J. S. Mill that the *initial* competence of the customer to choose education was inadequate. But he would have opposed Mill's conclusion that education should be taken out of the market for this reason. For the day-to-day experience of this market was *itself a medium of instruction,* and one which Smith thought superior for the purpose to any government authority.

However, J. S. Mill presents another case where undue emphasis on partial quotations from his works can only too easily give a misleading impression of his general and final judgement. For despite his doubts about the efficiency of the market mechanism in education, Mill in the end, like Smith, came down in favour of private schools. His main reason for this was not, however, quite the same as Smith's. It was Mill's adherence to his principle of liberty which was crucial to his final judgement on the subject. Liberty was required not only as an end in itself but because of certain consequences which Mill thought desirable such as spontaneity, variety and experiment. A state school system would swamp these:

> A general state education is a mere contrivance for moulding people to be exactly like one another: and as the mould in which it casts them is that which pleases the predominant power in the government, whether this be a monarch, a priesthood, an aristocracy, or the majority of the existing generation; in proportion as it

41. J. S. Mill's father, James Mill, was on the side of Adam Smith in this matter, supporting his opinion that 'all institutions for the education of those classes of people who are able to pay for it should be taken out of the hands of public bodies, and left to the natural operation of that free competition which the interests of the parties desiring to teach and to be taught would naturally create;—and it is easy to see that the same reasoning is applicable in a great degree even to the education of the poorest classes.' *Edinburgh Review,* Article IX, 1813.

is efficient and successful, it establishes a despotism over the mind, leading by natural tendency to one over the body.[42]

J. S. Mill, therefore, despite his misgivings about the ability of ordinary people to buy education themselves, eventually confined his proposals for state intervention to a law rendering only education (not schooling) compulsory. 'The instrument for enforcing the law should be no other than public examinations, extending to all children.'[43] Thus the place or source of their education was immaterial after all. To see how radical such a provision would be today we have only to imagine children obtaining their knowledge by television, correspondence courses, dame schools or part-time academies or even by being taught by their parents at home in the same manner that J. S. Mill himself was educated. There would even be no official pressure to supply people with teachers previously instructed in government training colleges. In the words of Adam Smith: 'They would soon find better teachers than any whom the state could provide for them.'[44]

In view of this general investigation of the writings of the classical economists one is bound to conclude with the speculation that these authors would be acutely disappointed with the subsequent development of education in their own country in the succeeding century, and not least with the 1944 Education Act. They would probably have challenged nearly every piece of educational legislation after Lord Sandon's Act of 1876. This Act met J. S. Mill's desire for compulsory *education* as against compulsory *schooling*. At the same time such compulsion was rein-

42. *On Liberty*, Fontana edition, 1962, p. 239.
43. *Ibid.*, p. 239.
44. *W.N.*, p. 796.

forced by examinations, as Mill had also advocated, whilst another of his conditions had been satisfied in the provision against individual cases of poverty by the granting of special financial concessions. The legislation which followed the 1876 Act, however, progressively undermined this position, and proceeded according to principles quite alien to the early writers. For there is indeed nothing in the evidence of their writings to suggest that any one of them would have supported the degree of state predominance in education that is experienced in our own times. Finally, their main case for any state intervention in the first place, the 'reduction of crime' thesis, would demand from them much rethinking in the twentieth-century setting in view of the evidence adduced in Chapter 3.

CHAPTER NINE

Literacy—Before and after 1870

Nineteenth-century advocates of state schooling continually referred to a serious educational deficiency in their own times. What was the nature of their evidence? Two indices in particular received important attention: the prevailing degree of literacy and the current quantity of schooling. This chapter will look at the evidence of literacy. The schooling position will be examined in Chapter 10. Special attention will be given to quantitative evidence prominent in the parliamentary debates which has gained a conspicuous place in subsequent discussion.

It should not be assumed, of course, that one should necessarily regard any single set of quantitative statistics as a satisfactory measure of education in itself. For one thing they provide only circumstantial evidence; for another no two people can agree on what comprises a good education. However, since such figures have been seriously put forward by others and have apparently influenced discussion and popular opinion, respectful and critical examination is called for in this book. But to help forestall the reader's impatience when the *quantitative* evidence is being examined, the author wishes to reassure him that he is well aware of the importance of the *quality* of education which the figures may conceal. Space will be left in both this and in Chapter 11, therefore, to give appropriate attention to this aspect. Since there is considerable interconnection between the evidence examined in this and next two chapters, the reader is advised to suspend his judgement until all three chapters have been read.

General Circumstantial Evidence of Literacy

Since the semantic niceties of the term have already been explored in Chapter 4 (p. 45) the word 'literacy' in this chapter will be taken to imply the most usual definition, that is, simply the ability to read and write. Before looking at the official statistics, it will be helpful to consider some important pieces of circumstantial evidence in order to establish some sort of background and perspective. The most salient fact about the first 33 years of the nineteenth century was that the effect of state activity upon individual efforts to become literate was one of deliberate hindrance.

On this subject most modern specialists seem to be agreed and the documentary evidence is abundant.[1] The frightened reactions of early nineteenth-century English governments against the spread of political literature among the 'lower orders' took the form of fiscal and legal action against the spread of newspapers, especially those critical of government. The fear of such political literature was not confined to the aristocracy. It was shared as early as 1803 by the political economist, Thomas Malthus, who had apprehensions about Tom Paine's *The Rights of Man*. It has since been claimed indeed that Tom Paine sold one and a half million copies of his book. William Cobbett, who incidentally was a strenuous opponent of the idea that ordinary workers needed the assistance of the state to educate them, sold

---

1. The best account is found in A. Aspinall, *Politics of the Press*, Home and Van Thal Ltd., 1949.

200,000 copies of his *Address to the Journeymen and Labourers* in only two months. The struggle of *Cobbett's Register* to find a working-class audience despite the closing down of public reading-rooms and the withdrawal of licences from public houses, inns and coffee houses receiving this newspaper was a result of the restrictive policy of the government of the time.

It remains true that the official energy displayed in suppressing such literature was based on the knowledge that reading ability was widespread. Mr H. J. Perkins quotes Samuel Bamford, the 'weaver-poet', as saying that the writings of Cobbett 'were read on nearly every cottage hearth in the manufacturing districts of South Lancashire . . . '[2]

Religious tracts enjoyed an even larger circulation, while the reading of the Bible at home was, of course, traditional and well established. Beyond this, there was an extensive market in popular literature from the 'penny magazine' and the serialised fiction such as *Pickwick Papers* down to almanacs, ballads and last, dying speeches. The innovation of steam printing in the 1830s caused revolutionary cost reductions in the production of newspapers, which then began steadily to increase their sales despite the restrictive taxes. The most rapid increase in newspaper sales, therefore, did not come until after the removal of the taxes; the advertising duties were removed in 1853, the stamp taxes in 1855 and the excise taxes on paper in 1861. That a mass newspaper-reading public was already in existence well before 1870 is now firmly acknowledged by specialist writers. Mr Perkins writes: 'no historical myth dies harder than the belief that the modern popular press grew up in direct response to the introduction of state education'.[3] Similarly Mr Raymond Williams: ' . . . there

2. *History Today,* July 1957, p. 426.

3. *Op. cit.,* p. 425.

was no sudden opening of the floodgates of literacy as the result of the 1870 Education Act'.[4]

Statistical Estimates of Literacy

In the more formal or statistical evidence of literacy in the nineteenth century, the first thing that stands out is the consistency of its testimony that the ability to read was always in advance of the ability to write. The schools generally taught reading before writing and this reflected the relative contemporary demand. Ordinary people wanted to read in order to enjoy the new excitements of magazines and newspapers, whereas they did not have quite the same need for writing and writing materials were expensive because of taxes upon them.[5]

Two sets of figures to demonstrate the extent of literacy have been used by educationists since the Victorian period. The first were the records of educational qualifications of criminals published by the Home Office from 1935. The second were the figures showing the number of persons signing the marriage register with marks.

As an example of the first type of figures I shall quote from the researches of Mr R. K. Webb.[6] Of the persons committed for trial between 1837 and 1939 44.6 percent were reported to be able to read and write. Such criminal tables, however, obviously suffered from not being properly representative of the whole population. Furthermore, since such averages mix older with younger persons, they do not adequately intimate the current education

---

4. *The Long Revolution*, Chatto and Windus, 1961, p. 166.

5. The introduction of the penny post in 1840 gave a vigorous boost to personally written communications.

6. R. K. Webb, 'Working Class Readers in Early Victorian England', *The English Historical Review*, 1950.

standards of juveniles. Criminals aged about 30 and over, for instance, would have been of school age in the difficult period of the Napoleonic war.

Webb's information can be supplemented with data relating to another public institution—the workhouse. A good sample of this can be obtained from the 1838 report on the Training of Pauper Children in workhouses by the Assistant Poor Law Commissioner, James Philip Kay. Kay was eventually the first Secretary to the Education Committee of the Privy Council (in a sense the first Minister of Education); we must assume that this measurement of literacy was particularly reliable. Table 5[7] refers to the children maintained in the workhouses of Suffolk and Norfolk. As shown in the table, 87 per cent of these children could already read to some extent. It is true that a smaller proportion of them could write but even this was 53 per cent.

It is interesting to compare this evidence with the extent of literacy as measured by UNESCO in some countries in 1950: Portugal 55–60 per cent, Egypt 20–25 per cent, Algeria 15–20 per cent. The UNESCO figures are percentages of the adult population, whereas the English example refers only to pauper children between 9 and 16 years. It is true that such children had received some educational benefit from being in a public institution for some part of their lives. Whether this was sufficient to give them equal opportunities with most children, however, is doubtful.

An estimate of literacy among miners in 1940 shown in Table 6 appeared in the report of an inspection into educational standards in the mining districts of Northumberland and Durham.[8] Such early Victorian figures show that 79 per cent of these miners were already able to read; also more than half of them had

7. From *The Report of the Poor Law Commissioners,* 1841.
8. *Minutes of the Committee of Council on Education,* 1840–41, Appendix III, p. 138.

TABLE 5

Workhouse Children in Norfolk and Suffolk, 1838

Youths from 9 to 16 years	Who can read—well	206
	—imperfectly	217
	Who cannot read	62

TABLE 6

Literacy among Northumberland and Durham Miners, 1840

Colliery	No. of Pitmen Employed	No. Who Can Read and Write	No. Who Can Read Only	No. Who Can neither Read nor Write
Wallsend	265	145	76	44
West Towneley	206	100	50	56
Benwell	153	89	29	35
Elswick	127	56	51	20
Backworth	92	55	14	23
Total	843	445	220	178

learned to write. This attainment must have been largely independent of state help which started in 1833, when most of these pitmen would have left school. In any case state subsidies were very small in the 1830s.

The Reports from the Assistant Handloom Weavers' Commissioners in 1839 indicated that handloom weavers were even more advanced. For instance, according to one inspector only 15 of 195 adults (shoploom weavers) in Gloucestershire could neither read nor write. A special survey of the reading and writing abilities of the people of Hull in 1839 found that of the 14,526 adults (people over 21) 14,109 had attended day or evening school and that only 1,054 of them could not read; in other words over 92 per cent *could* read.[9] Again hardly any of these people could have benefited from state subsidies to day-schools since the average school-leaving age in those days was eleven at most; most of these adults, therefore, were at least 15 when the state first began to subsidise schools in 1833.

Who then paid for the pre-state education? It is common to point to philanthropy and the Church. But to dwell on these sources is to conceal the part played by the ordinary people themselves. If we are to believe the evidence of Henry Brougham[10] most parents bought education by modest fee-paying. In many cases, the contribution from the so-called religious 'charity' derived from the church subscription of the ordinary working people who were using or were expecting to use the services of the schools for their own children. This was especially so in the growing and energetic Wesleyan day and Sunday schools in the north of England, and would account for instance for much of the attainment of the Northumberland pitmen quoted above.

To the possible objection that the statistics of literacy may conceal a too generous interpretation of the term 'reading ability' there are two important answers. First, there was a remarkable consistency between all the various surveys in different parts of the country and by different types of investigators. Second, there is evidence that the education inspectors who made some of the tests were so demanding that their figures were, if anything, underestimates.

9. 'Report on the State of Education in the Borough of Kingston upon Hull', *Journal of the Statistical Society of London*, July 1841, quoted by R. K. Webb, *op. cit.* See this same source for similar findings in Bristol and the Manchester areas.

10. See the quotation below, p. 173; and the last sentence from James Mill on pp. 170–1 below.

The testimony of inspectors is also apt to be 'ex parte'. Most of them were reformers, and an unconscious bias led them naturally to dwell on unsavoury aspects.[11]

A more important test of private responsibility for educational self-help in a developing country faced with an unprecedented population problem is the *rate of growth* of literacy compared with the growth of the national income per head. The period we are most interested in is that immediately before 1870. Mr Webb's general opinion of literacy in the late 1830s, a period sometimes described as the end of what is popularly known as the 'Industrial Revolution', was

> In so far as one dare generalise about a national average in an extraordinarily varied situation, the figure would seem to run between two-thirds and three-quarters of the working classes as literate, a group which included most of the respectable poor who were the great political potential in English life.[12]

By the middle of the 1860s, as will be explained below, the proportion was probably nearer nine-tenths.

The appreciable rate of growth in literacy is reflected in the fact that young persons were more and more accomplished than their elders. Thus a return of the educational requirements of men in the Navy and Marines in 1865 showed that 99 per cent of the boys could read compared with Seamen (89 per cent), Marines (80 per cent), Petty Officers (94 per cent).[13]

If we accept Mr Webb's estimate that at least two-thirds of the working classes were literate round about 1840, how far are we to attribute the improvement of much of the remaining third to

11. R. K. Webb, *op cit.*, p. 337.
12. R. K. Webb, 'The Victorian Reading Public' in *From Dickens to Hardy*, Pelican, 1963.
13. Reported in R. K. Webb, *op. cit.*, p. 149.

government intervention from that time down to 1870? It is certainly true that state subsidies played an increasing part at this time. Even so, as late as 1869, two-thirds of school expenditure was still coming from voluntary sources, especially from the parents, directly or indirectly. Even the state subsidies were derived from a tax system which was largely regressive, falling heavily as it did on food and tobacco, so it is not easy to demonstrate that had the state not raised the money through taxation to subsidise the schools the total expenditure on them would have been lower, or that the great impetus in the growth of literacy already established before state help would not have continued.

Marriage Signatures

Another set of statistics traditionally used as indices of nineteenth-century literacy are the figures showing the number of persons signing the marriage register with marks. One example of this kind of reasoning is found in the writing of Professor David Glass. Although conceding that the incidence of illiteracy in England[14] 'could not have been as high as it is in some underdeveloped countries today' he continues:

> Even so a third of the men marrying in 1840 in England and Wales, and half of the women, signed the registers by a mark; the proportions in 1870 were still 20 per cent and 27 per cent. The rate of change in the provision of education since 1870 has been so rapid that it must be taken into account when considering present day educational deficiencies.[15]

14. Professor J. L. Williams has argued that by 1870 there was almost universal literacy in Wales, but it was literacy in Welsh. What the post-1870 Board Schools did was to change this for literacy in English. (*Times Educational Supplement*, 22 May 1970, p. 20.)

15. David Glass, 'Education and Social Change in Modern England' in *Education, Economy and Society,* ed. A. H. Halsey, Free Press of Glencoe, 1962.

Accepting for the moment that such statistics are an adequate measure of writing ability, Professor Glass's concluding sentence seems odd. Is he implying that the rate of change in the provision of education was faster in the 90 years subsequent to 1870 than in the 30 years between 1840 and 1870? His figures suggest quite the opposite. An increase from 66⅔ to 80 per cent of men able to sign their names over a 30-year period of significant population increase is surely a most remarkable rate of change compared with an increase from 80 per cent to 100 per cent (at most) over a later 90-year period.

More important, this kind of argument as it stands does not show the absolute size of a schooling gap in 1870. The 20 per cent of men signing with a mark in 1870 had, on the average, left school 17 years before as the average age of marriage at this time, according to the Registrar General, was about 28 years.[16] If most people learn to read and write at school, an assumption which seems to be implied in this sort of reasoning, the 1870 marriage registers reflect the schooling of the early 1850s. A more appropriate figure to test the literacy rate at the time of the Forster provisions is that the 1891 Census. This showed that only 6.4 per cent of the men (7.3 per cent of the women) were signing the marriage register with a mark. Their average marrying age again being about 28 years and the typical school-leaving age being 11 years, these men must have left school on average round about 1874. They could, therefore, have barely benefited from Forster's 'gap filling' Board Schools since his building programme had scarcely got under way at this time. In other words if we are to accept the marriage signature test, and if we are to accept that illiteracy is mainly the result of a schooling gap, then we should

16. Registrar General Report in Vol. IV, Census of England and Wales for 1881.

conclude that 93 per cent of school leavers were already literate when the 1870 Board Schools first began to operate. Moreover, we should remember that this was not a state system as we now know it, for the 1870 Act, contrary to popular belief, did not establish universal compulsion, nor abolish fee-paying. The former came in 1880 and elementary school fees were not entirely abolished until 1918.

Not everybody, however, is willing to accept the marriage signature test of literacy. Some object that if for instance 60 out of 100 sign their names on this one important occasion in their lives, the figure may include many who perform the feat only as an isolated once-for-all gimmick designed to win social prestige. In other words we cannot be sure that many of the 60 could write more than their signature. Nevertheless, it is difficult to apply this objection to a time series of such statistics. If, for instance, with the passage of say 20 years it was found that the figure had increased from 60 to 80 out of 100 people signing their names it would be far more difficult to attribute such an increase to a growth in the average propensity to perform gimmicks. Table 7 shows the actual increase of male marriage signatures in the nineteenth century as well as figures of population increase to remind readers of the contemporary circumstances against which the educational enterprise had to struggle.

Commenting on the literacy figures, another prominent modern specialist, Professor R. D. Altick, gives what seems to be the latest word on the subject. After warning that the importance of the 1870 Act can easily be exaggerated he concludes:

> . . . The Forster Act did not significantly hasten the spread of literacy. What it did was to insure that the rate at which literacy had increased in 1851–71 would be maintained. Had the state not intervened at this point, it is likely that the progress of literacy would have considerably slowed in the last quarter of the century,

TABLE 7
Literacy and Population in Great Britain, 1841–1901

(1) Percentages of Literates (Males) Registrar General's Returns		(2) Percentage Increase	(3) Population Increase (percentage)
1841	67.3	2.0	12.5
1851	69.3		
1861	75.4	6.1	11.1
1871	80.6	5.2	12.7
1881	86.5	5.9	13.9
1891	93.6	7.1	11.2
1900	97.2	3.6	12.0
			10.3 (1901–11)
			4.6 (1911–21)
			4.7 (1921–31)

Sources: (1) and (2) R. D. Altick, *The English Common Reader,* University of Chicago Press, 1957, p. 171. (3) P. Deane and W. A. Cole, *British Economic Growth, 1688–1959,* Cambridge University Press, 1962, Table 75.

simply because illiteracy was by that time concentrated in those classes and regions that were hardest to provide for under the voluntary system of education. In short, the Forster Act was responsible for the mopping-up operation by which the very poor children, living in slums or in remote country regions, were taught to read.

Even Professor Altick, however, seems to be claiming too much for the Forster Act. For one thing, as explained earlier, such figures of literacy refer to people who were in their late twenties, not to young people of school-leaving age; in other words they overestimate the size of the 'mopping-up' operation which was called for from school provision. Further, he gives no evidence to show that the 'mopping-up' was in fact a complete success. Even by 1948 there were still in England and Wales 5 per cent of 14-year-old school-leavers officially classified as nearly or completely illiterate, and by the criterion not of writing but of reading ability (the easier of the two). More important, Professor Altick accepts too readily the assumption that the Forster Act with its Board School financed by local rates was the most appropriate means of meeting the family poverty which he seems to indicate is the chief cause of illiteracy. In Chapter 6 it was argued that the imposition of a rate system, since it is a regressive form of taxation, served to aggravate the poverty problem. This being so any champion of the Forster Act is faced with the insuperable problem of proving that much of the money so raised from poor people for public expenditure on education after 1870 would not have been spent on education anyway. But at this point the discussion leaves the question of literacy and raises questions about another index of education—the quantity of schooling—which is the subject of the next chapter.

CHAPTER TEN

The Rise and Fall of Nineteenth-Century Private Schools for the Masses

If most people were already literate in 1870, by what means was such a feat accomplished? First, the twentieth-century reader must be reminded of those private agencies which are no longer familiar: the Mechanics Institute, the Literary and Philosophic Societies, the Sunday schools. Moreover, systematic tuition in the home, often given by the parents themselves, was also quite common. Apart from all this, however, right from the early years of the century ordinary people were increasingly buying the services of ordinary schools for their children. Thus as early as the Napoleonic war period James Mill in an article in the *Edinburgh Review* (October 1813) asserted:

> From observation and inquiry assiduously directed to that object, we can ourselves speak decidedly as to the rapid progress which the love of education is making among the lower orders in England. Even around London, in a circle of fifty miles radius, which is far from the most instructed and virtuous part of the kingdom, there is hardly a village that has not something of a school; and not many children of either sex who are not taught more or less, reading and writing. We have met with families in which, for

weeks together, not an article of sustenance but potatoes had been used; yet for every child the hard-earned sum was provided to send them to school.[1]

Three years later, the third report of the Select Parliamentary Committee to enquire into the Education of the Lower Orders observed:

> There is the most unquestionable evidence that the anxiety of the poor for education continues not only unabated but daily increasing; that it extends to every part of the country, and is to be found equally prevalent in those smaller towns and country districts, where no means of gratifying it are provided by the charitable efforts of the richer classes.

The first comprehensive official statistics on schooling were provided by Henry Brougham's Select Committee in 1820. It stated that in 1818 about 1 in 14 or 15 of the population was being schooled. It claimed that this was a considerable improvement since the beginning of the century and reflected not only the energy and zealous ecclesiastical groups such as the National Society and the British and Foreign School Society in setting up schools, but also the increasing willingness of parents to send their children to them and indeed to pay the fees which were nearly always asked. In 1828 Brougham in his private capacity followed up this initial estimate with a 5 per cent sample survey of his own, using the same sources (the parochial clergy) as before. He was astonished when his findings indicated that the number of children in schools had doubled in ten years. In an age when the significance of statistical samples were not yet properly appreciated, it is not surprising that the advocates for a state system cursorily dismissed

1. See also *Westminster Review*, Vol. VI, October 1826, p. 271, where Mill asserts that reading, writing and accounts were the 'requirements now common to the lowest of the people'.

Brougham's figures. At the same time, although these persons could not offer any alternative estimate for the country as a whole, they seem to have readily accepted accounts of the educational deficiencies of particular places such as the towns in the North West. These towns, which included, for example, Manchester and Liverpool, were being daily flooded with new immigrants (especially from Ireland) and we can now see that they were not at all representative of the whole country.[2]

The principle of state subsidies to schools was accepted in 1833. The first annual grant which amounted only to £20,000 was handed to the two large voluntary school organisations for disposal. In the same year Parliament authorised another survey of the whole country but the figures were not available until 1835. The result of this official survey supported Brougham's own private estimate of the rate of growth. The numbers in schools had increased from 478,000 in 1818 to 1,294,000 in 1834 'without any interposition of the Government or public authorities'.[3] Although some people have claimed that these figures mis-reported the situation, as far as I know they have never supported their complaint with specific reasons or alternative evidence. But even if the inaccuracy were significant we must remember that so long as the series of statistics came from the same source, as was the case in the 1818 and 1828 estimates, and assuming the degree of misreporting, that is, exaggeration, were constant, the measure of *growth* in private schooling must have been tolerably reliable.

2. Writing of Manchester in *The Moral and Physical Condition of the Working Classes*, 1830, Dr J. Kay complained that Ireland had 'poured forth the most destitute of her hordes . . . ' and that they were spreading a 'fatal demoralisation of others'. At this time it was possible to get to Manchester from Ireland for as little as fivepence. Its population increased by 45 per cent between 1821 and 1831.

3. Speech in the House of Lords, 21 May 1835. Factory legislation attempted to compel education, but it only applied to a few sections of industry, and even then it was poorly administered.

It seems reasonable, therefore, to infer that when the government made its debut in education in 1833 mainly in the role of a subsidiser it was as if it jumped into the saddle of a horse that was already galloping. The question was: would the new rider improve its speed and if so, could this be done without injury? In 1835 Brougham expressed his fears very clearly. Referring to the doubling of the school population in ten years, which the official statistics had just confirmed, he urged:

> And surely this leads to the irresistible conclusion that, where we have such a number of schools and such means of education *furnished by the parents themselves from their own earnings,* and by the contributions of well-disposed individuals in aid of those whose earnings were insufficient, it behoves us to take the greatest care how we interfere with a system which prospers so well of itself; to think well and long and anxiously, and with all circumspection and all foresight, before we thrust our hands into a machinery which is now in such a steady, constant, and rapid movement; for if we do so in the least degree incautiously, we may occasion ourselves no little mischief, and may stop that movement which it is our wish to accelerate.[4] (My italics)

Brougham's fear was that the extent to which parents were faced with new rates and taxes to finance state subsidies for state education (three-fifths of taxation fell on food and tobacco at this time) would simply be matched by a reduction in their ability and willingness to pay fees. The same applied to others who supported the family. This in turn would discourage the existing expansion in private schooling. There would ultimately be no net increase in the growth of schooling but simply a change in the pattern of the existing provision. Moreover this change would do damage:

4. *Ibid.*

Let the tax-gatherer, or the county-assessor, or the parish collector, but once go his rounds for a school rate, and I will answer for
it, that the voluntary assistance of men in themselves benevolent,
and, indeed, munificent, instead of increasing, will soon vanish
away; that the 1,144,000 now educated at unendowed schools will
speedily fall down to almost nothing; and that the adoption of
such a fatal and heedless course will sweep away those establishments which, at present, reflect so much honour on the community, which do so much good and are calculated, with judicious
management, to do so much more.[5]

Over a century later, Brougham would no doubt look for support
for his prophecy in the fact that with a total population of nearly
four times bigger there were less than 500,000 pupils in unsubsidised and unendowed independent schools compared with the
1,144,000 in 1833.

The next estimates of schooling for the whole country came in
1851.[6] The Registrar General made a compilation with the aid of
his district enumerators who were conducting the ordinary population census in that year. They showed that there were
2,144,378 children attending day schools out of a total population
of adults and children of about 18 million, a proportion of 1 in
8.36.

One of the most striking sets of tables in this report gives some
clue about the *growth* of schools in the period (see Table 8 on
p. 175). Some of these tables relating to the period between 1801
and 1851 have already been given in Chapter 6 (see note 18, p. 104).

It is apparent that the vigorous growth of schools completely
independent both of official support and endowments, the
growth to which Brougham had referred, was developing into

5. *Ibid.*
6. There was a Select Committee Report on the conditions in towns in 1838. It
reported that 1 in 12 of the population were in receipt of some sort of schooling.

TABLE 8

Growth in Private Schools, 1841–51

Establishment of Existing Schools in Each of the Ten Years

	1841	1842	1843	1844	1845	1846
Private*	688	697	703	861	1,106	1,217
Public†	415	372	409	556	575	569

	1847	1848	1849	1850	1851	
					(3 months)	
Private*	1,521	1,987	2,735	3,754	1,491	
Public†	553	606	589	616	194	

Private—'All schools which derive their income solely from (fee) payments or which are maintained with a view to pecuniary advantage are to be considered private.'

†*Public*—The expression 'public' schools is intended to apply to all schools supported *in any degree* for other objects than pecuniary profit to the promoters.

Source: 1851 Census, p. CXXXIV–V.

what some would call a private school 'explosion'. What is more, many of these schools were apparently spurning the offer of treasury grants in return for state inspection.[7]

The Newcastle Commission Evidence

After the 1851 census information came the mammoth report of the Newcastle Commission on Popular Education. This body was set up in 1858 and included the economist, Nassau Senior; it

7. On the period 1800–40 a much more intensive study is now available in E. G. West, 'Resource Allocation and Growth in Early Nineteenth Century British Education', *Economic History Review*, April 1970.

reported in 1861. Its investigation deserves serious consideration because it was the first to be directed entirely and purposefully to a survey of schooling. Moreover it showed many improvements in statistical method, in particular the combination of an assessment of aggregated statistics with a cross-check of intensive sample examinations from selected areas. The first branch of the Commissioners' enquiry, which referred to the whole of England and Wales, was concerned with statistics obtained through the religious societies connected with education and through public departments. The second branch of their enquiry consisted of reports from specimen areas from the Assistant Commissioners 'who in many cases, either personally or by their clerks, assisted in filling up the forms issued from the office of the Commission':

> The result of the two branches of the inquiry has been, first that statistical information respecting the public week-day schools throughout England and Wales has been collected which may be regarded as approximately correct and complete: and secondly, that statistical details have been obtained from schools of all kinds in the specimen districts, which are not only exhaustive, so far as the districts are concerned, but which furnish proportions and averages which may be considered as representative of the rest of the country in relation to many subjects on which the statistics obtained through the societies and departments afforded no information.[8]

The specimen districts contained one-eighth of the whole population. The Assistant Commissioners' intensive surveys elicited the details of the non-inspected (i.e. non-subsidised) schools and their proportion to the inspected (i.e. subsidised)

8. Education Commission, *Report of the Commissioners appointed to enquire into The State of Popular Education in England,* Vol. I, 1861, p. 553.

schools. Assuming this proportion to hold good for the whole country, the Commissioners made the necessary addition to the total number of inspected schools in the country, figures of which were, of course, centrally available. The result at which they arrived, and which referred to 1858, was that in the country as a whole there were 2,535,462 scholars in day schools, a figure which seems quite compatible with the 1851 census which showed that the two million mark had already been topped. The next question was how many children did *not* receive a schooling. The Commission found that such general evidence as existed indicated that the bulk of the children who attended elementary schools had their names on the books of some school from six to ten years of age though a considerable number went before six and many remained until twelve. In order to calculate the number of children who ought to have been at school at a given time, the Commissioners assumed that the average period of attendance did not exceed six years. With this assumption they maintained that one-half of the total number of children between 3 years and 15 years should have been at school. This figure, obtainable from the Registrar General, was 2,655,767. Since the number actually on the books of all schools was 2,535,462, the shortfall was only 120,305. Much of this deficiency was accounted for by children who had bodily and mental infirmities, and also by children educated at home. Moreover, the Commissioners' information from the specimen districts (as against the general evidence) showed that the actual average duration at school was in fact 5.7 years. If this had been assumed in their general calculations instead of 6 years, the deficiency would have been almost negligible. In other words the figures indicated that nearly all the children were having some schooling.

These aggregate estimates were confirmed by the testimony of the ten Assistant Commissioners from their specimen districts.

Wherever the Assistant Commissioners went, they found schools of some sort, and failed to discover any considerable number of children who did not attend school for some time, at some period in their lives.[9]

Mr Cumin reported from the South West:

There are, I believe, very few cases indeed in which children have been at no school whatever.[10]

Mr Winder reported from Lancashire and Yorkshire:

My own enquiries, which were rather extensive, would lead me to believe that amongst the respectable working men in the towns, this absolute neglect is almost unknown, and that so much of it as there may be is confined almost exclusively to the lowest of the immigrant Irish, who prefer that their children should beg; to a few of the degraded class, brutalized by profligacy and poverty, and to the more ignorant of the colliers and miners.

At Rochdale, out of 1,825 scholars at evening schools, 2.85 per cent had never been to day school; and at Bradford, 6.34 per cent out of 2,006, but Mr Winder added:

I strongly suspect that these rates would be too high for the general population.[11]

Mr Foster reporting on Cumberland stated that 'There are few families without some kind of school within easy reach.'[12] Things were least satisfactory, as one would expect, in the larger and most feverishly growing towns. But even Dr Hodgson who reported on the South of London said that 'There are very few,

9. Report, p. 85.
10. *Ibid.*
11. *Ibid.*, p. 86.
12. *Ibid.*, p. 347.

perhaps, who do not "see the inside" of something that may be called a school . . . '[13]

The Commission concluded that there were no serious gaps in the provision of schools and apparently no call for state nationalised schools on the lines of Forster's later Board Schools. Certainly there was need for state aid to education but this should not take the form of state schools: it should consist of a still better system of direct grants to independent schools. The information collected in 1858:

> . . . points out the direction which future efforts for the improvement of popular education ought to assume. There is no large district entirely destitute of schools and requiring to be supplied with them on a large scale, nor is there any large section of the population sharply marked off from the rest, and capable of being separately dealt with, as requiring some special and stringent system of treatment.[14]

Because such an extensive framework of private schooling already existed, the Commission believed that the best policy for government was to avoid any general or local form of state schooling and to continue with an improved direct grant system and better inspection of the private schools. It did recommend that local boards be set up, not to run their own schools but to act as supervisors of local rate revenues designed to augment the existing central government grants. Naturally these grants were to have strings attached to them and the local boards were to perform school examining duties accordingly, but the general theme was the control and encouragement of the existing private framework rather than the political creation of new types of collectively organised schools.

13. *Ibid.*, p. 518.
14. *Ibid.*, p. 86.

As a final measure of the extent of the progress that had been made, the 1861 Commission stated that the proportion of scholars to the population in the middle of 1858 was 1 in 7.7 compared with 1 in 8.36 in the 1851 Census. Again the Commission cross-checked this estimate. Both the information gathered centrally through the societies connected with education and the returns collected by the Assistant Commissioners in their specimen districts confirmed the proportion of about 1 in 7.7. The Commission reported:

> The proportion of children receiving instruction to the whole population is, in our opinion, nearly as high as can be reasonably expected. In Prussia, where it is compulsory, it is 1 in 6.27; in England and Wales it is, as we have seen, 1 in 7.7; in Holland it is 1 in 8.11; in France it is 1 in 9.0. The presence of this proportion of the population in school implies (as is shown by the foregoing calculations) that almost every one receives some amount of school education at some period or other . . . [15]

Forster's 1870 Estimates

Nine years later Forster introduced his celebrated Education Bill of 1870. In presenting it he made hardly any reference to the Newcastle Commission's findings. Instead he seems to have relied upon information supplied by officials in his own department, and based on a special last-minute survey of four industrial towns (Liverpool, Manchester, Leeds and Birmingham). This survey, which was conducted by two inspectors in 1869 and took only a few months (the 1861 Report had been conducted by five Commissioners and ten Assistant Commissioners and had taken three years to produce), gave figures which seriously conflicted

15. *Ibid.,* p. 293.

with those of the Newcastle Report. Selecting from the 1869 survey the case of Liverpool, Forster told Parliament that it had been calculated that the number of children between 5 and 13 in that city (the ages that ought to receive an elementary education) was 80,000 while: ' . . . as far as we can ascertain, 20,000 of them attend no school whatever, while at least another 20,000 of them attend schools where they get an education not worth having.' In other words, if these towns were typical, then at least 25 per cent, but not more than 50 per cent, of the English school population was entirely without 'efficient' schooling.

Historians of education faced with some sort of choice between such conflicting estimates seem invariably to have preferred Forster's to those of the Newcastle Commission. Several writers suggested for instance that both the Newcastle Commission's composition and its terms of reference led to prejudice in its findings. The Commission was directed to 'Inquire into the Present State of Popular Education in England, and to Consider and Report what Measures, if any, are required for the Extension of *Sound and Cheap Elementary Instruction* to all classes of the People.' (My italics) My historians are quick to point out that, having spent 'alarming sums' on the Crimea War, the 1858 government was looking with apprehension at its expenditure programmes and not least the increasing cost of the annual education grant. The implication is that the authorities and their Popular Education Commission were looking for facts which would paint so favourable a picture as to relieve the government from too embarrassing a growth of educational expenditure in the future. Some writers also stress that the Commission was eager to present for the masses a class-based education designed to meet only the most elementary needs.

For those who seek objective facts such suspicions are not easy to handle. But if one is to discount the accuracy of one source of statistics on account of the personal bias of their compilers then objectivity demands that the same treatment should be accorded to all sources. One should at least consider a suspicion, for instance, that the figures produced by Forster's inspectors and departmental advisors in 1870 were exaggerated because they had a vested interest in the expansion of their own department in terms of the now classical principle of Parkinson's Law.

In the end, however, there is no need to dwell on such immeasurables, since there in one important technical comment to be made on Forster's figures which seems to resolve much of the argument. His departmental statisticians, for reasons best known to themselves, defined the term 'population of school age' as those between 5 and 13 years. But this was only as assumption, not a determined fact. If the length of schooling for the average child was in fact not eight years but something less, then Forster's conclusions must have been inaccurate; for if the *actual* school population was smaller, the deficiencies found in the survey would have been smaller too. The Newcastle Commission had gone to great lengths to discover the *de facto* school life of a typical child and they had found it to be 5.7 years. In other words the *actual* school age population as reported in 1861 was typically in the age range 5 to 11 years; it is unlikely that it had increased by more than six months by 1869.[16] Forster's advisors, it seems, in saying the 'school age population' consisted of those between 5 and 13 years, were asserting what it 'ought' to be and not what it was. Assuming for instance that by 1869 the average school duration had increased to six years from the 5.7 years reported by the Newcastle Commission, and readjusting Forster's figures accordingly, we have to multiply his 80,000 school age population for Liverpool by ⁶/₈; this produces a result of 60,000. Since this

16. Complete attendance up to 11 was not made compulsory until 1893. The school-leaving age was raised to 12 in all cases in 1899.

figure is the same as that of children actually found at school in the Liverpool survey, then on this interpretation such aggregate statistics provided no grounds for saying that there were some children without schooling at all. This being accepted, Forster's figures, far from conflicting with those of the Newcastle Commission, actually confirm them. Similarly the 1851 census information, properly interpreted, seems to be reasonably consistent with this kind of conclusion.[17]

Anyone today who, assuming that the 'proper' school-leaving age in England was 17 years, claimed that the difference between his 'school-age population' (i.e. those between 5 years and 17 years) and the numbers actually in school represented those who 'attend no school whatever' (to use Forster's words), would have great difficulty in finding a patient audience for such question-begging information. Yet such were the 'statistics' of school 'deficiencies' which issued from a zealous nineteenth-century education department for over 50 years, 'statistics' which have continued to mislead many a popular or general historian. Thus G. M. Trevelyan, author of *British History in the Nineteenth Century,* writes about conditions on the eve of the 1970 Act in the following terms:

> Only about half the children in the country were educated at all, and most of these very indifferently. England, for all her wealth, lagged far behind Scotland and several foreign countries. (p. 354)

17. See R. D. Altick's reassessment of Horace Mann's treatment of the 1851 statistics. Mann concluded from the 1851 Census Report that of the five million children in England and Wales between the ages of 3 and 15, almost three million were not at school. Altick points out that since masses of children spent much less than 12 years (i.e. the difference between 3 years and 15 years) in school, 'a larger proportion of the total population went to school *at some time or other* than is reflected by such figures'.—*The English Common Reader,* University of Chicago Press, p. 167. Even in 1965 much less than 100 per cent of those between 3 years and 15 years will be found in school!

Referring to the 1870 Act, Trevelyan continues:

> England had obtained, better late than never, a system of educa-
> tion without which she must soon have fallen to the rear among
> modern nations. (p. 355)

Again, Sir Arthur Bryant in his *English Saga* asserts:

> The great mass of the nation was illiterate. In 1869 only one Brit-
> ish child in two was receiving any education at all.

With the further reproduction of such inaccuracies in works
such as school textbooks which often use secondary sources, i.e.
other general historians, for their 'facts', it is not surprising that
popular opinion on this subject is still widely misinformed.

Was the 1870 Act a Stimulus?

Another misleading use of the nineteenth-century school statistics can be frequently found in evidence purporting to show the
progress of the supply of school places *after* the 1870 Act. First
referring to the supposed 1870 situation, Dr Pauline Gregg for
instance begins her argument thus:

> Of a population of over twenty-two million, estimating one-sixth
> as of school age, over three and a half million required schooling,
> whereas there was accommodation for only 1,878,000.[18]

Now there is no need to repeat that such an estimate of the
'school age population' tells us more about its author's personal

18. A *Social and Economic History of Great Britain, 1760–1950*, Harrap, 1954,
p. 513. There is no special reason for selecting this particular work in
preference to others. Most specialists in this field make the same kind of
argument as this author. See for instance footnote 21 on p. 185.

predilection than about the facts.[19] Consider then the second estimate in the above quotation which refers to available accommodation. The fact is that even in 1858, a decade before the Forster Act, there were over 2.5 million scholars belonging to public and private week-day schools.[20] Dr Gregg's figure of less than two million is only a measure of accommodation in the *subsidised* (i.e. inspected) *schools.* There must therefore have been additional accommodation for a considerable number of scholars in the non-subsidised (i.e. non-inspected) schools in 1870. The exclusion of any reference to the completely private sector is misleading.[21]

Consider next the way the argument proceeds:

> By 1886 the target had passed. There were then over five million school places for a population of nearly twenty-eight million.

19. One of the most respected nineteenth-century educationists, Sir J. K. Shuttleworth, thought one-eighth was the correct proportion agreed by 'most writers on the statistics of education' (*Public Education*, 1853). On this basis the school population of 1870 would be only two and three-quarter million.

20. Newcastle Commission, Vol. I, p. 573. Even the 1851 Census accounted for more than two million.

21. This criticism can be applied to several writers. Thus S. J. Curtis (1963, p. 275) is begging very big questions when he states: 'Taking the country as a whole, the schools under Government inspection had accommodation for 1,878,000 children, which was a little more than half that which was required.' This statement completely excludes the part played by non-inspected schools. Similarly C. Birchenough (*History of Elementary Education*, 1932, p. 123) reporting that only two-fifths of working-class children between 6 and 10 years of age and only one-third between the ages of 10 and 12 were in state-aided schools, continues: 'In other words there were 1,000,000 unprovided for between 6 and 10, and half a million between 10 and 12 years of age.' But those unprovided for in *inspected* schools include those provided for in non-inspected schools. If the reply is that *all* those in non-inspected schools were not *properly* provided for, this should be made clear. But it must be said at once that not even the most critical of nineteenth-century departmental reports were as severe as this about the quality of *non-inspected* schools. G. R. Porter makes the same error in *The Progress of the Nation*, 1912, p. 134.

The writer is apparently indicating first that a government could make education compulsory only after it had 'filled the gaps'; and second that this was in fact achieved in the 1880s.

One difficulty for the reader is that he is left without a guide to the precise contribution of the 1870 Act. Instead he is offered an argument of the crudest *post hoc ergo propter hoc* kind. To elicit the true *net* contribution of this Act proper account should be taken of the nineteenth-century growth rates that were already well established prior to 1870. The 'gaps' in 1870 were not a new phenomenon. There had been gaps in school provision from the beginning of the nineteenth century and, according to the evidence, they had been in a process of constant and progressive reduction, first because of private provision alone and then, after 1833, by private provision augmented in some cases by government subsidies. Only to the extent that the post-1870 'gap-filling' rates were in excess of those already established could it be clearly claimed that the Forster Act made any further improvement. Dr Pauline Gregg's figures of the growth of student places available between 1870 and 1886 should be compared with what was going on before. Table 9 indicates the pre-1870 trend and suggests that the gap-filling process was already well established.

But suppose we accept from Forster's departmental type of evidence that this growth suddenly slowed down between 1858 and 1870. How can we show clearly that the 1870 Act revived it? The first problem is that of identifying the parts of it which were supposed to be the most stimulating. Clearly they could not include any measures to make education universally free. In 1886 the majority of parents were still paying fees. Although it is true that the *relative* proportion of education costs covered by government expenditure (mostly subsidies) had increased by 1886 it is still true that ordinary fees had increased in absolute terms. Nor can we attribute any improvement after 1870 in any confident way to

TABLE 9
Growth in Private Schooling, 1818–58

Year	Population	Number of Day Scholars	Proportion of Scholars to Population: One to
1818	11,642,683	674,883	17.25
1833	14,386,415	1,276,947	11.27
1851	17,927,609	2,144,378	8.36
1858	19,523,103	2,535,462	7.7

Sources: The 1851 Census and the 1861 Newcastle Commission.

the introduction of universal compulsion since this came only in 1880 and even after that it had to be relaxed in certain cases.

Next, and this point is usually missed, much of the increase of schools in the public sector did not represent a net increase in school buildings in the country. A large part of the increase of accommodation in inspected schools between 1870 and 1886 was accounted for simply by a change over of many schools from the uninspected (i.e. unsubsidised) to the inspected (i.e. subsidised) category; 4,767 schools, accounting for over one and a quarter million 'new' places in Dr Gregg's terminology, had thus switched their colours.[22] Moreover this kind of government 'take-over' was already well under way *before* the 1870 Act.

The Board School and the Genesis of Nationalised Education

The most novel feature of the 1870 provision was the introduction of the Board School, by which the traditional subsidy/inspection principle was augmented by what may be called the

22. *Report of the Committee of Council on Education*, 1886, p. xi.

collectivist or nationalisation principle. To what extent then could this new creation have accounted for the net increase in school provision which has been postulated? Between 1870 and 1886, 4,402 Board Schools appeared. But not all of these were newly-built establishments: 1,124 of them consisted of previously subsidised schools which had simply been taken over and re-named Board Schools. (They included 792 Church, 15 Wesleyan and 223 British Schools.[23]) Furthermore there was an unknown but substantial number of other schools taken over consisting mainly of profit-making establishments, i.e. those which did not receive subsidies. The magnitude of these particular 'take-overs' was only hinted at in the Annual Report of the Education Committee for 1886. It explained (p. xii) that the boards had

> acquired a *considerable* number of schools, either by arrangement with private owners and managers, or, where the premises were held in trust for educational purposes, by transfer under the section of the Act of 1870, specially framed to meet such cases. (My italics)

The next difficulty is that, even if we do assume that there was a substantial number of genuinely new Board Schools, the nature of the 'gaps' they have were supposedly filling is not clear. Every year in which a child population increases there is in a sense a corresponding 'gap' to be filled whether it concerns food, clothing or education. For this reason it would be difficult to separate the extent to which the new Board Schools of the 1870–86 period filled the 'gaps' of 1870 from the extent to which they met the needs of 'gaps' which were subsequently caused by a rising population. This being so we enter once more into a hypothetical area of discussion as again we face the question of 'what would have happened had there been no 1870 Act?' Only if it can be shown

23. *Ibid.*, p. xii.

that the coming of the Board Schools did not discourage the setting up of new private school 'gap-fillers' after 1870 can their appearance be invariably and fully accepted as a net contribution to school provision. There are substantial grounds, however, for believing that the growth of the private sector was seriously curtailed by the coming of the Board Schools. The reasons for this will now be explained.

Effect of 1870 Act on Private School Establishment

By the 1870 Act the Education Department was empowered to have a survey made of each educational district. Where necessary a statement was issued warning that certain gaps in school provision existed and that, after a period of grace, any gaps which were still not being met privately could be filled with Board Schools. The size of the gaps was determined according to the usual departmental formula, that is by the difference between the local census return of *children of school age* (5–13 years) and the existing places available in schools thought to be *efficient*. We have seen already that the official definition of 'school age population' was based on accepted views on what it *should* be rather than what it was in reality. To this extent the 'gaps', as officially defined, were larger than would be filled voluntarily by the available number of children.[24] Moreover, where existing private

24. As a matter of fact it was later revealed that for purposes of their returns, the Education Department administrators defined 'school age population' to be between 3 years and 13 years, i.e. 2 years more than Forster's definition. The Secretary of this Department was questioned in 1886 by the Cross Commission whether he was aware that by acting on this rule he had compelled the London School Board, and school boards throughout the country, to supply an amount of accommodation which seemed likely to be much in excess of their real requirements.

At Midsummer 1885 the accommodation in elementary schools in London was 619,473; the highest number of scholars ever in attendance at any one

school places were *unreasonably* described as inefficient, the 'gap' was again overestimated and unnecessary duplication of places resulted. Excess capacity therefore inevitably appeared in many places. Because subsequent empty places in the new Board Schools proved an embarrassment, 'cut-throat' competition broke out between them and existing private establishments to secure the patronage of the prevailing student population.

Board Schools usually had overwhelming advantages over private schools in such struggles since they could call on overwhelming resources. We have already seen that the more the school boards wrote off existing private schools as 'inefficient' the higher the target 'gap' would be. But often this was due to extravagant notions about what efficiency really required in terms of buildings, playgrounds, etc. Witness Inspector Matthew Arnold's report on the London School Board in 1878:

> It cannot be right, it is extravagant and absurd, that the London boys' education should be so managed as to cost three times as much as that of the Paris one . . . Both in London and elsewhere, school boards are apt to conceive what is requisite in these respects rather as benevolent, intelligent, and scientific educationists in Utopia, than as practical school-managers. I am quite sure that their conception of what is requisite in the way of accommodations, studies, salaries, administration, is pitched too high.

With their advantage of rate aid the Board Schools could also afford to let their fees drop below those of private schools and

---

time was 539,307. Most of these superfluous places have no doubt been provided in consequence of the rule which you say the Department has acted upon. Every place in a school Board School in London has cost on the average £17 3s. 2d.; if you work that out you will see how large an expense the rule of the Department has put the ratepayers to?'

(*Answer*) That I daresay is correct; but I am only giving a statement of what the Department has done; I do not know that I am bound to defend it, whether right or wrong. (Question 1838, First Report.)

this also helped them to capture an increasing proportion of an otherwise private school clientele.

The burden of the rates was felt not only directly by those parents who paid them but also even by poorer parents who did not formally pay rates since the price of their accommodation was adjusted upwards to meet some of their landlord's higher costs. The result was that most parents had smaller net incomes after tax and were thus constrained to buy the education which was to be had at lower fees (i.e. at the Board Schools). Similarly, the effective ability (apart from the willingness) of those who normally made subscriptions to private schools was also restricted. Thus Inspector Fitch reported on the Lambeth district in 1878:

> During the few months in which I have had charge of the district several national and British schools have been closed, and there is no prospect of any school of either class. All the new schools 'in esse' or 'in posse', are those of the School Board for London. Nor can this occasion any surprise. In the densely-peopled districts of Walworth, Kennington, and North Camberwell there are few or no rich residents; the inhabitants are chiefly shopkeepers and others who form precisely the class most keenly sensible of the pressure of the rates, and most likely to regard the existence of the education rate as a reason for withholding all subscriptions from Church or other voluntary schools. The clergy of these parishes assure me of the increasing difficulty of obtaining local aid; and complain, not unnaturally, that as soon as they get a skilled and successful teacher he is tempted to leave them by the higher pay and more assured position offered by the Board.

It is interesting that although this inspector went on to regret

> the disappearance of different and interesting types of school, which, while all doing with success the same secular work, were

> adapted to the varied social requirements and religious convictions of different classes . . .

he thought the tendency was both desirable and inevitable:

> For schools which are contending with a declining subscription list and an increasing deficit are never efficient, and some of the expedients by which their managers seek to postpone the evil day are far from satisfactory.

In many cases he thought it was

> the clear duty of the managers to make the sacrifice of feeling, and perhaps of conviction, necessary for transferring their schools at once to the Board, rather than, on the one hand, to keep them working with a reduced staff and insufficient appliances; or on the other, to adopt the wasteful and selfish course of *closing excellent school buildings* and keeping them unused. (My italics)

Forster originally conceived the role of Board Schools as that of filling up gaps. These gaps were the wider the lower the efficiency of existing schools was alleged to be. But now it seems the mere presence of Board Schools was itself reducing the 'efficiency' of existing private schools. Board Schools were thus enlarging the gaps only to justify a further multiplication of their own species. The bitter complaints of those private schools which were being put out of business in the process were to the effect that the Board Schools were not real contributors to education but cancer cells in the hitherto healthily growing structure of private education.[25]

Some writers seem to suggest that the new 'competition' of Board Schools performed a necessary task of stimulating existing schools into greater efficiency. This argument reveals a misunderstanding of the nature of competition. Competition which is

25. For one example of this type of complaint see the appendix to this chapter.

socially useful requires that every single participant should be able to go bankrupt. Board Schools were in a specially protected position and they enjoyed the advantage of always being able to dip into public revenues to cover their costs even when they went above those of their competitors. The expenses of the school board were paid out of what was called the 'school fund', and the 1870 Act provided that: 'Any sum required to meet any deficiency in the school fund, whether for satisfying past or future liabilities, shall be paid by the rating authority out of the local rate.' (Section 54.) The absence of a market discipline on the costs themselves led to that situation of extravagance which called forth the protest of Matthew Arnold. Similarly G. R. Porter, in commenting on the growing expenditure burdens of a late nineteenth-century treasury, remarked:

> Unfortunately, expert knowledge of education and expert knowledge of finance are not often found in combination, and the greatest enthusiasm for educating the young is often accompanied by an utter carelessness of the money of the taxpayer . . . At present there is a vast amount of waste in unnecessary luxuries, in the building of ornamental palaces, in the multiplication of clerks, inspectors, and so forth.[26]

Altogether then, the 'competition' of the Board Schools with private schools was one which the latter could rarely hope to win. But if conditions were hostile to existing private schools they were even more discouraging for potential newcomers. Only the boldest of individuals were prepared to attempt to trade without a bounty in competition with those who traded with a considerable one (to use the words of Adam Smith). Moreover, because of the way the 1870 Act was interpreted by the administrators, the school boards soon emerged with more formidable

26. *Op. cit.,* p. 677.

power over the newcomers than was ever expected. For as the population grew and new schooling requirements arose, the Education Department took it upon itself to establish the rule that *where school boards existed, however small, they had the first right to supply the new deficiency.* If the board agreed to provide the necessary extensions additional private school accommodation would be deemed unnecessary, and therefore ineligible for any subsidy.[27] Thus it was that after 1870 the growing number of children demanding an education, a phenomenon consequent upon a rising population and a rising national income, were siphoned into Board Schools (later to be 'municipalised' by the 1902 Act and then called elementary schools) in order to fill 'gaps' which were largely of their own creation.

It would be difficult, of course, for anyone to deny that there were gaps of some sort in the provision of mid-nineteenth-century schools. What is debatable is their size and nature. What is even more open to question is the widespread belief that the Board School innovation was inevitably the most appropriate solution for filling the gaps after 1870. For it has not so far been adequately shown why the subsidy system of state aid could not, in some improved way, have achieved a better and more discriminating result, a result which did not include the wholesale de-

27. A still stronger rule which emerged from a minute issued by the Education Department in 1878 even brought a strong objection from its original instigator, Mr. Forster. At a Wesleyan meeting in 1878, he protested that those who ought to decide on new schools were those who were willing to build them. He thought that the Education Department would find that they had engaged in a most obnoxious business which they could only transact with odium if they tried to take upon themselves to decide whether any fresh school 'was necessary or not'. Forster interpreted the move to be directed at preventing 'unnecessary competition of schools throughout the kingdom'. He pointed out the disadvantage 'if schools thought they were free from competition'. Furthermore: 'The voluntary subscribers were compelled to pay their share of the rate towards the rate-schools, and if, notwithstanding that, they were anxious to have schools of their own, as tax-payers they had a right to their share of the taxes.'

struction and stunting of existing private schools and the discouragement of new ones.

Some may argue that nationalised schools were needed in the nineteenth century because they were better equipped to pursue all the various objectives of education. But this puts the question into a different category; the discussion now becomes centered on problems not of quantity but of quality. This chapter has simply been concerned with a study of the numerical estimates of the nineteenth-century school gaps and in particular those in the period of the 1870s. Such pieces of arithmetic having now been examined, the next chapter can devote itself to the problem of the quality of nineteenth-century schooling.

To recapitulate: according to government statistics it is true that in 1870 there was accommodation for 1,878,000 pupils in *inspected* schools compared with 5,145,292 places in 1886. But of this 3¼ million increase, over 1¼ million places were largely in existence before 1870 and merely transferred from the private (non-inspected) category to attain the status of inspected voluntary schools after that date. Much of the remaining increase came from the setting up of Board Schools. But again a considerable number of these represented establishments which had existed before 1870 but were taken over subsequently by school boards. For all these reasons the *net* increase of school places between 1870 and 1886 must have been very much less than 3¼ million taking all schools (public and private) together. Whatever this net increase, the credit for it can only begin to be attributed to the 1870 Act if it can be shown that it reflected a growth rate higher than that previously prevailing. This has yet to be done in a convincing way. In other words what remains clearly to be shown is that the increase of school places in the government sector was not completely offset by the damage done to the growth of the private sector.

Appendix—The Manchester Schools and the
'Menace' of the School Board Soon After 1870

The following letter to the Manchester School Board from the Rector of St Paul's, Hulme, on the question of the proposed transfer of the Mulberry Street Schools to the Manchester School Board, was written on 24 April 1876:[28]

Having carefully considered the proposition made to me several weeks since by the Chairman and Mr Hughes, desiring me to place the St Paul's C. of E. Schools . . . under the management of the School Board, I beg to submit the following for your consideration.

The reasons stated by you for making this proposal were that the Zion Chapel Schools, in the immediate neighbourhood, which could not succeed as denominational schools, having been placed under the Management of the School Board, are now in a prosperous condition, hence the present application to take them under the Management of the School Board.

'That the St. Paul's Schools', to quote from the 'remarks' in your published summary of 'school attendance', 'are not flourishing', I admit, and it was urged by your Chairman and Mr Hughes, as a reason for compliance, that still further injury must be done to them, by the erection of a new Board School, in the immediate neighbourhood, as the inevitable result of my refusing to hand over our Schools to the School Board.

But the statement that our schools are not flourishing requires explanation, and I am prepared to show that it is principally owing to the opening of the Zion Chapel Schools as Board Schools which offer advantages which few of the denominational schools can afford to give.

I refer, first of all, to the low fixed charge, by these Board Schools, of 3d. per week, for boys and girls, whereas in St Paul's, and in all the denominational schools in the neighbourhood there is a scale of fees, rising from 3d. to 6d. per week.

28. The letter is to be found in Appendix VIII of *The Manchester School Board*, M.Ed. Thesis, C. B. Dolton, Durham University, 1959.

I refer next to the Board Schools supplying free of charge Books, Copy Books, Slates, etc. for school use, and home lessons, which is not done in any of the denominational schools in the neighbourhood.

The case is simply one of under-selling, and it requires no argument to prove that any denominational Schools situated at a *reasonable* distance from these Board Schools must have a hard struggle to keep up their numbers under such favourable and unfair competition.

But in the case of St Paul's Schools the Board School is not placed at a reasonable distance but is in the *same street,* and is distant not more than a *hundred yards.* But I would ask, are the St Paul's Schools the only denominational Schools that are not flourishing?

What of the Radnor Street, Wesleyan Schools not distant from the Board Schools more than three minutes walk? I have it from a personal enquiry from the Master that the Board Schools have had the effect of diminishing the number of scholars by 150, many of whom were paying 6d. to 8d. per week.

I would therefore suggest that in the next published summary of School Attendance the Wesleyan denominational Schools, Radnor Street, should also be remarked upon as 'not flourishing'.

But the fact I perceive is admitted by you in 'The Summary of School Attendance', when a decrease is shown in that part of Hulme in which St Paul's and the Radnor Street Schools are situated, and which is accounted for by the increase in the part of Hulme adjoining, in which the low fee'd Board Schools are placed.

Let it not however be imagined that I am opposed to giving a cheap and good education to the people. If their circumstances require it, I would gladly aid to the utmost of my power in providing for the education of their children at the lowest possible charges. But I submit that their circumstances do not require it. They are well able to pay, as they have done heretofore, 6d. and 8d. per week. In the adjoining parish of St Michael's, where the circumstances of the parishioners are not near so good as in my parish, the parents are paying fees up to 8d. per week for their children. In the

Commercial Schools which are situated in my parish, and which are not more than 110 yards from the Board Schools, an arrangement has been made to receive boys of the same age, to be instructed in the same subjects as those in the Board Schools, at the rate of 30s. per quarter. An admission fee is also required and the parents have to pay for Books, etc.

Under these circumstances I would ask whether it is right to pay out of the public rates for the education of children where parents are well able to pay for themselves? And is it right to members of Christian Churches, which have made great sacrifices of time and money to erect schools in connection with their places of worship, to set up rival schools which, as ratepayers, they are compelled to support, in addition to their having to support their own denominational schools?

As to the lack of school accommodation, it is, I submit, quite a mistake to say any such thing. The total school accommodation for St Paul's Parish, which contains a population of about 8,000, is for 2,630 children, and they are not full by 800—a fact to be borne in mind before there is any more school building in the Parish.

The Conclusion, gentlemen, at which I have arrived, after mature deliberation and consultation with the principal contributors towards the erection of St Paul's Schools, is that we cannot accede to the proposition of the Chairman and Mr Hughes to hand over these Schools to the School Board, involving as it would a breach of trust.

They were subscribed for as Church of England Schools and the trust deed sets forth the same object, so that if even the menace, for so I regard it, to erect another Board School in the immediate neighbourhood takes effect, why then the only alternative remaining will be for us to close these Schools of ours.

(Rev.) Thomas Daniels,
Rector of St Paul's Church, Hulme.

CHAPTER ELEVEN

The Quality of Schooling before and after 1870

It must be said at once that most discussions on the quality of nineteenth-century schooling easily become involved with highly subjective statements which are rooted in value-judgements specially precious to individual participants. Discussion about this sort of problem has already been entered into in Chapter 6 which considered the 'religious difficulty'. The present chapter will confine itself to a commentary upon the more measurable aspects of the qualities of educational resources in the nineteenth century.

The first general point to be made arises quite naturally from the investigation of the preceding chapter. Any assessment of the extent of inferior quality education in the private sector will not be complete without an attempt to establish how far the situation was due to government intervention itself. It has been shown that private establishments were complaining about 'cut-throat' competition from government-aided schools well before 1870. After that date the coming of the Board School accentuated the process. Merely to chronicle the contemporary accounts of inspectors concerning the squalid conditions and poor facilities of private schools, as many history books do, is to present the situation incompletely. It is obvious from the documents (see the appendix to the preceding chapter, the inspector's report on pp. 152–3 and p. 95 of the 1861 Commission Report) that many of the private institutions were suffering their last death throes following the subsidised competition from schools in the public sector.

A very rough modern analogy may help the reader to appreciate the point. Assume that a government of today declared its opinion that there were marginal gaps in the provision of retail shops. Suppose that it set up its own shops and subsidised one or two 'gap-filling' private groups. Imagine that these shops, on the strength of revenues from rates and taxes, then started selling the goods at half their normal price and also proceeded to provide the highest wages and best conditions for their employees. Very soon other shops far and wide would be forced into cutting their prices to prevent the transfer of their customers to state shops. Their buildings would then fall into disrepair and they would lose the best shop assistants to the state shops. Would an historian of 100 years hence, in looking at the forlorn state of twentieth-century private shops, be justified in concluding that, with such bad quality service, the state was fully justified in subsequently entering the whole field of retailing as soon as was possible in order to make 'proper retail provision' for the people?

Most of the traditional complaints about nineteenth-century schooling seem to fall under four main headings: first, poor school attendance; second, a school-leaving age which was too low; third, poor quality premises; fourth, poor quality teaching. These will now be examined in turn.

School Attendance

In several nineteenth-century government reports the observation was made that school attendance was erratic, especially at certain periods of the year, such as harvest times. Modern writers may well be justified in using this testimony as criticism of nineteenth-century schooling; but how far should they go? One must guard against the temptation of applying too readily twentieth-century English standards to a nineteenth-century English setting. It must be remembered that in those days national income per head was much lower and agriculture was a relatively more important source of ordinary livelihoods. It is now a recognised world-wide phenomenon that absenteeism from schools is more common in agricultural areas, whether their education is compulsory or not, and whether they have state schooling or private schooling. Thus Professor T. W. Schultz, an American economist specialising in education, observed in 1963:

> The average daily school attendance of children from farm homes tends to be lower than that of children from non-farm homes. There is much work on farms that children can do and many farm families are relatively poor which makes the value of the work that children can do for them by missing a few days of school now and then rate comparatively high.[1]

Periodic absence from nineteenth-century schools was thus not necessarily a sign of parental negligence. It could have been the result of a judicious weighing of the expected sacrifice in family income against the expected educational benefits. This would have been a rational assessment, in other words, of what Professor Schultz considers to be an educational cost (opportunity cost) which is particularly important today in low income countries. It is significant that after education was made compulsory special holidays were frequently granted at harvest times. It is interesting too that in some Communist countries today

---

1. T. W. Schultz, *The Economic Value of Education,* Columbia University Press, 1963, p. 30.

school children are actively encouraged, and sometimes compelled, by government authorities to help with the harvest. Indeed all kinds of work on farms is often made part of the normal educational curriculum in these countries and is then of course included in the national statistics of education.

A Low School-Leaving Age

Besides the problem of spasmodic school attendance there was the question whether most parents should have postponed the time at which their children started full-time work in order that they could have had one or two extra years at school. Once again the argument becomes involved in particularities of costs and benefits. In England in the 1860s older children could usually earn over 6d. a day. According to one estimate the earnings of a 12-year-old boy averaged one-sixth of the wages of his father.[2] The weekly cost of sending a child to school therefore consisted not just of the amount of the school fee (which averaged 3d. a week) together with books and writing material, but also of the three or four shillings of potential family earnings which had to be sacrificed. In times of sickness or unemployment, such earnings must have been of agonising importance in parental decision-making, especially when there were many younger children to feed.

There can be no doubt that among some families poverty was frequently pleaded as an excuse for not sending children to school. Often, however, the problem was a genuine one. A child could never be happy in the environment of a distressed family. If he could relieve this distress by earning money, say at the age of 12, then it should be recognised that, to this extent, the happi-

2. Mr Belby, House of Commons, 11 July 1870.

ness of the child itself was being promoted. For this reason, although the claims of schooling can with justice often be pressed very far, they can never be absolute.

In retrospect one can argue that Forster's 1870 advisers were right in believing that the school-leaving age *should* have been 13 years and not 11 or 12 years, provided one is also prepared to argue that the money for such extra education could and should have been forthcoming. It is possible to begin to make a case on these lines by pointing out that the principle of 'progression' in taxation, that is the principle whereby taxation is designed to fall relatively less severely on the poor and relatively more severely on the rich, was never implemented at any time in the nineteenth century.[3] Developing this, it could equally be pointed out that nineteenth-century tax burdens on poor parents with large families were particularly severe. For since taxes fell heavily on articles of consumption, taxation increased with the number of mouths to be fed by any given wage-earner. Accordingly one can argue that if many of these taxes had been removed and progressive income tax substituted such families could have afforded to buy more education for their children. But once this position is taken up, the frontal complaint is not that the government did not decree a higher school-leaving age and provide education 'free' but that it did not correct a wrong distribution of income.[4]

If the net incomes of the poor had in fact been increased by

3. Apart from the exemption of a certain minimum from the income tax. This tax, which was *proportionate,* was not firmly established until 1846, and even then it accounted only for a small proportion of total government revenue.

4. Brian Simon (*Studies in the History of Education,* 1960) emphasises that nineteenth-century workers felt particularly grieved about, and demanded compensation for, the fact that the middle classes with the help of the 1868 Endowed Schools Commissioners diverted the educational endowments of the poor to their own use. In the terminology of the Marxist class war the 1870 Act was a victory of a newly enfranchised proletariat over a ruling class which had been exposed as expropriators of educational endowments for the poor.

such fiscal reform one must assume that much of it would inevitably have been used to buy more schooling and, therefore, for very many people the imposition of a compulsory school-leaving age would have been superfluous. The evidence shows that the number of years of voluntary schooling was indeed growing with those gradual increases in incomes that came with the economic growth of the nineteenth century. Once again the experience of Victorian England seems to be typical of low-income countries throughout the world today.

> People in low income countries . . . expect children to enter upon useful, regular work, say, at age 10; as countries rise on the income scale, the age at which children are expected to take jobs also rises.[5]

So much for the costs of nineteenth-century education; what about the benefits? The supply of education was not homogeneous; sometimes, because of low standards, parents may have kept their children away from school with good reason. Witness

---

There are difficulties in this reasoning, however. The endowments were not typically intended for the exclusive use of the poor but for the benefit of all children of a neighbourhood. Moreover, much activity in endowed schools was, by the nineteenth century, consisting of costly education in many subjects which early endowments did not cover. These had to be paid for by expensive fees and this naturally excluded many of the poor, especially when the burden of taxation on them was increasing. It seems that those who wish to argue the case of nineteenth-century injustice to the low income groups would seem to be on more substantial ground if they concentrated on the contemporary burden of taxation. If they did this they would also see that the 1870 Act was not the victory for the poor that is commonly assumed. For, as has been shown, it aggravated the burden of taxes on the poor and eventually saw to it that the extra money collected from them (rates and taxes) was spent less effectively (e.g. because of the extravagance of Board Schools) than they would have spent it themselves. In other words, the poor themselves paid for the 1870 Act and in more ways than one.

5. Schultz, *op. cit.*, p. 31.

the testimony of Assistant Commissioner Mr Coode as reported in the Newcastle Commission Report of 1861:

> It is a subject of wonder how people so destitute of education as labouring parents commonly are, can be such just judges as they also commonly are of the effective qualifications of a teacher. Good school buildings and the apparatus of education are found for years to be practically useless and deserted, when, if a master chance to be appointed who understands his work, a few weeks suffice to make the fact known, and his school is soon filled, and perhaps found inadequate to the demand of the neighbourhood, and a separate girls' school or infants' school is soon found to be necessary.

Mr Coode gives several instances of this. In one case a schoolmaster began with three pupils and raised the number in 15 months to 180; a strike took place and reduced the colliers to great distress:

> but such had now become the desire of the children to remain at school, and of their parents to keep them there, that the greater number remained during a time when the provision of the school fees must have encroached in most of the colliers' families on the very necessaries of life.[6]

It must be remembered that this was a period of flux. Considering the serious problem of population pressure, and the consequent dramatic increase in the demand for schooling, it would have been remarkable if unsatisfactory establishments, public or private, had never made their appearance. Therefore the judgement that all people in all places and under all circumstances could or should have all kept in step by withdrawing their chil-

6. *Royal Commission on Popular Education*, 1861, p. 175.

dren at some particular 'school-leaving age' is surely too peremptory.

Poor Quality Premises

Another common complaint was that private school premises were very inferior. But again one must remember that the effect of the 'cut-throat' competition of the state schools, as explained at the beginning of this chapter, was probably particularly severe on the ability of private schools to maintain their buildings, so this point should here especially be borne in mind. Further, it should be remembered that it was not only *school* buildings which were 'inferior' in the nineteenth century. There were also poor houses, hospitals, shops, offices, etc., simply because the national income per head was lower than it is today. Beyond this it should be noticed that every age seems always to be ashamed of its school buildings whether they are under private or public control. Thus, according to *The School Building Survey,* 1962, a high proportion of children in state schools today are to be found in 'ancient', 'ugly' schools with overcrowded classrooms and very poor sanitation and circulation. Half our schools today have mainbuildings erected before 1903. It is interesting that when people protest about children still being taught inside Victorian 'monstrosities' they are usually referring to the Board Schools which, as we have seen, were feverishly erected after 1870.

Poor Quality Teaching

The fourth type of criticism of the quality of education is that the schools were staffed by unqualified persons. Once again, those who argue that things could have been organised so very much better have to show how the necessary funds and resources could have been provided at the time. A demand for very high standards of qualification and schemes for prolonged teacher training paid for out of regressive taxes and rates, and at a time when a rapidly increasing population was endeavouring to protect its living standards, would certainly have been beyond reach. The annual supply of teachers would immediately have been reduced as more of them went to training colleges and others were discouraged by the prospect of postponed earnings. Classrooms would thus have become more crowded or the number of teaching hours per child reduced.

But just how bad was the situation? One should not accept eyewitness accounts too indiscriminately. It should be remembered for instance that the unfavourable reports on 'unqualified' teachers were often made by state inspectors who themselves had received formal training and who may therefore have sometimes felt prejudice against those 'amateurs', as they called them, who had not. In some cases, too, since the Victorian inspector was often regarded with fear, one cannot always be sure that all their reports on the performance of pupils of unqualified teachers were made under the best of conditions. Sir James Kay Shuttleworth, the first secretary of the Committee of Council on Education, himself admitted:

> All inspectors are not perfect either in manner, utterance, choice of words for poor children, method of examining them; nor in the skill, kindness and patience required to bring out the true state of the child's knowledge.[7]

A complaint that occurred with much repetition in the nineteenth-century education reports was that many persons had taken to the 'teaching trade' because other occupations had

7. Letter to Lord Granville, 4 November 1861.

failed. The difficulty with this kind of remark, of course, is that it can be made about nearly every occupation in turn. Some people, for instance, become actors after being unsuccessful as bank clerks; it does not necessarily follow, however, that they inevitably make bad actors too. Nevertheless it is easy to see that many charlatans did make their appearance amongst nineteenth-century teachers; as suggested above, this would not have been surprising considering the extremely buoyant demand for schooling at the time. What is more difficult to believe is that many such persons could have typically established themselves on any *permanent* basis. Mr Coode's evidence is testimony to the shrewdness of parents in detecting and effectively rejecting the 'quacks'. In other words, that some teachers were incompetent does not seem to have been one of those secrets known only to the learned![8]

Apart from this it would be ingenuous not to notice that the complaints about the new and motley array of 'unprofessional' teachers came more from suspicious 'professionals' than from parents. Consider the following protest of Mr Cumin concerning the 'mushroom growth' of schools in the 1850s. Many private teachers had appeared, he said, who had 'picked up' their knowledge 'promiscuously' or who were combining the trade of school-keeping with another:

Of the private school masters in Devonport, one had been a blacksmith and afterwards an exciseman, another was a journeyman tanner, a third a clerk in a solicitor's office, a fourth (who was very successful in preparing lads for the competitive examination in the dockyards) keeps an evening school and works as a

8. This testimony to the widespread sagacity of ordinary people would seem to be supported by the evidence (illustrated in Chapter 9) that most of them were at least managing to make themselves literate.

dockyard labourer, a fifth was a seaman, and others had been engaged in other callings.[9]

Again Dr Hodgson, regretting that 'the profession, as such, hardly exists', enumerated 'grocers, linen drapers, tailors, attorneys, painters, German, Polish and Italian refugees, bakers, widows or daughters of clergymen, barristers, surgeons, housekeepers and dressmakers as being found amongst the teachers of private schools.[10]

Whilst the average small schoolboy would today no doubt display wonder at the prospect of having such a colourful variety of experienced adults to teach him, the nineteenth-century professional teacher, it seems, saw them as nothing but a collection of uncolleged, and therefore untrained, individuals with no redeeming qualities of possible benefit to the schools.

One cannot make a proper historical assessment of these 'amateur' teachers without checking to see that their counterparts, the trained teachers in the inspected schools, were so much more competent. Investigation on this score does not raise much confidence. One unfortunately dominating element which persisted in the teacher training colleges, and which was perpetuated by the system of inspection, was the Victorian obsession with rote learning. Mr Altick writes:

> Having successfully memorised and parsed the hundreds of lines of verse set for the highest standards of the elementary school, prospective masters and mistresses became pupil teachers, and then, if they survived entrance examinations, went on to a normal college.[11]

9. The Royal Commission on Popular Education, Vol. I, 1861, p. 93.
10. *Ibid.,* p. 94.
11. *Op. cit.,* p. 161.

In the normal college (i.e. teacher training college) the process continued relentlessly:

> It was the same story to the very end of the nineteenth century; the institutions that fed teachers into the expanding elementary school system were pedant factories, whose machinery efficiently removed whatever traces of interest in human culture the scholars had somehow picked up earlier in their careers.[12]

The more one agrees with this description, the more one should presumably re-assess the traditional strictures about the relative shortcomings of untrained or 'non-professionals'. It seems at least arguable that the communication of the experiences of adults from varied occupations might, on average, have been more useful and inspiring to children in school rooms than their parroting of English literature before young school teachers who, in their own lives, had had little time to do anything else.

But even the contention that the trained teachers were on the whole to be preferred is separate from an argument to justify the predominant invention of the 1870 Act: the Board School. For it would have been quite feasible to have continued to depend on independent schools (with some receiving direct grants and others not), while legally forbidding the employment of uncertificated teachers in any of them. But when pressed this far some educationists fall back on the argument that what was really lacking before 1870 was an educational *system,* and that the real foundations of one was laid by the Forster act. But this line of argument associates such observers with the view that without a central plan there must always be chaos. To those who do not like central planning for its own sake and prefer to stress the need for liberty, variety, spontaneity, flexibility and experiment in education, the absence of a 'system' is an advantage rather

12. *Op. cit.*, p. 162.

than otherwise. Putting education more firmly into the grip of politics, as such 'systems' inevitably do, is regarded by the liberal as damaging to the general quality of education.

Quality Improvements Depend on the Choosers

All societies find themselves faced with the limitation that resources are both scarce and differentiated. The mere transference of control from the private to the public sector does not of itself alter this fact. Granted that the Victorian era was one of rapidly increasing population and therefore of inevitable hustle, in order to justify this transference what has to be shown is that the necessary weeding out of the growing supply of educational services was performed better by fallible *public officials* than by fallible *private individuals.* It must certainly not be assumed that the latter, if left by themselves, would have caused no improvements of quality at all.

The evidence of Mr Coode showed how, in his district, ordinary parents were ready to use the good schools and to withdraw their custom from the bad. But similar reports came from other districts and the Newcastle Commission in its overall reference to parents declared:

> they prefer paying a comparatively high fee to an efficient school to paying a low fee to an inefficient one. . . . There can be little doubt that a school which combined high fees with a reputation for inefficiency would soon lose its pupils.[13]

On this evidence it follows that there was a built-in mechanism ensuring that inefficient schools were already being weeded out. Parents were their own inspectors and, compared with official

13. *Op. cit.,* p. 74.

ones, they were not only much more numerous but exercised continuous rather than periodic check. Moreover the sanction exercised by the parents was of much more financial significance to a school than was an unfavourable inspector's report. For if parents withdrew their children, the school lost not only the government capitation grants but the parents' fee payments as well.

Because of the customary practice among writers of laying special emphasis upon the role of the church and of philanthropic bodies before large-scale government provision in education, many people are apt to underestimate this financial power of ordinary parents on the eve of the 1870 Act. In Leeds, according to the 1869 survey, for instance, it was not the government nor charity but parents who provided the largest single source of current revenue to the schools for working-class children (see Table 10).[14] Forster told Parliament in the following year that school fees by parents added up to £420,000 per annum for the whole country. He vouched that ' . . . generally speaking, the enormous majority of them are able, and will continue to be able, to pay these fees.'[15]

It is not surprising that with parents paying the piper so substantially it was they who were so effectively calling the tune. It seems too that they would not have it any other way; they mistrusted 'free' education:

Almost all the evidence goes to show that though the offer of gratuitous education might be accepted by a certain proportion of the parents, it would in general be otherwise. The sentiment of

14. Return to the Address of the House of Commons of 2 March 1870, dated 18 March 1869, p. 5

15. Education Bill, First Reading, 17 February 1870.

TABLE 10
Day Schools for the Poorer Classes of Children:
Leeds, 1869

Source	£	s.	d.
Taxation (including govt. grants)	6,036	4	2
Voluntary subscriptions	2,291	1	8
Congregational collection	425	3	6
Fees or payments by scholars	9,098	13	6
Endowment	266	8	8
Other	658	11	2
Total	£18,776	2	8

independence is strong, and it is wounded by the offer of an absolutely gratuitous education.[16]

Conclusion

That there was a considerable degree of unavoidable poverty in
the nineteenth century is a proposition with which many people
could easily agree. That this same poverty was the main reason
why the school life of many children was not as long as it should
have been can also be reasonably contended. But the argument
that the true remedy for this situation was for the government to
supply poor people with 'free' education out of taxes and rates

16. Newcastle Report, p. 73. Once again this conflicts with several accounts
in history books. It is true that in the 1860s certain trade unions and particularly
active groups like the Birmingham League were campaigning strongly for 'free'
education. But must we inevitably take as representative of all parents the
statements of such politically organised local pressure groups when the
systematic survey sponsored by the government in the shape of the Newcastle
Commission produced such contrary evidence?

which fell so heavily on themselves is a much more questionable form of logic. To supply through the political process something which people were already obtaining (often more effectively) for themselves was not so much to reform as merely to re-form. And even if it could be demonstrated satisfactorily that a substantial proportion of the state school finance in the latter part of the nineteenth century did not fall on poor families but came directly from the rich, it has still to be shown why such redistribution of wealth could not have been more effectively accomplished for most people by the earlier introduction of progressive income tax and the reduction of indirect tax.

Those who object that it would have been wrong to return to most families their 'cash' rather than 'free' schools, on the ground that the parents would have irresponsibly spent it on themselves or upon inferior education, are really rejecting the premise that the basic problem was poverty, and substituting the proposition that it was negligence or indulgence. But those who wish to enter this particular debate should be prepared to look at systematically collected evidence in order to gain a *typical* or *overall* impression; it is dangerous to rely on the isolated utterances of this or that novelist or poet as many writers have done.

CHAPTER TWELVE

Twentieth-Century Legislative Changes and the Struggle for Control

It was shown in the last chapter that up to 1870 the schools had three possible sources of income: subscriptions, fees and state subsidies or grants. After 1870 a fourth major source, the local rate (property tax), was introduced. By an Act of 1902 the Board Schools were taken over by 330 local authorities which became responsible for them in the same way that they were responsible for the water supply, roads and police.

Self-Propelling Legislation

Whereas the 1870 Act referred only to elementary education the Act of 1902 empowered the new education authorities to provide 'education other than elementary', that is, secondary and further education. This legislative enlargement should be interesting to those who have followed the argument about the protection-of-infants principle outlined in Chapter 1. It will be remembered that such reasoning established the state's responsibility for seeing that those of its members who were not capable of making decisions because they were below a given age were receiving at least a minimum level of education. Much of the public provision of technical colleges and adult education which the 1902 Act empowered local government to provide cannot be justified on the same grounds since these branches are services which are supplied to grown-up persons, many of them voters and taxpayers. One possible conclusion, therefore, is that modest educational legislation, once established, adopts some momentum of its own and spawns further legislation which despite the absence of any connection with the original principles on which it was based, is accepted without challenge by an electorate which has apparently become conditioned by its own institutions.

It is one thing to argue that children are not responsible agents and that they should be protected from ignorance by an intervening state which sometimes provides free of charge the necessary minimum of instruction. It is quite another thing for the state to intervene to give *further* education to *adults* whose fees are paid with the help of a forced contribution from other adults who have not the wish or the time to avail themselves of the subsidised service. It may be replied that the beneficiaries of such a scheme would be too poor to buy themselves the education in question. But, as has been constantly stressed, this is an argument not for protection but for less inequality of incomes and is best met by redistributive taxation which gives the minorities in question the *cash* rather than the *service*. But, in any case, the subsidised or 'free' further education service has rarely organised to discriminate in favour of the poor. For on the one hand the poor themselves pay taxes, e.g. on tobacco, sugar and rates, and, on the other, the 'free' services are made use of by people who are above the poverty line.

The only other way in which one can attempt to justify adult education by cross-subsidisation is by the external economies argument. In other words Mr A who pays the taxes but doesn't use the subsidised education may be consoled because he ultimately receives intangible economic benefits from Mr B who does use it. Since I have already tested this proposition in Chapter 7 I shall only make the further observation here that adult education financed from rates (property taxes), which the 1902 Act let in, includes much expenditure on courses, the benefits of which are largely confined to the immediate participants. Taxpayers whose consumption enjoyments do not include these particular educational courses (e.g. art appreciation, athletics, etc.) are net losers. If Mr A's leisure consumption, for instance, consists of listening to music at home, he will usually be content not to ask Mr B to subsidise this enjoyment. So when Mr B demands that *his* leisure pursuit in the form of a college course be subsidised out of general government revenue, some of which comes from taxes on Mr A's stereo equipment, the case is not easy to substantiate.

'Free' Schooling

The beginning of the twentieth century saw also the birth of another revolutionary principle, the establishment of 'free' schooling. H. C. Barnard describes the evolution of this principle as follows:

> . . . the question of compulsion was at last settled, but fees were not at the time entirely abolished . . . With the introduction of compulsory schooling, it naturally became increasingly difficult to collect them. In 1891, therefore, a special fee-grant of 10s. a head was introduced, and this measure made elementary education virtually free; other provisions secured that there should be no areas which were entirely without free schools. The Fisher Act of 1918 finally and definitely abolished fees in elementary schools.[1]

1. *History of Education*, 1947, p. 198.

That Barnard does not feel obliged to give reasons for his statement that it was 'naturally' more difficult to collect fees after compulsion illustrates the complete change of attitude that took place when the twentieth century took over from the nineteenth. Here again we have an example of the way in which legislation once started often evolves in a very different way from that intended by the original authors. For it will be remembered that Forster and his followers emphatically urged in 1870 that fee-paying should remain and that special cases of hardship should be met by free school tickets.

The lawyer, A. V. Dicey, seems to have been one of the few writers at the turn of the century to question the switch to 'free' education:

> This last change [the abolition of fees] completely harmonises with the ideas of collectivism. It means that A, who educates his children at his own expense, or has no children to educate, is compelled to pay for the education of the children of B, who though, it may be, having means to pay for it prefers that the payment should come from the pockets of his neighbours.[2]

Dicey contended that this latest development in educational legislation typically demonstrated how far the older arguments for individualism had become out of fashion. The individualists had maintained that the duty of the taxpayers to pay for the education of other people's children was no greater than their duty to pay for the feeding of children whose parents were not paupers.

> But this line of reasoning meets with no response except, indeed, either from some rigid economist who adheres to doctrines which, whether true or false, are derided as obsolete shibboleths; or from philanthropists, who, entertaining, whether consciously

2. A.V. Dicey, *Law and Public Opinion in England*, 1952 edition, p. 278.

or not, ideas belonging to socialism, accept the premises pressed upon them by individualists, but draw the inference that the State is bound to give the children, for whose education it is responsible, the breakfasts or dinners which will enable them to profit by instruction.[3]

To the classical economists the abolition of fees would have been seen primarily as a crucial severance between parents and the school authority. The fees were seen by Adam Smith, for instance, as a necessary instrument of dispersed control; to transfer a child, and therefore the fees, from one school to another was an effective means of communicating parental disapproval of a negligent school government or an unimaginative or torpid headmaster. Once this mechanism was removed, as it was after 1891, the older economists and indeed W. E. Forster, the architect of the 1870 Act, would have feared the growth of central authority and parental apathy or helplessness. The voice of the organised professional teacher and educationist would predominate, and that of the parent would be critically weakened. For the parent, having been accustomed to a powerful method of voting in the market would be relegated to the much less articulate method of voting through the political process at periodic elections.[4]

There were three major reasons why this exchange of voting methods was retrograde. First the system of political voting by the ballot box only took place at long intervals. Voting in the market, on the other hand, is a process whereby the wishes of the parent are immediately and more continually expressed, for the market mechanism is, in the words of Lord Robbins, 'a continuous general election on the principle of proportionate represen-

3. *Ibid.*
4. For the actual extent of the nineteenth-century parental power of 'voting' via the fees see again the evidence and argument of p. 211–12 above.

tation'. Second, the political process allows advantages to those who can organise themselves more readily into pressure groups; and because parents (especially mothers fully occupied at home) are less easily organisable in the political sense than others, much of their bargaining power is reduced. Third, voting through the ballot box is much less discriminating since it is less able to avoid the necessity of large 'package deals'. For instance, the selection of a local councillor involves voting not only for what he is expected to do in education but also for his policy in housing, roads, health, sewage, etc. In contrast, the fee-paying system, where it had developed as it had done in certain parts of the country and especially in Scotland, nicely discriminated not only between schools or schoolmasters but also between subjects. In Scotland, Robert Lowe once remarked, 'they sell education as a grocer sells figs'. The point was that the purchase of figs was not conditional upon the purchase of potatoes, apples or clothes, and by splitting the fee the parent could secure, say, less Latin and more arithmetic.

Apart from the disadvantages of the change in the 'voting' system the classical economists would have drawn attention to the accentuation of a tendency which was already well established: the driving out of business of existing independent schools and the discouragement of new ones. It will be remembered that after 1870 there were three categories of school: first, the Board School (which we may call the state school); second, the school which received state subsidies in return for inspection (which we may call the 'semi-state school'); third, the completely independent school. The financial advantages already possessed by the Board Schools over the completely independent schools before 1891 were of course sharpened more than ever when fees were abolished. But the subsidised schools (the 'semi-state schools') were also to suffer when the Act of 1902 reorganised the system of grants to these establishments. For under the new system of rate aid, which was established by this Act, public support proved to be much less generous in financial terms.

Such decisive foundations having been laid at the beginning of the century, there is not need to elaborate the developments of the next 30 or so years within the main structure. In any event, since many of the *ad hoc* provisions of this interim period were consolidated in the epoch-making 1944 Act, it will be more convenient to review next this landmark legislation.

The 1944 Act

The Education Act of 1944 seems, in many ways, to have been the logical fulfilment of the legislative momentum described earlier. The following were among some of its most important provisions:

Fees were abolished in secondary schools;
the school-leaving age was raised to 15;
new facilities for children above and below school age were to
     be provided by government out of taxes;
there were to be nursery schools for children under five years
     and 'country colleges' for young people aged between 15 and
     18 years, and part-time attendance was to be compulsory;
all children were to have secondary education from the age of
     11 years.

New generations had now appeared who had never experienced the exercise of choice by the payment of fees for their children's education. One can easily conjecture that by 1944 many people had been so conditioned by long experience of state dependence that they had begun to believe in the image of a beneficent state, which gave them services for which they did not have to pay. This, of course, was an illusion. Certainly many people recognised that the money had to come from taxation. But for some peculiar reason, when most people think of taxation they think primarily of personal income tax. Yet (to risk offending the reader with repetition) this tax supplies only a little more than one-third of government revenue; many people forget that they are paying taxes every time they buy such things as beer, tobacco, television, stereo equipment, cosmetics, sugar and petrol, and that, as their incomes and spending increase with the progress of time, so does the revenue received by governments. The point is that nobody has yet shown that the 'free' education services provided for typical families today are not substantially paid for out of revenues collected also from the same typical families.

It was probably because of this increased popular susceptibility that the 1944 legislation could be written in bolder and more positive terminology. It was now thought to be insufficient to express the state's responsibility merely in terms of seeing that a child was not deprived of a *minimum* of education. *All* children were now to be 'given' an education which was to develop them 'up to their full capacity', or to use the words of the Act, according to their 'age, ability and aptitude'. Thus, a movement which had started with the modest aim of filling up gaps, first by government subsidies to private schools, then by government-run schools, had gathered such momentum and achieved such proportions that it finally became an expression of full government educational paternalism for all; the only 'gaps' which remained seemed to be those in the government's own system of universal education, those being 'filled' by a few remaining independent schools, and tolerated it seems only by virtue of political expediency.

Education According to 'Needs'

Education has now become a 'social service' in which, as in other social services, the confident modern terminology includes frequent reference to what is called the satisfaction of people's 'needs'. Now some people speak of 'needs' with such felicity as to give the impression that all one has to do is to state them. If people 'need' bread, then give them bread; if they 'need' council houses, then give them council houses; and if cars are another 'need' then presumably it is again sufficient just to discover it and state it.

In education the 'needs' approach is more than usually plausible and appealing to the man in the street. Education is 'different' because not only do people have 'needs' but they are of a very special sort. First, since children are not responsible persons, their 'needs' have to be fulfilled under a special climate of trust and responsibility. Second, since each child is a separate personality his 'needs' are unique, that is to say, different from those of all other children. These points seem to have been acknowledged in the 1944 legislation in impressive terms, the most striking instance being the pronouncement that each child was to be educated according to its 'age, ability and aptitude'.

Many an ordinary person no doubt breathed a sigh of relief and wonder at these words; relief because he or she seemed to have a great moral and economic responsibility transferred from him as a parent; wonder because the phraseology seemed to reflect the authority and prestige of the highest professional advisers. It probably did not occur to these parents that in their own homes they, too, had for years been feeding, clothing and generally nurturing their children according to their age, ability and aptitude, and that they, too, had been using professionals and experts in their everyday purchases for their children. Of course most parents did not always presume to know better than the best of the professionals or better, say, than a government inspector of shops. But when, for instance, they bought shoes for their child they obviously did not get each shoe fitted without reference to the child's 'age and aptitude', a reference which reflected a combination of their own opinion with that of professionals, the manufacturers and retailers. The parent usually did, however, presume to have enough common sense to be able to recognise and avoid the offerings of the *worst of the suppliers.*[5] Their complaints immediately after 1945 about their prolonged captivity in a war-time system of rationing in which they often felt themselves too much at the mercy of their assigned retailers did, of course, eventually lead to an abandonment of these controls perhaps because the restrictive legislation had not been imposed long enough to condition people in the same way that it had done in education.

Thus, the surrender of free adult choice in schooling and its transference to government cannot be supported on the grounds that there were inadequate *technical* means of education available before government intervention. The evidence, as I have shown, does not demonstrate that most parents were originally failing to send their children to school. The argument therefore narrows down to the proposition that a centrally provided and centrally administered system is *qualitatively* preferable to any other. On what grounds is this proposition supported in the twentieth century? W. O. Lester Smith answers a similar question as follows:

> What apart from the change in our political theory, were the particular motives that led Parliament to make the centre so strong?

5. Judging by the 1861 Report on Popular Education, they certainly exercised this kind of common sense in the nineteenth century when they had complete freedom to choose teachers for their children. See the quotation on p. 205 above.

Two stand out prominently, . . . (1) a belief that you cannot approach equality of opportunity unless someone is able to insist that all local authorities, and all promoters of voluntary schools observe and maintain certain standards, (2) a recognition of the fact that you cannot hope to distribute fairly available man-power and materials unless the Minister has an effective voice in planning and in the determination of priorities.[6]

I examined at length the first of these (the equality of opportunity argument) in Chapter 5 (see p. 58) and I reached the conclusion that, if anything, the working of the legislation has made for less equality of opportunity than before; whilst in Chapter 7 it was shown that the central planning of manpower has so far met with little, if any, success. In this chapter I shall try to make a closer assessment of the 1944 Act in terms of its own specific objectives. In so doing I shall go over some ground already covered in Chapter 2, but in a way which will, I hope, place the earlier material in another perspective.

Did the 1944 Act Do What It Promised?

Despite the frequent reference in the 1944 Act to educational 'needs', reference to several of them in subsequent practice was downplayed, presumably because of the scarcity of resources in real life. For instance, nursery schools and 'country colleges' did not develop as promised. As another example, the reduction in the size of classes was not achieved as planned. The more formal administrative re-shuffling of the system that the Act prescribed was, of course, carried out. Primary schools, for instance, were separated from secondary schools. Secondary education was now provided for all, after an original re-naming process, following their hiving-off from the elementary or central schools. In addition, the school-leaving age was raised as intended.

6. *Education*, Pelican, 1961.

Among the administrative failures of the Act, one of the most conspicuous was the inability to fulfil Section 76. This laid down that subject to certain conditions, pupils were to be educated according to their parents' wishes. I have already examined the reasons for this failure, and in particular I have referred to the subsequent administrative practice called 'zoning'. If a parent lives almost on the boundary of one of these 'zones' he can procure his child's shoes or food from either area, but usually not his state education (Chapter 2, p. 24). Here it will be fitting to look at one particular avenue of escape for parents which has been severely discouraged. Local authorities are empowered, where they see fit, to use rate funds to enable parents to get free entry into independent or direct grant schools. In practice most local authorities, it seems, jealous for the promotion and expansion of their own schools, have shown no enthusiasm when parents have asked for such 'privileges', which, of course, allow them to break through the 'Berlin Walls' of the zoned state system. The London County Council, deliberately cut down the number of free places in independent schools. To the suggestion by some parents that the LCC was trying to force children into its comprehensive schools, the authority replied in effect that free places in independent schools have only been used in the past as a 'safety valve' to ease the pressure of school population bulges.

This example illustrates clearly the dramatic dilemmas, frustrations and upheavals which characterise a mixed education system, a system wherein collectivist institutions try to exist side by side with subsidised ones. That local authorities can so peremptorily withdraw support from direct-grant schools places such schools in a position of uncertainty which in any ordinary business would be quite intolerable. From the community's point of view this state of affairs is wasteful in at least two ways. First, if, in order to obtain sufficient funds to finance a large new comprehensive school building programme, a local authority is forced to cut down its support to direct-grant (independent) schools, many of the latter will be forced to close down. This means not only the destruction of long-standing and well-tried educational institutions but also that, at a time when school buildings are supposed to be scarce, several existing ones may be forced out of the sphere of education altogether. Second, if, at a subsequent local election, a different political majority gains power, the decision to create a comprehensive school system may be reversed.[7]

Discussion about the merits or demerits of a comprehensive system will be undertaken late in this chapter. The issue here is the objective of Section 76 of the 1944 Act which refers to parental wishes. It is obvious that the greater the variety of schools, which the direct-grant or state bursary system allows, the easier it will be to cater to a variety of parental wishes. Conversely, the more that available schools become merged into monolithic institutions drawing upon zoned 'catchment' areas, the smaller the range of parental choice between schools.[8]

The Case of Mrs Baker

A series of legal actions[9] which started in 1952 and did not end until 1962 demonstrated how barren in practice were some of the more ambitious phrases of the 1944 Act. In particular this litigation, which was the only example of its kind and therefore something of a test case, showed how far, at least in some local

7. Thus Middlesex after the war with a Labour majority decided on comprehensive schools. In 1949 a Conservative majority reversed the decision. Pupils and staff surely suffer considerably from this kind of 'stop-go' education policy.

8. In Bristol the fact that 28,500 parents petitioned against their local authority in 1964 showed how substantial the number of rejected parental wishes had become.

9. See *The Times*, Law Report, 6 February 1960, p. 10; *Eastern Daily Press*, 16 March, 15 July, 14 October, 16 November 1961, 18 July 1962.

authorities, government had reduced parental freedom of choice, and how far the 'age, ability and aptitude' thesis had turned into a verbal defence of local officials and away from the magnanimous edict that many people had once believed it to be.

Mrs J. Baker, mother of several children, expressed the wish in 1952 to educate her children at home. In the course of her expensive ten-year struggle she was twice fined, once sentenced to two months' imprisonment, and described as being 'plainly contumacious'. Some of her children were made, and then un-made, wards of court. At the end of a long struggle, an appeal court at last found that, as she had maintained all along, she *was* giving her children an education which was suitable for them.

The main interest in the Baker case for the purpose of this book lies in the way in which the authorities claimed that they were giving a more efficient education than the parent. The School Attendance orders served on Mrs Baker announced the decision of the Education Authority that one particular village school was suitable for her four children. Mrs Baker, conducting her own defence, asked how the committee had arrived at this decision in view of the fact that they had never seen the children. In reply she was told that the school was just over a mile from Mrs Baker's home and it was the school which children living in that area were normally expected to attend.

> Mrs Baker: 'The question of considering age, ability and aptitude is therefore pure nonsense? In fact all the Authority care about is not that the children should receive suitable education, but that they should attend the nearest school?'
> Mr Earl, Senior Welfare Officer: 'Yaxham school is regarded by the Education Authority as the proper school for children up to the age of eleven in that area. It is considered suitable for the ability and aptitude of these children.'

Mrs Baker: 'Although their actual individual ability is not known to the Authority?'

Mr Earl: 'It is considered suitable.'[10]

Mrs Baker was accused of not being 'properly qualified'. Whereas the Authority had no objection to the moral and spiritual aspects of the education she was giving her children at home, they thought their mental development was being retarded. Yet it seems that everyone who sat in judgement on her proved less qualified. One court decided to examine one of her sons themselves. It had been explained that this boy was interested in farming and that his 'countryfied' education at home had so far been in this direction. One barrister apparently thought it a test of this sort of 'education' to ask the boy the dates of George III. The magistrates, during their formal examination, asked what was in a camel's hump: when the boy gave the answer 'fat', they rejected it, saying it was 'water'. The boy asked them to look it up. The magistrates had to admit he was right. Despite all this, this court still found that Mrs Baker was not satisfactorily educating her son.

THE MORAL OF THE BAKER CASE

This example is significant because it shows how far we can become slaves of conformity and suppress individuality and spontaneity by our mistake of concentrating power instead of dispersing it. In reading this case one gets the distinct impression that Mrs Baker's main shortcoming in the eyes of the local authorities was not her 'failure' to educate her children according to their needs but her refusal to obey official commands and to show exact equality with other parents. One is reminded of de

10. As reported in J. Baker, *Children in Chancery*, Hutchinson, 1964, pp. 53, 54.

Tocqueville's general remarks on the natural progressiveness of collective power:

> Every central power, which follows its natural tendencies, courts and encourages the principle of equality; for equality singularly facilitates, extends, and secures the influence of a central power.
>
> In like manner, it may be said that every central government worships uniformity: uniformity relieves it from inquiry into an infinity of details, which must be attended to if rules have to be adapted to different men, instead of indiscriminately subjecting all men to the same rule . . . The faults of the government are pardoned for the sake of its tastes; public confidence is only reluctantly withdrawn in the midst even of its excesses and its errors; and it is restored at the first call.[11]

The case of Mrs Baker also provides still more evidence of the subsequent neglect of Section 76 of the 1944 Act respecting parents' wishes. If parents are really intended to be partners with the state it is important that they should be well informed about the schools that are available. According to her own account, Mrs Baker was ordered to send her children to a school of which she knew nothing. Because of her ignorance she eventually wrote to the authorities asking permission for her to visit it and to see the children at work and to inspect such things as the building and the preparation of meals. One would have thought that the initiative in this matter would ordinarily come from the supplier of the service. One would normally expect them to see to it that the facts about the services which they are supplying should be widely known. This could be done, for instance, by direct invitation to parents to make personal visits to schools, and by the issue of brochures; it is impossible for parents to

11. de Tocqueville, Alexis, *Democracy in America*, New American Library, 1956, p. 123.

make suitable choices if such information is kept from them until after their child is placed in a school.

Judging from a 1964 survey of the literature supplied by local authorities for parents,[12] the experience of Mrs Baker seems to be quite common. The authors of this enquiry asked every education department to send them copies of booklets, etc. sent to parents in its area. Much variation was found in the frequency and the style of the material. Many of the leaflets showed the desire of the local authority to remove parents' anxiety about the 11-plus examination or about the secondary modern schools selected for their children. Such schools were typically depicted in the leaflets as giving the 'right sort of education for most children'; 'the schools that give the best chance of happiness for four-fifths'. There is obviously here a frequent attempt to placate disappointed parents.

The same investigators also carried out an enquiry among a cross-section of parents. They found that 'Basically, what they wanted was less propaganda and more facts':

> They would have liked something on the lines of the traditional private school prospectus, stating the educational aims of the head, listing the staff with their qualifications, the number of children and the streams into which they were divided, subjects taught and examinations taken, facilities for games, languages and outside activities, library, laboratory and workshop space, with the actual numbers of pupils in each class and the numbers taking certain courses and going on to certain careers . . . They thought these descriptions should include all schools in an area, irrespective of type, and should go direct to parents automatically, before

12. 'Partners or customers?' Shirley Korner, *Where?*, Summer 1964, p. 29. This article is introduced by the caption: 'Are parents a nuisance? You might think so if you read some of the material local authorities send out to parents. How rarely parents find themselves regarded as equal partners in the educational process!'

any selection had been made. (Many areas that do send separate prospectuses only send them once the children have been allocated, so that parents have no way of knowing beforehand what the schools are like.) [13,14]

The Seventies, Eighties and Nineties

The strengthening monopoly of public education resulted in the emasculation of parental choice in more ways than those described so far. Of the most significant post-war changes, perhaps the most striking was the eventual conversion of what, following the 1944 Act, became a tripartite system of selective schools (secondary grammar, secondary modern and technical schools) into a single kind of institution, the comprehensive school. Whereas in the late 1960s such establishments accommodated about only 10 per cent of British state school children, by the late 1970s the proportion in comprehensive schools had risen to 90 per cent.

Sucessive opinion polls, nevertheless, indicated that such radical reorganization was not desired by a large majority of the public. In 1957, for example, a poll specially commissioned by the

13. *Ibid.*
14. Some critics are not in favour of widespread private market provision of many goods or services because they fear that the ordinary purchaser will be duped by advertisers. It is in the interests of those who want to get and to hold customers, and who are confident in what they have to offer, to broadcast as much information about themselves as possible. There is good advertising and bad (propaganda) advertising but one can make reasonably strong arguments to the effect that *normally* it is only the good advertising that pays and survives. Those who think that legislation which causes public institutions to supersede private ones will inevitably dispense with the need to advertise are mistaken. In the end advertising of some sort will emerge whatever the institutional setting. Ultimately, therefore, citizens must compare for themselves the advertising of public with that of private institutions and judge the relative 'goodness' and 'badness' accordingly. And if they suspect the existence of 'hidden persuaders' at all it seems that they should look for them no less in the public than in the private sector.

Labour Party indicated that the majority of the public was basically satisfied with the existing selective (tripartite) system of schooling and that only 10 per cent believed that selective education was socially undesirable.

Furthermore:

> . . . while there was a strong desire for traditional changes, such as the reduction of class sizes, there was practically none for radical reorganization.[15]

In 1967, two years after local education authorities had been ordered to submit plans for comprehensive reorganization, another poll showed 76 per cent of the public in favour of retaining grammar schools. In July 1987 yet another opinion poll revealed that 62 per cent of the population was in favour of returning to a system of grammar and secondary modern schools. A second poll in October found 50 per cent supportive of the same proposed change.[16]

Other signs that the ordinary public had lost control of its state education system included the insinuation of what to the layman appeared to be strange new philosophies expressed in terms of incomprehensible vocabularies. Consider for example the language of the reviewer of a recent book, emerging from the London University Institute of Education. He praises the authors because they subscribe

> to one version or another of the real books approach if only in that they consider code-learning as something that can happen incidently in the course of worthwhile reading enterprises.[17]

15. M. Parkinson, *The Labour Party and the Organization of Secondary Education*, Routledge and Kegan Paul, 1970, p. 31.

16. John Marks, *Standards in Schools*, The Social Market Foundation, London 1991, p. 40.

17. John Marks, 'The National Curriculum and Primary School Method', Centre for Policy Studies, London, November 1932, p. 8.

The newly imposed philosophy described itself as 'child centred' and emphasised 'projects', 'discovery methods' and 'self-expression'. Individual children, it claimed, would develop spontaneously and acquire the skills they needed if only they were left to themselves. 'Didactic teaching, which means the transmission by teachers of systematic bodies of knowledge, was to be avoided, while examinations and assessment of all kinds should be downplayed if not abolished altogether. Unfamiliar but 'trendy' courses began to crowd out the traditional subjects of history, mathematics, English literature and geography. The newcomers to the curriculum included 'peace studies', 'world studies', 'life skills', and 'social awareness'. In several cases the purpose of such innovations seemed clearly political.

By the 1980s the resultant reduction of time spent on the more rigorous traditional subjects was showing up in international comparisons of student achievement. The comparisons revealed, for instance, that the average 15-year-old Japanese child was being better educated in maths and other testable subjects than the top one-quarter of British 16-year-olds who were passing at O-level. Also 30 per cent of all 16-year-old school-leavers in Germany were attaining the equivalent of O-level passes in at least four core subjects compared with 12 per cent of 16-year-olds in England. Meanwhile universities as well as businesses were complaining more and more about what was being perceived as an alarming growth of illiteracy.

As for the performance of the comprehensive schools, by 1986 the National Council for Education Standards and senior statisticians at the Department of Education and Science were agreeing that districts with selective schools (grammar and secondary moderns) had better expectations of good examination results at O-level than districts with comprehensives. Furthermore, having been established with the aim of decreasing inequality, the comprehensive school clearly had not succeeded in its objective. But to democrats and libertarians the most crucial failure was the continual snubbing of parents and, indeed, the disregard of the preferences of the majority of the public as a whole.

The Legislation of 1980, 1986 and 1988

In view of the litany of problems and deficiencies just outlined, it is not surprising that some strong public resistance was becoming manifest by the mid-1980s. One result was the attempt by political leaders to introduce a series of 'once and for all' fundamental reforms.

IMPROVED PARENTAL CHOICE

Since 1980, the central government has repeatedly declared its intention of widening parental choice and generally restoring taxpayer/citizen influence and control. Reversing the burden of proof in favour of parents, the Education Act of 1980 obliged local education authorities (LEAs) to show why a parent's preference for a school should not be satisfied. Local appeal committees have since been established to hear the complaints of aggrieved parents on behalf of their children. The same principle infused the Education (No. 2) Act of 1986, which gave parents a much greater involvement in the running of schools through their direct participation in new governing bodies with substantial powers. Meanwhile the Education Reform Act of 1988, through its open enrolment provisions, secured more choice for parents, requiring schools to admit pupils up to the limits of their physical capacity. By specifying that the allocation of delegated budgets should be primarily student-based, the Education Reform Act of 1988 has ensured that parental choice influences individual schools directly in the sense that the more pupils a school attracts, the larger its budget becomes.

GREATER SCHOOL AUTONOMY

The 1980s saw the emergence of the individual school's governing body as an independent unit and the movement to greater
school autonomy at the expense of the Education Committee of
the LEA. It was the Education (No. 2) Act 1986 that defined for
the first time a clear and distinctive job for each separate school's
governing body on which parents and teachers would always be
represented. The Education Reform Act of 1988 carried this process further through delegation via local management of schools.

GREATER ACCOUNTABILITY

By the 1990s schools had been made more accountable to parents,
employers and the wider community. The Education Act of 1980
had taken the first step towards requiring the publication of performance data in school prospectuses.

> That requirement was strengthened in 1986; again in 1988; and
> was completed in the Education (Schools) Act of 1992 which, in
> line with the Citizen's Charter, made provision for the publica-
> tion of data about performance and school attendance, as well as
> four-yearly inspection reports. Annual meetings with parents to
> consider a report from the governing body and the publication of
> financial data under the local management of schools are part of
> the same process.[18]

The government also now insists that examinations and testing
are the main keys to monitoring, raising standards and informing
parents.

A New Social Contract?

At first sight the reforms just described look impressive and they
have certainly drawn enthusiastic praise from many observers.

18. *Choice and Diversity: A New Framework for Schools*, Department for
Education, London: HMSO, July 1992, p. 5.

According to Martin McLean, Britain's Education Act of 1988 shifted the role of central government from provider and manager of public education to legal arbiter and protector of consumer rights.[19] As is well known, given a stipulated minimum in favour, parents in England and Wales can now opt out of the current local education system by reorganizing their schools under individual trusts run by managements of parent-governors. The trusts are directly financed by the central government. This pressure to bypass local authorities is seen by McLean, not as a new departure, but a resuscitation of the social-contract philosophy of governmental responsibility for social services that prevailed between 1830 and 1870, a philosophy, according to him, that derives largely from Bentham, J.S. Mill and Nassau Senior (and to which list could no doubt be added Robert Lowe).

McLean appears wrong in some respects and right in others. He is mistaken in linking the nineteenth-century period to a social contract. The masses appear to have been manipulated rather than consulted by the nineteenth-century Utilitarians and others; and consultation, after all, is the essence of any social contract. On the other hand, McLean is undoubtedly correct in drawing some parallel between nineteenth-century Benthamism and the structure of the 1988 British Education Act. For despite its claim to be a movement largely for parental choice, the initial four clauses of this Act place extraordinary, and in some cases unprecedented, powers with the Secretary of State.

The second clause provides that for every grant-maintained (GM) school the methods of teaching shall follow precisely those laid down by the central government. This clause fulfils the

19. Martin McLean, 'The Conservative Education Policy in Comparative Perspective: Return to an English Golden Age or Harbinger of International Policy Change?', *British Journal of Educational Studies* 36.3 (October 1988), pp. 200-17.

highest aspiration of the nineteenth-century founder of the English public system, James Kay. The first and third clauses establish and describe a national curriculum such that government leaders will determine, for instance, whether French is better than German, or the new math is better than the old, an arrangement that, in principle, was close to the heart of John Stuart Mill. Bentham would have been pleased that nowhere in the description of the national curriculum is there any mention of religious education. Finally, Robert Lowe would no doubt approve of the provision whereby methods of assessment (examination) will follow those laid down by the central government. He would have been disappointed, however, by the absence of any payment by results. In addition he (and Senior) might have been somewhat surprised that, over a century after he had expressed the need 'to compel our future masters to learn their letters', government compulsion and provision still dominate.

Parents who, under the new British legislation, opt out in order to have their school controlled by themselves will face many problems. Generally they are better consumers than managers. And consumers prefer wide and meaningful choice. But this in turn requires competition via a positive-priced system. Modern British authorities, just like the nineteenth-century Benthamites, however, dislike this. The charging of fees by maintained schools is forbidden under the 1988 Act. It is this fact more than any other that brings into question McLean's argument that the British central government has now become a protector of consumer rights.

Clearly many aspects of Benthamism in education retain a firm hold. It certainly seems to have ingrained itself into the very bones of the British civil service from which successive ministries of education receive constant advice and guidance. This is not to say that there is at present any obvious official desire to promulgate or implement Bentham's central pleasure/pain philosophy. What remains is the *machinery* of Benthamism—the mechanisms of central administration, curricula selection and examination. Many writers in the field of public choice conclude that those who benefit most from a government school system are the suppliers of education since they have been granted the privileges of protected income and jobs. The Benthamites did not want free trade in working-class education. But the absence of internal free trade implies monopoly. And to the economist at least, this and the survival of a strong and ambitious central bureaucracy is still the chief inherited legacy.

The Bureaucracy Struggle

The recent legislative thrust in Britain has amounted to a struggle for power between two types of bureaucracy, local and central, with the latter emerging triumphant. The new powers the bureaucracy enjoys are not likely to be reduced dramatically in the near future. Indeed the economics literature predicts a strong *growth* of a bureaucracy's budget once it has removed or reduced the power of competing bureaus. But it is the growth of the budget that provides senior bureaucrats with greater income and job security prospects.

Evidence potentially supporting such predictions is contained in yet another education bill introduced in Parliament towards the end of 1992. The main context of its proposals relates to the opting-out by parents of the control of local education authorities. The danger is that parents will merely be switched from the dominance of one form of government to the greater one of another. It is certainly pertinent that the 'opted out' GM schools come under the continuous watchful eye of the Secretary of State. Indeed, in addition to his powers over the curriculum he has discretion to put forward his own proposals concerning changes to the character of any GM school 'if he judges it appropriate'.

The power and budget size of the central government bureaucracies can be expected to increase in proportion to the number of schools that transfer from LEA to GM status. By mid-1992 only about 300 schools had made this transfer and this situation was obviously disappointing to the government. As a result plans were afoot to make the ballot procedures simpler and to achieve more flexibility and perhaps generosity in financial support for GM schools in the future. The government expressed hopes in 1992 that the total of GM schools would reach 1,500 by April 1994.

Some potentially significant influence in reaching this total will occur through central government action to close what are deemed to be very inefficient schools in the LEA sector. More precisely such schools will be given the blunt option of closing down or opting out. When a school is judged by inspectors to 'require special measures', the local authority will have the right to appoint additional governors and suspend the school's right to run its own budget. If these measures fail, the Education Secretary will send in a 'hit squad' in the shape of a temporary body of at least five outside managers to prepare the school for GM status—and all this *without* parental ballot.

Returning now to the bill before Parliament at the end of 1992: It proposes a powerful new bureaucracy to take control of education as schools opt out of the LEA control. It will take the form of what is called the 'Funding Agency for Schools'. This body, comprised of 15 members appointed by the Education Secretary, will monitor the finances and management of the GM schools. It will also gain powers over the allocation of places and admissions in the LEA sector once 10 per cent of its pupils are taught in GM schools. Clearly there is considerable scope for central government contained in this planned legislation. Indeed the Education Secretary is hoping to gain as much as 44 new powers from it.[20]

The argument of the bill is that the cost of the new agency will be met by savings in the Education Department. The skeptic, however, will believe this when he sees it. One is reminded of the education bureaucracy in New Zealand in 1988 after it had been given the task of implementing a prestigious report that had recommended strong decentralisation. Legislation was subsequently passed replacing the Department of Education with a small ministry, but, in effect, the old department soon reappeared under five new labels. At the end of the exercise, moreover, most civil servants in education had benefited financially.[21]

Assisted Places Scheme

There is one relatively neglected aspect of the legislation of the 1980s that has interesting parallels with the British system of direct grants to independent schools that was employed between 1833 and 1870. The system lingered after 1870 and remained in a very attenuated form right down to 1976, by which time it was confined to a few superior, mainly secondary schools. When in 1976 the direct grant system was terminated, 59 of the existing direct grant schools entered the state system, while 119 became completely independent schools. These latter schools subsequently benefited from the resuscitation of the direct grant principle when, in 1981, the Assisted Places Scheme was established. The objective was to provide a ladder of opportunity for able but poor students. Under the scheme today, low-income parents can obtain assistance with independent school tuition fees if the

20. 'Patten Unveils More Bureaucracy to Run Opt-Out Schools', *The Times*, October 31 1992, p. 6.

21. Stuart Sexton, *New Zealand Schools: An Evaluation of Recent Reforms and Future Directions*, New Zealand Business Roundtable, Wellington, N.Z., 1990.

school has been approved by the Department of Education and Science.

In 1992 there were about 27,000 students receiving assisted places at 295 specified independent schools in all parts of England and Wales (there is a separate system for Scotland). About 5,000 new pupils enter the scheme every year, but mainly at the ages of 11 or 13.

One consequence of the scheme is that 'funds follow the child', a principle that today's government insists it wishes to follow because it encourages 'market discipline'.[22] The question arises, therefore, why the Assisted Places method cannot be relied on much more than it is. Why are the places limited mainly to 'able pupils' who can show that they have the potential for high academic achievement? Such pupils can expect a higher than average life-time income whether they are in Assisted Places or whether they remain in government schools. Such discrimination does not evidently square with the objective of promoting equality of opportunity. But this embarrassment would be removed if the Assisted Places Scheme were extended to the whole population of school-age children. The demand for independent places would of course, vastly expand, but with reasonably free entry the supply of new schools could also increase, and often perhaps via the transfer or renting of assets of state schools that are closing down.

The economist would see the main virtue of such a change to be the return to the price system in education. For without positive prices competition and market discipline is never really effective. If, moreover, the government is serious in its stated quest for more market discipline and competition, it must recall another key condition: freedom of entry. But nowhere in the

22. See *Choice and Diversity*, Department of Education, 1992.

current white papers or official announcements is this point emphasised. Continuing silence on it will only encourage the view that the unspoken objective is not to encourage newcomers but to protect the existing state schools (which includes the GM establishments). And this objective, of course, is consistent with maintaining, if not expanding, the power and the incomes of present members of the bureaucracy.

The present system of 'opting out' simultaneously obliges a family to 'opt in' to another form of government-provided school. The question of why parents should not be given the fullest of options as just described is never addressed.

PART FOUR

New Patterns in
State Responsibility

CHAPTER THIRTEEN

An Educational Model in Political Economy

In this section (Part IV) I shall look again at the two principles around which political economists have established a case for state intervention in education: the 'protection principle' and the 'neighbourhood effect' principle. To state principles is one thing; to choose appropriate policies is another. Modern discussion is hindered because of the failure to bring to the surface all the background assumptions on which it is based. Since principles operate in different settings, yesterday's policy may be inappropriate today. It is important, therefore, first to clarify one's assumptions about settings and circumstances. In order to crystallise the arguments of the various parts of this book it will be helpful first to conduct a discussion on the assumption that we are about to establish our state intervention policy for the very first time and under explicit conditions. It is hoped that such a hypothetical exercise will serve as a peg on which to hang most of the more important findings of earlier chapters. The more practical problem of how best to modify an old and traditional framework of state intervention will be explored later.

Parental Choice: Liberation versus Emasculation

To many twentieth-century Americans the public school may have become a 'necessary' institution simply because it is one of those institutions to which they have become accustomed. It may be salutary to remember that the original American common school was not 'free', and indeed that most early Americans were educated outside of public schools. It should be helpful therefore to rehearse the basic arguments that have led to the present system. To do this I shall first present a simple model that will illuminate most of the basic issues. After that, I shall relate the discussion to the real world and show the effects of the emergence of the U.S. public school system upon education costs and upon individual rights under the First Amendment.

The Initial Model

I shall make the following three explicit assumptions: first, that state education has not so far been established in the country; second, that taxation is therefore correspondingly much lower than 'normal' so that ordinary people for instance are expecting 'customary' amounts of taxation on daily purchases and thus have more disposable money in their purses; third, that out of every 1,000 families with children only 50 families are on the borderline of sending or not sending their children to school whilst the other 950 are so doing. Lest anyone considers this third assumption as too unrealistic let him consider that it fits in reasonably with the historical evidence of family behaviour documented in this book.

To elaborate the model further, imagine that a campaign has for a long time been organised by a pressure group, on which the teaching unions are well represented, in order to complain that because education is not yet universal, that is, 100 per cent of children are not yet being compelled by their parents to go to school, and because some parents are sending their children to inferior schools, government intervention should immediately take place.[1] Assume that this campaign succeeds and the machinery of government is now called upon to operate. The minimum education in which the state is interested is first defined; it is normally, say, to consist of eight years of schooling (a provision which, in fact, at least the 950 families are already making voluntarily for their children).

Because the state is not satisfied about the quality of some existing schools it can lay down and police minimum standards. What level these should be will have to be carefully considered because it is possible that they could be set *too* high in relation to available resources. More important, it will be necessary to examine thoroughly the reasons why existing standards are thought to be unsatisfactory in places. One reason may be that competition between schools is imperfect. The most direct way to meet this problem, of course, is to concentrate on breaking down local monopoly positions; this cannot successfully be accomplished by the introduction of government schools that are under no obligation to cover their costs. Where the imperfection of competition is due to a lack of knowledge among parents the state can temporarily establish agencies to provide them with as much information both on the alternatives available and on the minimum standards that the state recommends. Given the maximum of parental free choice, pressure will be brought to bear on the least satisfactory schools so that they are constantly prodded into matching the services of competitors threatening to attract or already attracting their clientele. In these conditions there

1. This assumption also includes the historical evidence. See Chapter 17.

would be every reason to expect efficiency in schools to continue rising until they all exceeded and made superfluous the minimum standards originally specified by the state.

Beyond laying down minimum standards and the establishment of an inspectorate, further intervention should clearly be seen in three distinct steps: first, the provision of legislated compulsion; second, covering the costs of education by government, i.e. government provision only of educational *finance* to families; third, the actual provision of education by government authorities. I shall follow Professors Milton Friedman, A. T. Peacock and Jack Wiseman[2] in their argument that the third of these steps (state schooling) is not a necessary one; beyond this I shall, I think, go further than these writers in outlining qualifications upon the other two.

To continue with the illustration, the next task should be to find out as accurately as possible the reasons which account for the behaviour of the doubtful 50 families in every 1,000. Suppose, first, that investigation indicates that 20 of these families, even though they can normally be expected to act responsibly, are in danger of not sending their children to school not because they are unwilling but because they are too poor. What is the most direct way in which government can meet their case? Obviously by concentrating on the direct alleviation of the root of their problem and relieving their poverty. But how best to increase the net incomes of these families?

Reduced Taxation

The state may see its first duty as that of discovering to what extent the poverty is due to the existence of government itself. It

2. Milton Friedman, *Capitalism and Freedom,* University of Chicago Press, 1962; A. T. Peacock and J. Wiseman, *Education for Democrats,* Hobart Paper 25, Institute of Economic Affairs, 1964.

may take the view, for instance, that the best way to cure the trouble is to obtain a more equitable system of taxation. Although an average school education may cost $x on the market, a typical poor family in our group of 20 may be paying $x + 1 in taxation because of regressive taxes or rates on, say, tobacco, housing and fuel. The more these taxes are reduced the 'richer' these families become since they will have larger net disposable incomes. Therefore, after experimental reductions of such taxes on the poor and a suitable time-lag, it may well transpire (since I have assumed them to be responsible) that the 20 families in the example will begin to buy education for their children like all other families. Such a program can be augmented, if desired, by a system of government inspection of schools so that the state can ensure that minimum standards of schooling exist everywhere.

Selective Money Grants

But suppose that existing taxation is already deemed to be equitable. No readjustments to reduce the revenue from indirect taxes are, therefore, considered justified. The payment of such taxes by the poor families is regarded as their proper contribution to services such as defence and justice, services from which they like everybody else benefit. The question of removing the poverty which remains the chief educational obstacle in the 20 families can still be met, but this time, by the provision of *direct money grants* from the state. The most practicable way of doing this would be to convert much of the apparatus of indirect taxation into a comprehensive system of income tax in which all heads of households were coded. Beyond a stated code, taxation would become negative: the government would automatically pay out more to the needy minorities so that an efficient and impersonal means test would constantly operate.

Giving these families the cash rather than the education is defensible on several grounds. One danger of the third governmental step, the direct provision by the state of a 'free' service, is that to judge from nineteenth-century experience those who are just above the poverty level will begin to request entry into it and that the service will very quickly fall into the hands of a majority which does not need it. In comparison, the administration of a negative income tax system will be cheaper because the basic administrative apparatus is already established and well tried. Moreover, this method will be more efficient because the authority will be making disinterested judgements and it will discriminate on the basis of a less ambiguous set of rules which are based on the measures of money costs and money incomes. In contrast an Education Department in charge of subsidising or providing schools will always be tempted to be more and more generous in its ideas of the cost of a minimum education. And if its own notions are to be the chief criteria, it will constantly be subject to pressure by new candidates to revise the definition of poverty so as to let them qualify for subsidies or other aid. This process will probably become cumulative since the extra provision of subsidised or 'free' places will necessitate the raising of tax revenues, so impoverishing others. The result will be the rapid decline or take-over of the existing private schools and the conversion of most of the parents of the 950 families from an independent, fee-paying class to a politically supplicant one, dependent on government discretion and decisions and subject to all the other attendant disadvantages examined in this book. Such will be the probable outcome of a cure originally directed to the needs of not more than 50 in 1,000 families. Furthermore, because the switching of education into the political process will entail the necessity of substantial taxation to pay for the 'free' state education, then there is a danger of significant disincentive effects upon work and savings that are summarized in modern economics literature by the term 'deadweight costs', or 'excess burden' of taxation.

Selective Compulsion

Twenty out of the 50 doubtful starters having thus been accounted for, what of the other 30? Assume that 15 of the remaining 30 are also poor but it is expected that they may well be irresponsible too. In other words, assume that they cannot be trusted to spend refunded taxes or state grants on education. One method to meet this situation would be to institute a system of what one may call *selective* state compulsion. Such compulsion, which would not, of course, apply to the vast majority of families, could be designed exclusively to affect the 15 families from the moment they received the state grants. Even this restricted and discriminating form of compulsion need only be regarded as a last resort. It could be withheld until evidence was shown that a family was still not spending from the state grants and refunds on education. A period of grace would have the advantage of giving a presumption in favour of the family, and some initial respect for it as a decision-making unit.

A parallel can be seen in the way in which we protect infants from physical neglect such as malnutrition. The state has means to see to it that no family is without the purchasing power necessary to feed and clothe a child to a certain standard. The total apparatus of protection is then strengthened by the provision whereby health visitors are allowed periodic access to children in their own homes. Such persons have the duty to report clear cases of parental neglect. They can appeal to Child Abuse Laws to instigate what amounts to legal compulsion of the parents. In other words there are two sorts of compulsion: first, formal compulsion as legislated for education; second, what may here be called selective or contingent compulsion, as in the case of malnutrition. This second kind of compulsion is brought into force only with discrimination; that is, it applies selectively where the case warrants. There seems to be no overwhelming argument to show that the first type (formal compulsion) is any more efficient than the second type (contingent compulsion) in meeting the needs of neglected children. If there were such an argument it is surprising that, in the case of health protection, which is needed to prevent damage likely to have equally serious consequences to children, we use the least efficient available form of compulsion.

Selective Vouchers

One way to augment the combined policy of redistribution of tax burdens and selective compulsion would be to earmark money grants to the 15 families in the form of education vouchers. These are defined as financial instruments allocated to families that can be spent only on the education of their children. Thus selective vouchers (to be distinguished from the more usually advocated *universal* vouchers) could be spent by the poor families only in the schools of their choice, providing that they had been approved by government inspectors. Such vouchers would have the advantage of the free state-school method of giving the family powerful support in the choice of a school. It is necessary to repeat that proposals for vouchers can be (and usually are) coupled with the provision of state approval of those schools which cash them. Such approval can be effected by periodic state inspection, and in so far as this is efficient the complaint of those who suspect that the average family if given much freer choice is in danger of making a seriously bad one will be substantially met.[3]

3. A selective voucher system was established in Milwaukee, Wisconsin, in 1990. Eligibility to participate in the program is restricted to students whose family income does not exceed 1.75 times the federal poverty level. The value of

Universal Vouchers

So far I have accounted for 35 of the 50 doubtful families. Suppose that the remaining 15, although able to afford it, would not in fact educate their children adequately in the absence of official pressure. In other words, having accounted for 20 poor but potentially responsible families and 15 poor but potentially irresponsible families, we finally have to deal with 15 'rich' but potentially irresponsible (or neglectful) families. It will be remembered that any proposal for intervention, beyond the laying down and policing of minimum standards, involves two major questions: first, whether the government should provide the finance for the education; second, whether it should go further and provide the education itself.

To some economists, the addition of this assumption about the possible existence of 'rich' but negligent parents (the existence of some parents who are irresponsible despite income sufficient to afford at least a minimum education) is so important as to swing the balance in favour of *universal* provision, if not of state schools, at least of state finance, that is, the provision of universal vouchers. The argument of Professors Peacock and Wiseman is that the state, having made education compulsory, cannot escape the obligation to provide all the necessary finance for compulsory education. Their main reason is that:

> . . . there is no operational way to distinguish the families upon whom financial assistance should be concentrated, if the criterion is the amount of education that would have been bought in the absence of compulsion. A means test, for example, would meet the need only if there were a high correlation between means and

---

the voucher is equal to 53 percent of average per-pupil costs in government schools. The system continues to do well four years later in 1994.

demand for education, and if this were so many of the problems of education policy would be much simpler.[4]

It is only because they have implicitly accepted that formal (universal) compulsion is preferable to what I have called contingent (selective) compulsion that they have placed themselves in the position of having to accept the corollary that vouchers should be universal too. To pursue the logic of the present model, however, I would argue that there is no more reason for announcing to *all* parents that education is to be formally compulsory and 'free' because of the possibility of a *few* negligent parents, than for announcing that for the same reason child feeding is to be formally compulsory and 'free' too. In other words, the accepted policy under which we protect children from malnutrition seems to challenge the claim that there is no operational way of distinguishing the cases where state aid is needed most. Moreover, even if a minimum education were to be made *formally* compulsory (i.e. compulsory in the universal, as against the selective, sense), there is no clear reason why the state should provide the finance. There are many administrative precedents for this in real life. Thus the state makes it compulsory for car users to undertake third-party insurance but leaves the individuals to finance it. It may be argued that this case is different because if the owner of a car becomes poor he can divest himself of the compulsory obligation only by selling the vehicle. In our situation, however, this point is met by government provision of the finance to any needy minority.

In trying to assuage what may reveal itself as a kind of community guilt complex about the educational neglect of children, we are in obvious danger of over-reaching ourselves. To bring into existence the vast, costly and cumbrous machinery of state-

4. *Education for Democrats, op. cit.,* p. 28.

administered finance for the 'benefit' of 1,000 families, just because of the shortcomings of less than 50, would be inappropriate. Because these elaborate methods will involve such a vast drain on resources, children as a whole will undoubtedly be made worse off than otherwise. For where there is only selective treatment the saving in resources means that more can be concentrated where the need is largest, while the smaller scale of taxation would mean stronger incentives to work and save out of which *all* children would benefit.

So much for the hypothetical model with its own explicit assumptions. In this particular case I have argued that the most appropriate policy to fit the 'protection' principle would be governmental responsibility for some *selective* compulsion together with some *selective* grants or vouchers, thorough attention having previously been paid to the removal of that kind of poverty which stems from inequitable taxation.

The Real World

I shall end this chapter by qualifying my initial model with important practical considerations that arise in the real world of U.S. experience. Suppose that the 950 families out of the 1,000 who would normally buy education now find themselves *in fact* in a situation where the government 'does their spending for them'. Instead of purchasing schooling directly, their money is collected in taxes in return for which they are given 'free' education. Their position is now worsened because a public school system is less efficient, as late twentieth-century experience shows. From the school years 1971–72 to 1976–77, the total professional staff in U.S. public schools went up 8 per cent. The money cost of education increased by 68 per cent (or 21 per cent allowing for inflation). But as inputs thus increased output *decreased*. The number of students fell by 4 per cent as did the number of schools. The educational testing scores of all kinds (SAT, college board examinations and school common tests) showed declining student performance. Pronounced centralization has increased the distance between the consumers of education and the suppliers (the administration). In addition it has introduced substantial deadweight costs of taxation.

Similar remarks could be made about the practical experience of government (state) schools in the United Kingdom. The struggle of many parents to 'opt out' of local-authority schools into what are called grant-maintained (GM) schools financed by the central government is just one symptom of attempted 'consumer' resistance to a long-standing monopoly. Comparing this real world with the 'ideal' model previously outlined reveals the full price that society has to pay for its current school system: that price covers the substantial costs of the monopoly that accompanies it and also the significant excess burden of taxation.

CHAPTER FOURTEEN

Are Twentieth-Century Parents Competent to Choose?

The usefulness of the model employed in the last chapter depends on how close its assumptions are to the real world, but it has been deliberately constructed to bring to the forefront any substantial differences of opinion there may be concerning average family responsibility in real life. Are they typical or exceptional?

Are Irresponsible Families Typical or Exceptional?

The more it can be shown that the irresponsible or 'problem' families are not a small minority in the real world, as assumed in the model illustration, but are very typical of our society, the more erroneous my conclusions would seem to be. The problem, of course, goes deeper than this. The existence of some degree of incompetence among families is a necessary but not a sufficient ground for intervention. The final test is whether such incompetence is more serious than the potential incompetence of government officials appointed to carry out state policy. We have now a wealth of experience of the performance of the fallible administrators and other government appointees to set beside that of the fallible heads of families, and I have attempted in this book to put some of it on record. This extra knowledge is an advantage we hold over those of our great-grandfathers who had to debate on the threshold of an untried system. It is our duty now to make full use of it.

How can we tell how many 'doubtful families' there will in fact be in every 1,000? One way of trying to get our bearings on this is to make a thorough investigation into actual family behaviour before state intervention. My enquiry on this score was summarised in Chapter II. There I reached the conclusion that on a reasonable assessment of the evidence, the behaviour of most families in the nineteenth century seems to have been much more commendable than we have often been led to suspect. What is more, it seems to have been improving with experience and with the growth of private incomes. The exceptions to this rule are always in danger of receiving such a disproportionate amount of public attention that the unwary are constantly in danger of being blinded by them. The widely read Dickensian caricatures of some nineteenth-century families, for instance, may be rich in literary appeal but in them lies the danger that they may too easily be taken as dispassionate and representative social commentary.

An attempt to judge *present-day* family educational responsibility is made more difficult because it must involve questions about what people would do if things were different. Nevertheless, such speculation yields interesting results. Suppose, for instance, that the state were to abolish universal compulsion and were gradually to contract out of most of their system of universal education and to 'return' the money so saved by way of reduced indirect taxes. Assume that this was done in such a way that the disposable cash in every family purse increased in direct proportion to the diminution of government 'free' services. The question now is whether *most* parents would spend the extra money in their purses on themselves regardless of the fact that the state no longer educated their children, or whether they would use the money to buy at least the same quantity of education for their children as before. The criterion is the amount of education obtained before and after, not the amount of money spent on it; for it is possible, especially in view of the expectation of increased competition, that parents could, for instance, purchase for themselves the same amount of education that the government now provides, but at a lower total cost.

There are two major problems awaiting those who would conjecture that most parents would not buy the 'normal' amount of education in these circumstances. First, the onus is upon them to explain why, after more than half a century of 'free' and 'universal' schooling, the state system should be producing parents who are not only widely irresponsible but who are also much less responsible than their Victorian forefathers who did not have these 'benefits'. It is not sufficient to quote sociological studies which are alleged to show that the family is no longer the basic unit in society. For such information purports to tell us only what is, not what ought to be.[1] If most people ideally *want* the family to be a basic unit, and this seems to be assumed in the reports of contemporary education commissions, they will be more interested in the reasons why the family has allegedly lost its central place. The circumstances of this decline could not exclude the wave of state intervention which has been a predominant feature of the last 100 years of history. We should therefore be anxious to ascertain how much this intervention was the effect, and how much the cause, of the weakness of the individual and his family. To the extent that it was the cause, then these

1. Thus J. Vaisey asserts that reliance on the family as the basic unit of society 'is not one that would readily stand up to sociological analysis'. *The Economics of Education*, 1962, p. 28.

circumstances are within our own control and a policy of restoring the family as one of the most important units in society can be consciously selected to meet our desires.

The second problem which confronts those who do not think most families can be trusted to spend on education for themselves directly is a political one. This can be sharply outlined by a further use of the previous model but this time with modified assumptions. Suppose the figures were reversed and that without government intervention only 50 families would educate their children and 950 would not. Assume also that the whole electorate consisted exclusively of the adult members of families. Why should the majority of 950 families in every 1,000 appoint the government to do something for them which they are not prepared to do in private, and which, when collectively provided, will be much more expensive? In other words those who argue that the average adult member of a family is not competent to employ or choose a schoolmaster directly are obliged to explain why he is presumed to be competent enough to select the right political representative to choose the schoolmaster for him indirectly, through the authority of the government he elects. It is not solely parents to whom I refer (although parents as a class constitute a substantial proportion of the electorate themselves) but adult family members; the proposition is about families and it therefore brings in grandparents, uncles and aunts and grown-up brothers and sisters, many of whom share the responsibility towards their younger relatives.

It is indeed sometimes contended that parents and other relatives are somehow different people when they are at the ballot box than when they are at home. But this phenomenon may be explainable along the lines of ignorance. For instance, Mr A may acquiesce in the present state system because he secretly believes that Messrs B and C would not educate their children without it.

Yet B and C may, in turn, think likewise about the other two. In this case, what is needed primarily is the dissemination of more accurate knowledge of people's own neighbours rather than seeking refuge in a state school system which only perpetuates such hallucinations. Again, Messrs A and B may accept the present system because they think that it is only C who is paying for it. This, again, is erroneous. In reality, the average user of the state service is a taxpayer; the sooner such facts are properly disseminated and digested, the sooner these ballot-box mirages will dissolve.[2]

Does the Evidence on 'Early Leaving' Discredit the Average Parent?

In most discussions about the competence of parents to make wise educational decisions for their children, educationists are anxious to refer to evidence about what they term 'early leaving'.[3] This shows that on average the children of manual workers leave school earlier than others, i.e. that there is less voluntary staying on at school among this large group beyond the statutory leaving age. It is often inferred from such evidence that there is a widespread deficiency in family perspicacity and responsibility, and that it is just these kinds of circumstances which warrant the government in continuing with universal compulsion and provision.

It will be appropriate here to analyse an exposition of this ar-

2. According to *Choice in Welfare,* a survey by Mass Observation commissioned by the Institute of Economic Affairs in 1963, 18 per cent of the sample of heads of households interviewed thought state education was entirely free and that people did not have to pay for it either directly or indirectly through rates and taxes.

3. The main source is the White Paper *Early Leaving: A Report of the Central Advisory Council for Education,* Ministry of Education, 1954.

gument which recently appeared in a reaction to the published proposals of Professors Peacock and Wiseman for the establishment of parental free choice via a system of universal vouchers. The official organ of the Association of Education Committees, *Education,* in rejecting this system[4] contended:

> To argue against it in principle you must show (as anyone acquainted with the current school-leaving statistics could easily do) that free choice—if it has to be backed, even marginally, with cash—is likely to be exercised to the detriment of children of manual working class groups

and that

> the same principle which makes it necessary to fix a statutory school leaving age makes it necessary also to relieve parents of economic choice in education as much as possible.

What is the validity of such reasoning? First, a question of definition. Generalisations about 'parents' as if they were a separate species with uniform behaviour are imprecise and misleading. The evidence about 'early leaving', since it concerns relative and not absolute data, must be broken down and related to different types of families and to different parental circumstances. It is important first to notice that the evidence is always presented as a contrast between some children who leave 'early' and some who do not. Since at least some parents of 'late' leavers are presumably beyond reproach, any action by the state to compel *them* to educate their children up to a certain minimum duration will obviously be superfluous. We must, therefore, first estimate the size of this group and then deduct it from the gross total of parents before we can begin to argue whether it is a majority or a

4. 28 February 1964, p. 384. This journal was reviewing *Education for Democrats, op. cit.,* published the same month.

minority of parents who are 'potentially unreliable'. And this latter question is the really important one.

Suppose next that the 'early school-leavers' are in fact found to be in the majority. To what extent does it follow that their parents are 'unreliable'? There are several cautionary observations to make. If we are resigned to the existence of at least some income differentials and also to the impossibility or undesirability of making private expenditure on education illegal (as it is on harmful drugs), then there should be no cause for surprise when the average 'rich' proceed to secure more education than the average 'poor'. Among the ways that this will manifest itself will be the practice of richer parents giving their children an education of above-average duration. However high the statutory leaving age is placed, therefore, there will always be some leavers who are 'later' than others. Thus the 'phenomenon' of 'early leaving' will always be with us, if only for the reason that some families will always be able to keep their children at school longer than others. Whilst a few Utopian educationists will always greet the practice of 'early leaving' with sadness or reproach, what will irritate the egalitarian most is the 'problem' of 'late leaving', a problem caused primarily by the 'anti-social rich'. It seems, then, that if incomes are never to be equal, the Utopian and the egalitarian will have an argument for further government intervention to raise school-leaving ages which will last them indefinitely; or until they see that their most direct approach is to argue openly for redistribution of wealth and income.

Some Utopian paternalists, however, will have another argument which will certainly preoccupy *them* indefinitely. For even if all parents withdrew their children simultaneously at the age of, say, 17 years, these 'experts' will produce reasons why it should be 18; and if 18 is the prevailing norm they will want 19, and so on. Thus all children, except presumably those who belong to the educationist himself, will be 'early leavers' simply because they do not conform to particular standards set by the Utopian. It was suggested in Chapter 10 that it was this kind of sophistry which led to the statistical invention of much of the so-called 'gaps' in nineteenth-century history and which often enabled some paternalists to produce initial self-justification for their own subsequent role in government intervention to fill them.

But even if everyone earned equal incomes, i.e. incomes which did not give some families such purchasing-power differences that they could secure more education than others, it would still not follow that instances of 'early-leaving' could always be equated with family irresponsibility. A condition which would be necessary before this could be established is that there were no cases of inferior state schooling from which parents were seeking to protect their children. This must be a matter of honest difference of opinion, but at least nobody would deny that there are significant variations in standards. Indeed the official acknowledgement of the practice of zoning bears testimony to the need for the 'less good' schools to be protected against loss of customers by zonal walls. Thus it is more than likely that the educationists' concern for the 'early leaver' will often be based on his own idealised vision of what education ought to be, or is about to become, rather than what it happens to be at any particular moment in this or that particular district secondary school.

Judging by the criticisms of the boredom and purposelessness in the 1960s in many secondary modern schools reflected in the 1963 Newsom Report,[5] we must now assume that it is at least possible that some parents, in the knowledge that any planned improvement will be too late for their children, are often *right* in

5. *Half Our Future, op. cit.*

ending their captivity in such schools as soon as possible. And in so far as these parents have in mind the prospect of their children making a quick transference to some alternative form of education, such as part-time technical college or apprenticeships (many of which must start as early as 15) it is also possible that in particular circumstances the educational judgement of the parents is wider and therefore more reliable than that of educationists. The latter are often far too dogmatic; to them 'the best education' seems so often to be visualised in terms of something which is always homogeneous, full-time, and state-provided, a view which is far too rigid. Furthermore, the desire of the parents of the large and poor family that, pending any tax reforms to its benefit, its young members should contribute earnings to it as soon as possible is not always reprehensible.

But whatever the particular significance of the above observations on the view that 'early leaving' is conclusive evidence of average parental incompetence, there remains another reply to it which is much more fundamental. This switches the attention momentarily away from the question of demand to that of supply, and focuses upon the competence of public authorities themselves to expand educational services to keep up with demand.

In 1959 the Crowther Report[6] asked the following question:

> Is it lack of opportunity or lack of desire which decides that more than four-fifths of the boys and girls in England should have left school before they are 16?

In the evidence collected it was found that very many schools were indeed catering so inefficiently for those who wanted to stay on that a very large number of children were being discouraged. Local authorities were so spending rates and taxes that sup-

6. Para. 93.

ply was typically never catching up with demand. Sixth forms were only slowly being catered to because the school buildings were grossly unsuitable or because the size of the staffs was inadequate. The Crowther Committee, then, after investigation, answered its own question thus:

> The evidence seems to us to establish that it is insufficient opportunity, at least for a very large number of children, and not lack of desire for more education, that makes them leave school at 15. Given the chance, it looks as if parents would soon see to it that the proportion of 15 year-olds at school was doubled. The evidence goes to show that good educational facilities, once provided, are not left unused; they discover or create a demand that public opinion in the past has been slow to believe existed. If this is so, then it follows that many boys and girls are at present deprived of educational facilities which they would use well and which they are legally entitled to receive. (Para. 100)

It is difficult not to conclude from such a serious verdict that, in some ironic and tortuous way, the need for compulsion in the fixing of a statutory school-leaving age is designed to meet not the negligence of typical parents but the tardiness of local authorities to keep up with parental enthusiasm. Indeed the announcement in Parliament (27 January 1964) that the statutory leaving age was to be raised to 16 was coupled with the explanation that it could not be implemented before 1970 because of the necessary stepping up of teacher supply, building programmes and curriculum planning.[7] In the transition from one emergency to another, from, for instance, a building supply crisis in the past to a massive teaching shortage in the present, the authorities it

7. A conference of the National Association of Schoolmasters on 24 April 1965 approved by an overwhelming majority a resolution urging the Government not to raise the school-leaving age until staffing, accommodation and equipment allowed the step to be taken without damaging the quality of education.

seems, are one step behind current demands. Thus, although it may be natural, it is quite unscrupulous for them to try to divert attention away from their own inefficient 'choice making' by constantly insisting that the 'early leaving' statistics demonstrate the justification of continuing to 'relieve parents of the making of economic choices in education'.

It is not irrelevant, either, to point out that those economic choices which parents are still allowed to exercise freely in other fields do not seem to have been met with the same convulsions that their elected representatives have produced in education. Those agencies which, following the expressed wishes or choices of parents, privately provide food and clothing for their children, do not seem to have *their* careers punctuated by alarming shortages of supplies, employees or premises. And ordinary companies engaged in publishing, the production of sports equipment, entertainment, insurance, seem to have coped with the various 'bulges' in their school-age market without any of the 'stop-go' upheavals and crises that characterise the schools.

The type of evidence and judgement about inefficient school supply put forward by the Crowther Committee therefore seriously weakens the argument in *Education* that we have been examining. But more than this: these findings make the 'early leaving' argument against parents recoil to the embarrassment of state educationists themselves. For, accepting their own framework of logic, the Crowther evidence alone could suggest that it is the local authorities, not the parents, who need to be 'relieved of economic choices in education as much as possible'.[8]

8. The same review in *Education* admits: 'After all, a parent who wants to cannot spend ten shillings or a pound a week on education over and above his rates and taxes. He has got to be right in or right out of the private system unless he is lucky enough to get his child into a direct-grant school. Moreover, he pays the same (more or less) if his child goes to a good or not-so-good maintained

In the final analysis, therefore, those adults who cannot clearly be placed in the category of 'irresponsible parents' should include most of those whose children are 'late leavers', those who are in certain special economic circumstances, those who remove their children as soon as possible because the schools are genuinely inferior or because they wish to transfer to an alternative form of education such as apprenticeship, and those very large numbers who, according to Crowther, are parents of children who are at present deprived of educational facilities by the failure of their local authorities to supply them. In view of all these exceptions it seems that those critics who suggest that the 'irresponsibles' account for a substantial majority of parents still have a difficult task of substantiation before them.

Even if the evidence of 'early leaving' will indeed one day be shown to discredit average parents, it will still be difficult to accept the argument that their choices should be reduced throughout the whole field of education. For it is not at all clear that because parents may be deficient in one particular choice (i.e. in the quantity of education) they will also be incompetent to make other economic choices (e.g. in the *quality* of schooling given by one primary school compared with another). If it *was* clear, then we should equally expect people to argue that because the state makes a stipulated minimum quantity of insurance compulsory for motorists it should also 'relieve' them of the problem of choosing their particular insurance company.

Are Independent School Parents Competent Choosers?

Another way of forming an opinion about how most families would behave if given much more freedom to choose their

school, irrespective of the pupil-teacher ratio and the capitation grant and all the rest of it.'

schools is to examine the behaviour of the minority who still use the private sector. The distaste which some people have for what they think of as the average independent school of today is sufficient to make them opposed to any extension of choice to other families. There are several problems here. First, if they are comparing a 'typical' present-day independent school with one in the public sector, how do they select a 'typical' present-day state school for comparison? Since, for instance, comprehensive schools dominate the public sector, should we compare the independent schooling of an average 12-year-old with that of a comprehensive school boy or girl? To find faults with independent schools is not enough. These faults have to be compared with those of their state counterparts. The judgement must be relative, not absolute.

Second, have the persons who use this kind of argument to object to *universal* parental freedom of choice failed to consider the scale of the change implied? A vast and active demand for schools would release new energies and certainly lead to a wide variety of new and experimental schools unhampered by traditions or bureaucratic inhibitions. In this new situation the few independent schools that now exist may not all be representative of the future educational scene. Indeed those who at the moment care for neither the state nor the independent schools (but who settle for the former as a choice of evils) could be the persons who would have the most influence on what the new institutions would be like.

Some writers who disliked independent schools used to complain at the same time that the state education system had capitulated to or was dominated by 'middle-class' influences. These influences were alleged to have insinuated themselves not only through the personalities of those who got themselves elected to serve on education committees and boards of governors but even also through the ulterior academic and 'bourgeois' ambitions of headmasters and teachers of secondary modern schools. Since parents and children of working-class environments do not even begin to speak or understand this middle-class language, so it was argued, state education is frustrated by a conflict of cultures. The working-class customers of education become apathetic and ride out their years of formal and compulsory schooling in a state of uncomprehending captivity. In this way, the argument concluded working-class culture was left to atrophy or to disintegrate, lacking the nourishment of its own natural and genuine leadership.[9]

The degree of accuracy in this kind of sociological comment leaves room for debate, of course, but its authors at least should welcome the opportunity inherent in any proposals to extend the choices of ordinary families. The same applies to those who believe that religion has been weakened by the system of collective provision of education. It is surely too hasty to dismiss any proposed reform in the direction of further parental independence as a plan 'to turn still more people into snobs'. If ordinary people had the same freedom to spend money or vouchers on education as they do now on ordinary goods and services one would expect to see schools emerging which reflect all kinds of cultures, aspirations and classes. Ordinary families would be in a much stronger position to influence the developing character of the institutions they patronise. The ability to buy this or that education directly is the easiest, most convenient and most direct way of applauding or encouraging this or that quality, tendency, innovation or experiment. Less ancient history in the school curriculum and more modern craftmanship is one example of the

9. Dr Michael Young seems to have been the writer who expressed himself most forcefully on this subject: *The Rise of the Meritocracy,* Pelican, 1958.

change that would probably be the first to occur to meet the wishes of those families, for instance, which identify themselves with local industrial traditions and skills. Any scheme which widens family choices is surely to be welcomed by the defenders of 'working-class culture' who see the present system as one in which apathetic parents are manipulated by alien committees which in turn are trying, through the political process, to administer a teaching profession seeking its own separate goals or 'images'.

To reply that when ordinary people are allowed to buy their own education they will be at the mercy of 'commercial pressures', especially advertising, is to lose a sense of proportion and to miss the burden of much previous discussion. Accepting for the sake of argument that advertising is the 'evil' it is so often presented to be, such a proposition points only to a need to control advertising, not to the need to nationalise the schools. In any case it seems that the citizen cannot escape the pressure of 'propaganda' advertising even under the present state system (see p. 231).

But even though many families may be duped temporarily by one commercial advertiser it is difficult to believe that they will not promptly use their opportunity to transfer their attentions to other suppliers and other advertisers after unsatisfactory experience with the first. The trouble with the state education system is that it offers the worst of all possible worlds. For it is a system under which the citizen is not allowed normal commercial freedom to change his local authority supplier, while the latter is allowed to continue to advertise the 'virtues' of its service in a similar manner to a political party propagandising itself in a one-party authoritarian state.

A third question to those who would speculate gloomily on the results of universal free choice for parents on the basis of their own critical verdicts on present-day 'typical' independent schools is: how reasonable and objective is their judgement? It is certainly insufficient to condemn an independent school, for instance, simply because of some superficiality such as the accents of its scholars or the type of games it encourages. To be consistent and fair objectors should at least take into account the views of the same inspectors who test for general efficiency throughout the *state* schools. It is not perhaps widely enough known that these officials have been given opportunities to make periodic and systematic reports on private schools.

In this connection it is interesting to study the official reply that was made to those people who were for many years suspicious that very many independent schools were full of 'unsuitable' teachers. After the 1944 Act such people were constantly pressing for an official investigation of the private sector which Part III of the 1944 Act had empowered. The ultimate evidence, collected by inspectors and others in 1958, was received with surprise:

> One of the main reasons for bringing Part III of the Act into force as soon as possible was anxiety about the possible presence of undesirable teachers in independent schools. With the co-operation of the schools, however, extensive checks had already been carried out each year since 1954 and the new statistical return of particulars of the teaching-staff in independent schools brought to light only 9 such teachers.[10]

Finally, the arguments of those who disapprove of 'typical' independent schools call for some reconciliation with the fact that 60 per cent of independent school children are now in schools recognised by the Department of Education, via its inspectors, as efficient. And it will be remembered that even the remainder,

10. Ministry of Education Annual Report, *Education in 1958*.

which include large numbers of nursery school children, are in schools which have succeeded in becoming registered and have therefore passed some minimum test.

The Costs of Decision-Making

There is yet one other type of reasoning which is sometimes used to support state-provided education. Even conceding that most heads of families are responsible and well informed, so this argument goes, they may yet agree to a collectivised education system because of what are called the costs or disutilities of making up one's mind or taking decisions. To quote Professor R. G. Lipsey:

> The head of a low-income household, faced with making a choice between a very expensive operation with only 25 per cent chance of curing his crippled daughter, and further education for his son, might not agree that choices were made without disutility and that the necessity for making such choices was not a degrading one. If there is a loss in making such critical choices—balancing health and welfare of one member of a household against that of another, then providing education, medical care, etc. free may make people happier *because* it takes such choices out of their hands.[11]

In this quotation it is not entirely clear what the author has in mind. On one interpretation, the transference of the problem to the state may be thought to be better because then the needs of both the crippled daughter and the son will be met. Accordingly, there will be a redistribution of wealth within the 'common pool' to meet such hard cases. If this is so, then it does not establish a

11. *An Introduction to Positive Economics,* Weidenfeld and Nicolson, 1963, p. 543.

case for collective provision of education at all, since in the end this problem is not of 'choice', but of poverty. And, poverty can be relieved more directly by government grants, either in the form of money vouchers or otherwise. Moreover, even this application of the 'club' principle need not necessarily involve the state; insurance companies provide protection against being crippled as against other contingencies.

On a second interpretation of Professor Lipsey's illustration, the emphasis is on the burden not of poverty but of *choice*. To illustrate from another field: a women's organisation recently argued in favour of price-fixing in shops (resale price maintenance) because it saved them the bother of shopping around. They argued in effect that others such as retailers and manufacturers should make their choices for them. These women were more concerned about having to make a choice than having to pay higher prices. Similarly in the present case the argument could be that others should do the choosing, but this time it is not retailers and manufacturers but government officials. That is, to return to the quoted illustration, the state, in taking over by taxation the relevant part of the limited income of this family, itself makes the choice between the crippled daughter and the son, one of whom still cannot escape suffering. The 'degrading' necessity for making a choice has not vanished but has simply changed hands in order that the head of the family can enjoy perhaps the comforts of an ostrich-like detachment.

But although the head of the family undoubtedly has a burden (or cost) associated with the choosing, the proposed solution does not banish these decision-making burdens from society; indeed they may be increased. For the number of decisions necessary will now increase in this more complex situation. Even now the head of the family himself will not really be able to avoid decision-taking altogether since he has to decide which government to vote for. One political party may be generally more 'health-minded' and less 'education-minded' than another, and he will have to choose between them. Apart from him, the decision-making units *within* the elected government will next have to make choices and reach compromises between government leaders or officials who have different opinions especially in such a hard case as is postulated in the quotation. Only in a government which consists of persons all keeping in step with one another in the frictionless pursuit of something called 'the common good' will there be no costs of collective decision-making connected with the relative treatment of the crippled girl and the educable son.

Even if this difficulty did not exist, there is another which demands an answer. Suppose Mr A is the head of a household who for reasons mentioned in the quotation opts for state provision while Mr B estimates that the costs of such a system itself (including the equally 'degrading' cost of loss of independence) so outweigh other considerations as to make him opt for a private system. If A wants a *universal* system of state provision, then it follows that it must be one into which B is coerced. Only if everybody thought alike and there were no 'awkward' people such as Mr B can there be a truly universal demand for universal state education. On what basis then should a government agree to ignore the additional costs to those of its members such as Mr B whose choices are thwarted at least to the extent that, even if he is legally allowed to buy private education, his power of so doing is severely reduced because he is forced to pay through taxes for a service he will not use?

Before we enter once more the debate whether we should settle for majority rule on this sort of question or not, it is essential that we first elicit people's true feelings on the subject. Professor Lipsey's hypothesis is one which can easily be tested. He himself is particularly insistent that:

> A vast advance in the use of economics in policy matters would be achieved if people accepted the statements of economists only after they had asked 'what is the evidence' . . . [12]

Important evidence on family choice in education which is relevant to this particular discussion was in fact obtained for the first time in 1963 in the form of a sample survey.[13] In brief, it showed that only one-half of those interviewed, a proportion which included a wide range of social classes and groups, really wanted state education to go on expanding. The other half wanted it either to be concentrated on people in need (i.e. the rest having to pay privately) or to continue on the understanding that individuals were allowed to contract out of state education and to buy education privately if they wished (by a voucher or comparable means). On such evidence, it is clear, even with the most generous interpretation, that Professor Lipsey's 'decision-making cost' thesis cannot rationally account for or justify the present state education system in England.

12. *Op. cit.*, p. 545.
13. *Choice in Welfare, op. cit.* especially Table XII.

CHAPTER FIFTEEN

'Neighbourhood Effects' in Perspective

The upshot of the discussion so far is that on the grounds of the protection of minors' principle it is very doubtful whether there is a case for government intervention beyond measures applied exclusively to 'problem families'. Such measures need not go beyond selective compulsion and the provision of finance in cases of poverty; in other words the protection principle does not justify the present system of 'free' state schools. What about the second broad principle, based on the argument about 'neighbourhood effects'?

On this additional argument it is contended that, although most people may indeed exercise private responsibility and educate themselves, at least to an extent which will satisfy the protection principle, it is possible that there would still be some 'under-investment' in education since there are 'spillover' benefits to society as a whole which would not be taken into account by people acting privately. The extra spillover effects in question range from postulated further *economic* benefits to society, including the presumed stimulus to innovation and invention, to wider and more intangible *social* benefits such as the attainment of certain desired social goals such as equality of opportunity, social cohesion and the establishment of law and order.

This is the area in current discussion which needs much more work both in the presentation of hypotheses and in the task of empirical research. It must be remembered that proof of external economies from schooling is only a necessary, not a sufficient, condition for state financial provision. Such proof does not simultaneously demonstrate that people will privately underinvest in schooling. It may be helpful to illustrate this point from another sphere, that of health.

Suppose that medical research has established the probability that if the average person eats one orange per month he will benefit, not only himself, but also other persons in his environment. For example, research may have indicated that he is much less likely to be the carrier of certain infectious diseases if he consumes oranges at the rate of one per month. What is the relevance of such findings for government policy? Clearly much depends upon established consumption habits. If people are on average already eating *two* oranges per month then nothing further is to be gained from government intervention.[1] If on the other hand people are consuming on average just under one orange every month there is a *prima facie* case for some government intervention. Thus it is important continually to establish facts about private behaviour. And if the government has intervened at one time it does not follow that the intervention should be permanent, because the circumstances of private behaviour may alter.

To apply this kind of reasoning to schooling: while it is constructive to put forward hypotheses about external (spillover) benefits and then to check them with the facts, it is equally important to take each postulated neighbourhood benefit in turn

1. See the technical distinction between Pareto relevant and non-relevant externalities above, page 52, footnote 9.

and to ask whether there would be underinvestment in the absence of government-provided finance, and if so how much. Consider for instance those external benefits which are associated with one aspect of schooling: the attainment of literacy. What evidence have we that the average family's private expenditure would result in underinvestment? One kind of answer to this question was attempted previously in this book when it was shown that most people had become literate well before the finance of average schooling was fully provided by governments. In the absence of any other data, therefore, it cannot be assumed that average people need government finance today for this purpose.

Of course it does not follow that evidence on this one question of literacy alone settles everything. Other aspects of schooling may involve such predominant external effects as to be the crucial ones. Thus considerations of economic growth through acquisition of those skills which are acquired beyond literacy may be the really important ones in modern times. Even so, it is still not sufficient merely to postulate that there would be underinvestment in the absence of government finance; empirical testing is required to show *how much* private underinvestment would be involved. In this connection the Robbins Committee Report, which attached so much importance to the connection between education and economic progress, is of particular interest. On the assumption that the national income will grow at $3\frac{1}{4}$ per cent per annum, it argued:

> One may buy less of services such as bus travel if one's income rises, but surely not less education. To spend more on higher education would almost certainly be the average family's individual response. Why should it not be assumed to be true of the community of families considered collectively? (Para. 635, p. 208)

This argument that 'they would do it in private, so why can't we do it in public?' is one of a very different emphasis from 'we must do it in public because they wouldn't do it sufficiently in private'. The Robbins Committee's contention that the average family would voluntarily spend more on higher education if their incomes were increased carries with it the implication that in the entire absence of the government finance of higher education the private investment of most families would be very positive and progressive. In so far as empirical enquiry supports this view the case for government intervention must again be argued in terms of a marginal, not an absolute, instrument in the finance of higher education. Indeed the more marginal such justified support is, the less need there is to enter the debate whether the government should help students to finance themselves at universities, technical and teacher training colleges with the aid of loans, a debate on which the Robbins Committee declared itself almost evenly balanced.[2]

The purpose of this chapter is not to claim dogmatically that the case for 100 per cent government provision of educational finance (through vouchers) is under all circumstances entirely unfounded. Rather it is to draw attention to the kind of research that remains to be done before 100 per cent government finance can be permanently justified on the grounds of pure logic.[3] Of

2. The argument for student loans for higher education will thus become centred not on the question of external economies but upon the need to do something about the obvious imperfection of the capital market in the sphere of personal or human investment. The reader is recommended to consult Professors A. T. Peacock and J. Wiseman, *Education for Democrats,* Hobart Paper 25, IEA, 1964, for a full discussion on these lines.

3. In his review of the First Edition of this book ('Economic Aspects of Vouchers for Education' an essay appearing in E. G. West, *et. al., Education: A Framework for Choice,* Readings in Political Economy 1, IEA, 1967 [Second Edition, 1970], p. 31), Professor Mark Blaug made the criticism that it argued away the case for intervention on neighbourhood-effects grounds because

course, some economists would argue that for the moment it is revolutionary enough to establish the principle that the government provision of finance in the form of universal vouchers is preferable to the present method of supplying the education direct in the form of 'free' state schools. Nevertheless the proper test of any theory is to try in as many ways as possible to refute it. To do this one should be prepared to consider all sorts of qualifications or alternative hypotheses, however outrageous they may seem.

In this spirit therefore let us imagine a situation where, after some further growth of affluence, it was generally felt that if the government were gradually to reduce taxes and eventually to leave the average person to find his own finance for education he would not fall far short of both personal requirements and those arising from neighbourhood effects. In terms of the health example, imagine that the average person can at last be expected to buy almost the 'right' quantity of oranges from purely personal motives and private expenditure. Would there be any advantages in the government withdrawing fairly promptly, so giving individuals the benefit of any doubt? One can think of at least four which would demand consideration.

First, it will be remembered that the main advantage of the voucher system is that it promotes wider choice and greater competition. We should now ask ourselves whether the spending of direct cash will make choice and competition even keener. It may be for instance that the psychology of consumers is such that they are much more alert when they are spending their own money directly than when they are 'spending' a government voucher only. In other words many spenders of vouchers may

externalities were minimised to vanishing point. Close reading of this part of the book (as in the original edition) will dispose of this misunderstanding.

still be under the illusion that the money to finance them could not possibly have come from taxes paid by themselves and may therefore be taking less trouble in seeing that they are spent as wisely as personal income.

Second, where there is vigorous competition, costs can be expected to fall from time to time and in different places or circumstances. But the presence of customers who possess vouchers of fixed amounts which 'must be spent' may restrain the full benefits of competition since it may unnecessarily prolong a seller's market. Moreover, if the financial value of vouchers is fixed at discrete intervals, then, in a situation which is one of potential cost reduction, the authorities will always be several steps behind.

Third, the longer the government continues to provide the finance the greater the expansion of the government sector. In the words of Professor Friedman:

> If, as now, the government pays for all or most schooling, a rise in income simply leads to a still larger circular flow of funds through the tax mechanism, and an expansion in the role of government.[4]

To those who are particularly sensitive about personal freedoms the avoidance of unnecessary growth of government functions is a very desirable neighbourhood effect in itself.

Fourth, the reduction in taxes may have such incentive effects as to raise the rate of income growth. The same will be true of the removal of the administrative costs which are incidental to the vast two-way traffic of tax collection and voucher allocation.

The subjection of the universal voucher scheme to the test of these kinds of considerations is surely constructive. For such a scheme after all is only a means to an end and like any other

4. *Op. cit.,* p. 87.

means it involves costs of operation. These costs of course may well be worth paying; but the full vigour of argument demands that they should at least be taken into account. Special attention has been drawn to them here because they seem to be commonly neglected in ordinary discussion.

CHAPTER SIXTEEN

Conclusion to the Second Edition

W hile some people may accept most of the reasoning of this book simply as a piece of logic, they may still reject it on the grounds of irrelevance. They may argue that it is based on incomplete analysis or wrong assumptions. They may hold that certain aspects of education (which may or may not fit into the category of neighbourhood effects) are so unique as to make the entire discussion seem hopelessly academic. For their very definition of education may be one which is so bound up with their political philosophy that the absence of a central role of government is inconceivable to them. They will argue that because the state is the mother institution and because it is interested in achieving 'social harmony', it alone is capable of reconciling man with the social pressures that surround him. They will contend that the family is not competent to fulfil this role since it is not sufficiently outward-looking to see it. Indeed the family is more often an obstacle to the fulfilment of 'social harmony', they will insist, since its objectives are too exclusive, too egoistic. What is the significance of this kind of reasoning for the analysis in this book?

At this point one is forced openly to suggest that the differences here come to rest upon conflicting value judgements. The writer who has conducted his examination on the assumption that it is the individual who constitutes the basic philosophic unit will have to confess that any reverential reference to an 'organic' entity called 'The State' and to such a term as 'social harmony' belongs to a language which he finds difficult to accept. If the individualist sees any collectivity as no more than the sum total of its individuals he will always be reluctant to acknowledge a hierarchy of collectivities which is not of his own choosing. The liberal will not be convinced that a person should be discouraged from joining and supporting those groups of his choice on any other ground than his harm to the freedom of others. This being so he is averse to opposing the interests of the family, for instance, to those of any other institution, and certainly he cannot accept that true education is something from which the family, the church, the friendly association, the private trust, or any other law-abiding institution should be deliberately excluded. Moreover, the individualist's concept of liberty precludes the possibility of his being 'liberated' by collective organisations, or by other individuals, into any mental state of 'harmony' with something called 'society'. And when it is suggested that the state should go further than merely provide people with the finance for education because state schooling is an integral part of 'government for the people and by the people', the liberal can only reply that he prefers libertarian to totalitarian democracy.

This forcing into the open of a discussion on the value-judgements of those who participate in economic debate, as was done in Chapter 6, should give no cause for regret to the economist. For it enables him to take a more cautious attitude to the application of economic theorems to subjects which might have the deceptive air of value neutrality. Consider again for instance the proposition that state education will secure the desirable 'neighbourhood effect' of reduced crime. To those who think of the state in 'organic' terms, in the form of some super moral entity, it is axiomatic that the longer people can live in close proximity to it (as in state education) the more favourable its influence will be on ordinary behaviour. This 'neighbourhood effect' thus appears as a hypothesis which apparently needs no verification by the facts. Indeed it is strictly not a hypothesis at all but a tautology based on something of the nature of a categorical moral imperative. The individualist, on the other hand, will not think of the 'State' in the abstract, but of politicians, administrators, education officers, state school teachers; in other words he will picture ordinary individuals, subject to average human fallibility, who happen to be placed in a particular organisational setting. He will therefore not be at all indifferent to the testing of this particular 'neighbourhood effect' by an appeal to the accumulated facts of experience. And if he finds (as was suggested in Chapter 3) that the facts do not support the 'reduction of crime' hypothesis, or that they even suggest its reversal (i.e. that there is an *adverse* neighbourhood effect, the result will occasion less surprise to him than to others.

It is not enough for economists to put forward concepts, models and hypotheses. All such theoretical work should be continually tested for concealed value-judgements and for relevance to the facts; if economists themselves do not bother to do this then one danger is that by 'fond repetition' the hypotheses themselves will eventually masquerade as evidence. Another danger is that theorems will be used to rationalise existing policy at one moment only to be dropped when it is inconvenient.

The notions of equality and quality of opportunity again need to be treated with particular care. While others will vigorously and automatically associate them with state education, the instinctive reaction of the individualist will be to demand definition and proof. He will wish first to analyse the egalitarian terminology and then to test it for its consistency. It was from this standpoint that Chapter 5 of this book was written. The investigation therein, which ranged over the false hopes and conflicting notions about equality which abound in present-day popular discussion, brought forth conclusions which like all others must only be tentative. But the enquiry in that chapter certainly indicated that the hypothesis that equality or equality of opportunity, however defined, is a goal which can best be pursued by a government-supplied education (as distinct, say, from a voucher scheme) is extremely questionable. Meanwhile those economists who continue to treat imprecise egalitarian aspirations as desirable 'neighbourhood effects' may once more be the victims of their own untested or ambitious terminology.

It is hoped that this volume has served at least the minimum purpose of providing an outline of the intricacies of the education debate and a panoramic glimpse of the central issues which divide the participants. Everybody, of course, is continually involved in some sort of educational decision-making throughout his life, but very few will have had the time for enough reflection to enable them to grasp with any clarity all the choices of means and ends before them. The present contribution has thus been confined mainly to an attempt to illuminate the scene for them. It would be premature to conclude with any prescriptions for very specific policies, for it is obvious that these first demand more clarification of goals than at present exists.

One of the most important functions of the economist is to examine the consistency of chosen means to achieve given objectives. Once the objectives are reasonably clear and once the economist finds, by a strict review of the hypotheses and evidence, that there are other means capable of achieving them with more efficiency, it is his duty to put them forward for consideration.

There is one objective or goal upon which it seems from ordinary discussion there is already general agreement. That is that children should receive an education which is in close accordance with the desires of their families. From their writings and speeches it seems that legislators, politicians, educationists, the members of government enquiries, church dignitaries all want the family to be a strong institution with important decision-making powers.[1] Indeed, to the British reader at least, this desire seems to have been enshrined in Section 76 of the 1944 Education Act and even more clearly in the subsequent acts of 1980, 1986 and 1988. Since therefore the evidence indicates that current legislation has almost entirely failed to achieve this objective, the writer has felt obliged not only to draw attention to particular defects, such as those associated with the practice of zoning, but to examine alternative means that may help people to achieve this goal more effectively. To this end it has been shown that there are no *technical* grounds which support collectivist assumptions in education. The fact that we still have a private sector in education is testimony to that. Discussion has been centred therefore not on the *possibility* but on the *desirability* of giving an increased number of people access to it. As has been shown, however, some people object to an extension of the private sector since, much as they want wider parental freedom, they think that such an extension will lead to less equality of opportunity than now prevails. It seems, in other words, that for some people there are here two major objectives in education which seem to be opposed. For such people it is hoped that the investigation of the earlier chapter of this book (Chapter 5), where it was argued that a large part of such apparent conflict is unfounded, will be of special interest.

Whatever the final judgement there seems to be no special in-

---

1. See for instance the Robbins Report, para. 28, and its reference to partnership with the family.

evitability about the continuance of the present type of government role in education. To claim as many do that 'history' supports the prevailing structure because the trend has been unquestionably set in favour of such a public sector in education throughout the world seems to be a surrender of all rational judgement to the simplest type of historical determinism. W. E. Forster would have resisted such a view in 1870. Over a hundred years later he would have repeated his complaint that our present type of system is 'too logical a piece of machinery'. This was not the system he first intended; indeed he would presumably now be urging reform to recapture the real vision of his original scheme, a scheme which really could fill the gaps in education—even those as serious as to-day's.

PART FIVE

A Further Case Study
of Public Intervention

The Political Economy of American Public School Legislation

The previous chapters of this book will remind the reader that new legislation cannot abolish the problem of scarcity; all it can do is to rearrange our institutions that seek to resolve it. Neither can new legislation liquidate the social conflict that accompanies scarcity; all it can do is to change its pattern according to the prevailing circumstances of political power. Generally most economists, by nature of their trade, have for a long time espoused this non-romantic attitude to lawmaking and lawmakers.

A different attitude seems to predominate, however, in the field of education. Here there seems to be general agreement that legislation can do, and has done, much more than merely reallocate. A widespread belief seems to prevail that in this case the effect of legislation has been much more than marginal; that without it very few educational resources would exist; and that, in consequence, society would be engulfed in crime, ignorance, and economic catastrophe. That view may be justified, but it is based more on intuition than on empirical verification. Certainly economists seem to have been much less demanding in terms of evidence when faced with popular histories of the evolution of the public school system than they are when presented with historical claims about the special achievements of say agricultural or labour legislation. And views seem to be especially inflexible about the particular pattern of legislation that happens to have evolved. For instance, although there are possible alternatives to a nationalised school system, alternatives that might redistribute income and protect the poor more effectively, there is a widespread reluctance to discuss their relative merits.

Economists have often "justified" parts of our inherited educational legislation by arguing that originally they must have been built upon the basis of "scientific" propositions in welfare economics. Compulsory laws, to take one instance, are sometimes considered to have arisen as the logical outcome of the recognition of external benefits in education. Such a view betrays excessive rationalization. The mere fact of legislation does not presuppose "scientific" legislators. In other fields, economists are quick to recognize that we do not have an "ideal" political process and that instead of problems being resolved according to "optimal welfare criteria," they are usually settled crudely according to the distribution of political power. Since it is typically assumed that self-interest motivates representative politicians no less than others, it is clear that normally it must be only by coincidence that political decisions will truly reflect the economist's "ideal" welfare prescriptions.

Has such a coincidence indeed occurred in the field of educational legislation? Has the political process been "purer" in this area than in others? If so, it would be worthwhile to know more about those responsible for passing the original legislation. Furthermore, it would be interesting to see whether the special sequence of economic circumstances of those times can throw light upon our present attitudes and adherence to particular institutions. It is the business of the present discussion to attempt such an investigation. Attention will be focused especially upon the emergence of the nationalisation principle in American schooling and upon the genesis of the three particular features described in the terms universal, free, and compulsory. Problems of manageability suggested that the investigation should, in the first instance, be confined to a single state. New York State was chosen for special study because it is considered to be reasonably representative.

The first part of the present discussion will outline the history of New York State education between 1800 and 1840. The second part will examine the Free School Campaign of 1840–50. That will be followed by a brief review of propositions from the newly developed economic theory of politics, whose relevance is suggested by the data. The final part of the discussion in pursuing particular questions suggested by those propositions, will draw out further details from the history after 1850 in an attempt more fully to interpret the events of the remainder of the nineteenth century.

Public School Legislation before 1850

After the 1776 Revolution, the first government intervention in education in New York State was an Act in 1795, "for the encouragement of schools." By that legislation, $50,000 a year was appropriated for five years, "for the purpose of encouraging and maintaining schools in the several cities and towns in this State . . ." The Act was operative for the first five years but was discontinued thereafter. In 1804 another Act was passed providing that the net proceeds of the sale of five hundred thousand acres of the vacant and unappropriated lands owned by the State be appropriated as a permanent fund for the support of schools.

The interest of that fund (known as the school fund) was to be distributed to the schools once it had grown to the figure of $50,000 per annum. The first distribution was not made until 1814.

In 1811 five Commissioners were authorised to report on a system for the establishment and organisation of Common Schools. Their report appeared in 1812 accompanied by the draft of a bill that was the basis of the Act passed later in that year. It is interesting to compare the terms of the bill with the rationale of state aid as argued in the report. The Commissioners contended that while public education was not indispensable to a monarchical government, it was so to a republic; where every act of the government was an act of the people, it was absolutely necessary that people be enlightened. Education was also essential for prosperity.

> The Commissioners think it unnecessary to represent in a stronger point of view the importance and absolute necessity of education, as connected either with the cause of religion and morality, or with the prosperity and existence of our political institutions.[1]

For state aid to be completely justified, however, it was further necessary to establish in what respects the people were not already securing sufficient education for their children. The Commissioners acknowledged that schooling was indeed already widespread:

> In a free government, where political equality is established, and where the road to preferment is open to all, there is a natural stimulus to education; and accordingly *we find it generally resorted to, unless some great local impediments* interfere.[2]

1. Randall, *History of The Common School System of the State of New York*, Ivison, Blakeman, Taylor, & Co., 1871, p. 18. See *ibid.*, pp. 17–23.
2. *Ibid.*, p. 18. My italics.

Poverty was in some cases an impediment; but the biggest obstacle was bad geographic location:

> In populous cities, and the parts of the country thickly settled, *schools are generally established by individual exertion.* In these cases, the means of education are facilitated, as the expenses of schools are divided among a great many. It is in the remote and thinly populated parts of the State, where the inhabitants are scattered over a large extent, that education stands greatly in need of encouragement. The people here living far from each other, makes it difficult so to establish schools as to render them convenient or accessible to all. Every family therefore, must either educate its own children, or the children must forego the advantages of education.[3]

The problem was thus presented in the same terms as those later to be used in England by W. E. Forster, the architect of the 1870 English Education Act; it was largely a problem, to use Forster's words, of "filling up the gaps." The logic of such argument, of course, called mainly for discriminating and marginal government intervention. To this end three methods were available. First, the government could assist families, but only the needy ones, by way of educational subsidies. Second, it could subsidise the promoters of schools in the special areas where they were needed. Third, the government itself could set up schools, but only in the "gap" areas. The Commissioners, without discussing possible alternatives, recommended that the inconveniences could generally best be remedied "by the establishment of Common Schools, under the direction and patronage of the State."

The report, having stressed the plight of the rural areas, leads the reader to expect special attention to be paid to them in the general plan of intervention. No such priority appears, however.

---

3. *Ibid.,* My italics.

The main features of the plan suggested by the Commissioners were: that the several towns of the State be divided into school districts by three commissioners, elected by the citizens to vote for town offices; that three trustees be elected in each district, to whom shall be confined the care and superintendence of the school to be established therein; that the interest of the school fund be divided among the different counties and towns, according not to the distribution but to the size of their respective populations, as ascertained by the current census of the United States.

Thus, in place of discrimination in favour of poor and thinly populated districts, a flat equality of treatment was decreed for *all* areas; the public monies were to be distributed on a per capita basis according to the number of children between five and fifteen in each district, whether its population was dense or sparse. Beyond this, each town, at its own discretion, was to raise by tax, annually, as much money as it received from the school fund.

The 1812 Act, in addition to incorporating all the points mentioned above, created the offices of trustee, clerk, and collector for school districts. The three Commissioners of Common Schools, whose first duty was to form the school districts, were the financial officers of the schools, to whom was paid the public money for distribution to the districts, and to whom the trustees were required to report. The Act also provided for the election of from one to six inspectors of schools, who, together with the Commissioners, had the supervision of Common Schools and the examination of their teachers. The office of State Superintendent of Common Schools was also created.

The State Superintendent himself submitted a draft of an amending law in 1814. His amendments were designed to correct what he considered to be administrative defects in the operation of the 1812 Act. An amending Act of 1814 embodying the Superintendent's proposals made it compulsory for the boards of supervisors to levy on each town a sum equal to its distributive share of the school monies. Such a levy, it will be remembered, had previously been left to the discretion of the towns. Since many of them had not done this, the Superintendent apparently assumed that they were negligent in providing education. The 1814 Act also authorised the levy of a like sum, *in addition*, if voted by the town. Furthermore, the new law required the trustees to see that a school be kept open at least three months.

Two further details of this early legislation are worthy of observation. First, there seems to have been no announced intention of making education free. Pointing out that the public monies alone would never be adequate to maintain the Common Schools, the Commissioners of 1812 observed:

> But it is hardly to be imagined the Legislature intended that the State should support the whole expense of so great an establishment. The object of the Legislature, as understood by the Commissioners, was to rouse the public attention to the important subject of education and by adopting a system of Common Schools in the expense of which the State would largely participate, to bring instruction within the reach and means of the humblest citizen.[4]

Even with the addition of the revenues from the town taxes there were far from sufficient monies to cover expenses. The substantial balance was presented in the form of rate bills (fees) to the parents, who were required to pay in proportion to the attendance of their children. For instance, in 1830 parental fees contributed $346,807 toward the total sum for teachers' wages of $586,520.[5]

4. *Ibid.*, p. 21.
5. *Ibid.*, p. 66. Teachers' wages constituted about one-half of total expenses. More detailed estimates of the proportionate contribution of rate bills will be given below.

The second detail of the early legislation worth noticing is that religion was regarded as an integral part of school education. The Commissioners observed: "Morality and religion are the foundation of all that is truly great and good; and consequently, of primary importance."[6] The Bible, in Common Schools, was to be treated as more than a literary work. The Commissioners particularly recommended the practice of the New York Free Schools (the charitable establishments) in "presuming the religious regard which is due to the sacred writings."[7]

Subsequently the annual reports of the Superintendents revealed a steady growth in the number of school districts organised. In some cases, entirely new schools were built; in others the personnel of existing private schools allowed themselves to become socialized, that is, to become Common Schools, in order to qualify for the public monies. In the report of 1821 it was stated that the whole number of children between the ages of five and sixteen residing in the State was 380,000; and the total number of all ages taught during the year was 342,479.[8] Thus, according to this evidence, schooling in the early nineteenth century was already almost universal without being compulsory. Moreover, although it was subsidised, it was not free except to the very poor.

Charity schools had existed well before 1812. But the new legislation seems to have caused much subsequent quarrelling among them. The city of New York had special arrangements. The Free School Society, by the General School Act of 1812, became entitled to a distributive share of the Common School Fund in proportion to the average number of pupils under instruction. By an Act of the following year, incorporated religious

6. *Ibid.*, p. 19.
7. *Ibid.*, p. 22.
8. *Ibid.*, p. 39.

societies in the city that "supported or should establish Charity Schools" were also entitled to apply for a similar share. The vigorous response to the latter concession led the Free School Society to become alarmed at the competition for its clientele that the religious bodies began to make. The Society began to make strong objections and among other things accused some of the religious bodies of perversion of the funds to purposes not contemplated by the Act. The Legislature thereupon passed an Act transferring the local distribution of the fund to the Common Council, who immediately referred the subject to a special committee. This committee recommended the cessation of distribution of public money to the schools of religious societies, arguing that the school fund of the State was purely of a civil character, designed for civil purposes, and that "the entrusting of it to religious or ecclesiastical bodies was a violation of an elementary principle in the politics of State and country." Thereupon an ordinance was introduced directing distribution to be made exclusively to the secular free school societies.[9]

In the first half of the century figures of private schooling throughout the State were hard to come by. But it will be remembered that the 1811 Commissioners observed that in thickly populated areas the means of education were already well provided for. The Superintendent's Report of 1830 contained an account of a census of the schools of the city of New York for the year 1829. It showed that of the 24,952 children attending school in the city, the great majority, 18,945, were in private schools.[10] In 1832 the Superintendent of Common Schools estimated that in the State as a whole there were annually instructed in private schools about 43,000 scholars—compared with 512,000 in the

9. *Ibid.,* pp. 43–48.
10. 1830 *Ann. Rep. N.Y. Supt. Common Schools,* p. 17.

Common Schools. By this time the Superintendents were expressing complete satisfaction with the whole system. On the quantity of education the Report of 1836 asserted:

> Under any view of the subject, it is reasonable to believe, that in the common schools, private schools and academies, the number of children actually receiving instruction is equal to the whole number between five and sixteen years of age.[11]

The fact that education could continue to be universal without being free and without compulsion seems to have been readily acknowledged. Where there were scholars who had poor parents, the trustees had authority to release them from the payment of fees entirely, and this was done "at the close of the term, in such a manner as to divest the transaction of all the circumstances calculated to wound the feelings of scholars."[12] It was felt that too large a sum of public money distributed among Common Schools had no salutary effect. After a certain point the voluntary contribution of the inhabitants declined with almost uniform regularity, as the contributions from the public fund increased.

> In almost every case, in which a town possesses a local fund [that is, a local tax to *augment* the state contribution], the amount paid for teachers' wages, above the public money [that is, collected in fees] is about as much less, compared with other towns having no local fund, as the amount received from that source.[13]

The Superintendents of the 1830s argued that it was better to allow individuals to make an appreciable contribution in direct

11. 1836 *Ann. Rep. N.Y. Supt. Common Schools*, p. 8.
12. 1831 *Ann. Rep. N.Y. Supt. Common Schools*, p. 16.
13. 1834 *Ann. Rep. N.Y. Supt. Common Schools*, p. 13.

payments because this would keep awake their energies and interests. Since most children of school age were now being educated, the pressing requirement was acknowledged to be the necessity of improving the quality of schools.

> The mere distribution of money, however abundant, will not produce good schools. They can only be established and kept up by the continued exertion, and much painstaking on the part of a number of the inhabitants of each district.[14]

Comparison with other states was claimed to bear this out. For instance while the annual apportionment from the New York State treasury amounted to 20 cents to each child in the state between five and sixteen, the apportionment in Connecticut gave about 85 cents per child.

> If the mere distribution of money from a state fund, would produce good schools, it might be inferred that those in Connecticut were much superior to our own. But even there, with an ample fund, there is much complaint in regard to the low state of common school education.[15]

On the next page of the 1831 Report the Superintendent observed:

> Of the three modes of providing for popular instruction—that in which the scholars pay everything and the public nothing—that in which the public pays everything and the scholars nothing— and that in which the burden is shared by both; the exposition given by Dr. Chalmers, in the "Considerations on the System of Parochial Schools in Scotland," Edinburgh Review, No. 91 in favour of the last, appears to us unanswerable.

14. 1833 *Ann. Rep. N.Y. Supt. Common Schools*, p. 18.
15. 1831 *Ann. Rep. N.Y. Supt. Common Schools*, p. 17.

This was an interesting connection with the views of the British classical economists. Adam Smith, of course, had expressed his approval of Scottish practice long before Chalmers.[16]

The Free School Campaign 1840–50

In the following decade there was a remarkable switch in the tone of public discussion. Official sentiment suddenly turned against the rate bills (fees), which were now declared a serious enemy of the system. The opposition, mainly by teachers and government officials, stressed first the administrative difficulties of collection and second the discouraging effects upon poor families. There were indeed strong grounds for complaint on the administrative score. Teachers were employed for stipulated wages, and at the close of the term they were given orders upon the town superintendent for such portion of the public money as was their due. The residue was collected in the form of rate bills upon the parent or guardian according to the number of days' attendance of his children; poor parents were exempted. After the rate bills were completed, thirty days' notice was given by the trustees, one of whom had to be in attendance on a day and at a place appointed, once a week for two successive weeks, to receive payment. After the expiration of thirty days, if all the persons named in the rate bill had not voluntarily paid, the trustees put it, with their warrant, into the hands of the district collector. He was allowed thirty days to make his return to the trustees. Thus, the teacher was obliged to wait thirty or sixty days for his pay after having fulfilled his contract. The remedy demanded by

16. West, "Private Versus Public Education: A Classical Economic Dispute," 72 *Journal of Political Economy*, 465 (1964). The work of Chalmers was first published in 1819. It was reviewed in the *Edinburgh Review*, June 1827, pp. 107–14.

the teachers, however, was not a reform of the administrative machinery, a reform that was obviously feasible, but the substitution of a "Free School System" that completely relieved the trustees from the duty of making out rate bills.[17]

The campaign for free schools seems to have originated in the teachers' institutes. These were first held in 1843, and they received legislative recognition in 1847. The first step in the campaign seems to have come from the Onondaga County Teachers' Institute. In 1844 it presented a committee report on the subject, which gave three reasons why the Free School System was favoured. First, it argued, every human being has a right to intellectual and moral education; "it is the duty of government to provide the means of such education to *every* child under its jurisdiction." Second, the Free School System was a means for the prevention of crime. "It will be found universally true that the *minimum* of crime exists where the *maximum* of moral education is found." The Committee did not elaborate on the meaning of "moral education"; it did not for instance mention the relevance of religion and the church. Neither did it present any formal evidence of the general proposition that state education reduces crime. Third, the Free School System, it was argued, by overcoming the impediment of poverty, would benefit and develop the latent talents of the lower classes.[18]

In the following year (1845), the County Superintendent of Genesee also presented (to the State Convention of Superintendents) a report in favour of free schools. He argued that "we have reason to believe" there were children in every county who did not attend school because the self-respect and pride of their

17. Randall, *op. cit.* note 1, pp. 250–52.
18. *Ibid.*, pp. 215–16.

parents prevented them from being relieved of payment of fees by the trustees."[19]

During the next session, in 1846, an animated speech on the subject was delivered by the celebrated champion of education, Horace Mann. Since he was such an influential figure, it will be useful to have a special look at his arguments. Mann contended:

> The individual no longer exists as an individual merely, but as a citizen among citizens . . .
>
> Society must be preserved; and in order to preserve it, we must look not only to what one family needs, but to what the *whole community* needs; not merely to what one generation needs, but to the wants of a succession of generations.[20]

Much of Mann's reasoning, and that of the other protagonists, could be taken as constituting an early formulation of what has today become known as the "neighbourhood effects" argument. But if so, they do not seem to have appreciated that the onus was upon them to give evidence and measurement demonstrating how deficient was the existing supply of education. Proof of positive neighbourhood effects even if it is unambiguously established, is only a necessary, not a sufficient, condition for state provision. Such proof does not simultaneously demonstrate that every person, acting individually, will underinvest in schooling. And even if underinvestment could be shown, it would be a coincidence if this called for exactly 100 per cent or 60 per cent; or for an equal subsidy to every family regardless of its income. Requi-

19. *Ibid.*, p. 217. Eventually a select committee (in 1850) reported to the State Government that the evidence, although imperfect, was enough "to authorize the opinion that, in all the State, over 46,000 children were thus deprived of a participation in the benefits of our common schools." Finegan, *Free Schools*, New York, 1921, p. 293. This figure amounted to 6% of the common-school population of that year of 742,000.

20. Randall, *op. cit.* note 1, p. 221.

site conditions for government intervention, moreover, include a consideration of all the costs of such interventions.[21]

But Mann's oratory on this occasion[22] swept past such precise considerations:

> If education, then, be the most important interest of society, it must be placed upon the most permanent and immovable basis that society can supply. It should not be found upon the shifting sands of popular caprice or passion, or upon individual benevolence: but if there be a rock anywhere, it should be founded upon that rock. What is the most permanent basis—that which survives all changes—which retains its identity amid all vicissitudes? It is PROPERTY. I mean the great, common, universal elements, which constitute the *basis* of all property—the riches of the soil, the treasures of the sea, the light and warmth of the sun, the fertilizing clouds, and streams, and dews, the winds, the electric and vegetative agencies of nature. Individuals come and go; but these great bounties of heaven abide.[23]

Thus, not only was there a failure more precisely to quantify the external benefits (neighbourhood effects) from education; proposals for the imposition of the costs were equally nebulous,

21. See above, pp. 281–7. See also Pauly, "Mixed Public and Private Financing of Education: Efficiency and Feasibility," 57 *Am. Econ. Rev.* 120 (1967). Pauly argues that there are inefficiencies inherent in *equal* provision of public support to each student, whether facilities be publicly or privately operated.

22. On other occasions, Mann did attempt to examine these questions; but even then he relied more upon assertion than upon concrete evidence. Thus, in the *12th Annual Report of the Secretary of the Massachusetts Board of Education,* he simply asserted "the opposition" to the Massachusetts system of free schools, would, should it prevail, "doom to remediless ignorance and vice, a great majority of all the children of this land." Mann did not refer to the evidence of New York State which showed that the majority of children there were being educated in "nonfree" schools. Contemporary evidence showed indeed that wherever there was a relative decline in expenditure on the New England public schools in the 1830s and 1840s, private-school expenditure increased.

23. Randall, *op. cit.* note 1, p. 222.

which implies some idea of the incidence of the requisite taxes.

In his secretarial reports to the Massachusetts Board of Education, Mann proclaimed repetitively the classical economic theme that education was a good public investment because by reducing crime and disorder it reduced public police expenditure and increased output. He insisted that such an educational investment should be made primarily in Common Schools. He eventually offered as proof the replies to a questionnaire that he had circulated to teachers selected "from the sobriety of their judgment and from their freedom from any motive to overstate facts."[24] In the circular, Mann asked the teachers

> how much of improvement, in the upright conduct and good morals of the community, might we reasonably hope and expect, if all our Common Schools were what they should be, what some of them now are, and what all of them, by means which the public is perfectly able to command, may soon be made to become?
>
> Should all our schools be kept by teachers of high intellect and moral qualifications, and should all the children be brought within these schools, for ten months in a year, from the age of four to that of sixteen years; then what percentage, of such children as you have had under your care, could in your opinion, be so educated and trained, that their existence, or going out into the world, would be a benefit and not a detriment, an honor and not a shame to society?[25]

The respondents, each of whom was later described by Mann as being a "sincere believer in such innate natural condition of the human heart as opposes the most formidable obstacles to success in moral training," replied that Mann's policy would be between

24. 11 *Ann. Rep. of Sec. Mass. Bd. Educ.* 48–49 (1848).

25. The Circular is printed in 11th *Ann. Rep. of Sec. Mass. Bd. Educ.*, pp. 49–58 (1848). The sections quoted will be found pp. 49–56.

99 to 100 per cent successful. It should be added that such "evidence" of the profitability of government investment was qualified by Mann's important proviso that the persons of "highest talent and morality" could only be attracted into education by very substantial increases in the wages of Common-School teachers.

Mann did concede that, besides property, there was another "rock" upon which education was naturally founded: the natural fidelity of the family. An "all-mastering instinct" prompted parents to accept willingly the duty of educating their children. Observation on these lines led to the conclusion, as it did for John Stuart Mill, that the state's educational powers are to be regarded as powers of last resort. Mann accordingly concluded that society succeeds to the place of parents only where the latter cannot provide the sustenance and care.

> If in any period previous to the age of discretion the parents are removed, or parental ability fails, society, at that point, is bound to step in and fill the parents' place.[26]

But Mann did not seem to want to grasp the implications of this reasoning. For, in practice, his observations were relevant only to the problem of what to do with the *minority* of families that was neglecting to educate its children. His proposals to provide free schools for *all* implied that he was willing for the majority of parents to reduce their existing *direct* payments. This further step required the support of extra argument. For, in so far as other people (non-parents) were now expected to shoulder the burden of school finance, this amounted to a free gift of money to the average parents, and a gift spendable upon anything but schooling. On the other hand, insofar as most parents were

26. Randall, *op. cit.* note 1, p. 225.

intended to contribute to *free* schools via the incidence of the new taxes, the change merely amounted to the substitution of an indirect for a direct payment.

The New York State Free School Campaign, to which Mann's arguments made a significant contribution, almost achieved its goal in 1849. The Legislature passed an Act in that year establishing free schools, abolishing the rate bills (fees) and leaving the deficiency of teachers' wages to be made up by district taxation. It is interesting, however, that the legislation proved to be unworkable and that the Act was met with immediate and widespread hostility. The new law had made it compulsory upon the local districts to supply any deficiencies beyond the state allocation so that their schools could be kept open for a statutory minimum of four months. In some districts, especially those that were poor or had a large proportion of non-parents, the majority of voting taxpayers grudgingly provided only enough revenue to keep the schools open for the legal minimum of four months. Parents, who were typically accustomed to using the schools for up to eight months, now found the school doors closed to them after four.[27]

The new legislative provision, therefore, far from facilitating the supply of schooling, actually reduced it. Moreover, the parents' direct means of action to encourage supply, the payment of rate bills, was now removed. After only two or three months in operation there was a torrent of petitions from all parts of the State demanding a repeal of the Act. The controversy was eventually settled by a repeal of the law in 1851. The rate bills were

27. Ample evidence is given in the *Report* of the select committee on the petitions for the amendment or repeal of the free school law in 1850. For a reproduction of the report see Finegan, *op. cit.* note 19, pp. 286–308: "Not only are our schools thus closed for a portion of the year, during which they were before taught, but this diminution is accompanied by much ill-feeling on the part of those who were intended to be benefited by the act in question." *Ibid.,* p. 295.

restored in this year and at the same time the public monies for the Common Schools were augmented by the revenue from a state tax amounting to $800,000. The rate bills were not successfully removed until 1867 with the "Free School Act" of that year.

Between 1828 and 1867, the rate bills had returned on an average $410,685 per annum. In 1849, the climax year of the first "free school controversy," they had risen to $508,725, which amounted to 29 per cent of the total expenditure on schools ($1,766,668). Until 1849 they provided the largest single source of revenue for most rural school districts. The other three major sources were the federal funds, the town and county tax, and the school district tax. For the year ending 1866, the year before their abolition, the rate bills were still yielding the significant sum of $709,025.[28] Parents of ordinary means, therefore, were still directly buying education for their children in New York State a century ago, an education which, to repeat, although almost universal, was not yet compulsory.

Whatever the attitude of a minority of negligent or poor families, there is no systematic evidence to show that average parents, as distinct from public-school teachers and administrators, preferred the method of paying for schooling through increased taxes to that of the rate bill system.[29] The teaching organisations insisted that "society" basically demanded the change because the electorate voted for the 1849 Act with a firm majority.[30] But it is clear, from people's immediate hostility to the practical operation of the Act, that the political spokesmen had not presented them with all the issues.[31] The decision process that was involved

28. 13 *Ann. Rep. Supt. Pub. Instruction*, p. 17 (1867).

29. Finegan, *op. cit.* note 19, p. 305. The select committee reported that the rate bills were "willingly paid."

30. *Ibid.*, pp. 239–43.

31. The 1850 select committee stated: "It is useless to say that the law was adopted by a majority of thousands, of hundreds of thousands. . . . This law has

in the legislation consisted of two parts: the demand choice and the supply choice. These two parts had become arbitrarily separated at the ballot box. The voting issue, of course, as it presented itself to each individual voter, appeared mainly as a demand choice. People would have been irrational indeed if, believing that they could really obtain something free merely by voting for it, they did not in fact do so.[32]

In retrospect, the "best" economic solution of the mid-nineteenth-century problem of financing schools demanded much stricter comparisons of all the costs that were implicit in any proposed change. These would have included, for instance, a comparison between the costs of operating some improved administration of the existing rate bill system[33] on the one hand, and the various costs of switching to and maintaining a free school system on the other. The latter would include not only a consideration of the burdens of inequity caused by the tax change, but also the costs implied by a reduction of parental choice.

To obtain deeper understanding of the reasons why contemporary political discussion so readily brushed aside considerations of administrative improvement as an alternative to the revolutionary step of complete abolition of the rate bills, we obviously need further study of the facts. But here, of course, we openly confront the familiar dictum that facts by themselves are inadequate. Since, as always, deductive and inductive reasoning

---

now been in operation some four months only, and yet we are already daily receiving petitions for its amendment, or its total and entire repeal." *Ibid.,* p. 294.

32. On the separation between demand and supply choices in the political process see Buchanan, *The Inconsistencies of the National Health Service* (1964). See also Buchanan, *Public Finance in the Democratic Process* (1967).

33. Finegan, *op. cit.* note 19, p. 149. The first obvious improvement needed was to make the parental contributions payable in advance. Only one superintendent seems to have advocated this, however. *Ibid.,* p. 152.

should preferably go hand in hand, our next immediate requirement is for suitable hypotheses that, when combined with the facts, will more fully illuminate the scene.

School Legislation and the Economic Theory of Democracy

The study of the new evidence so far strongly suggests the relevance of that new branch of economics which has come to be known as the economic theory of democracy.[34] It will be remembered that this theory distinguishes itself by an application of the self-interest axiom ("the profit motive") to the actions of voters, governments, public agencies, and to all aspects of political activity in general. In other words, the maximisation hypothesis, which is the traditional foundation of analysis concerning *private* economic agents, is extended to apply to those in the political process also. There are many important corollaries to this hypothesis but three of them seem to be particularly relevant here.

Since it is postulated first that every government seeks to maximise political support, it follows that in order to do this it has to be constantly informed about the wishes of the majority of voters. Second, in the real world, the existence of uncertainty creates barriers to communication. On the one hand it is costly for government to keep constantly in touch with voters; on the other hand, the electorate is not fully aware of all the issues. Such a situation is favourable to the emergence of special interest groups claiming that they are representatives of the popular will. Propaganda put out by them will serve to create real public opinion at the same time that it attempts to persuade government of the existence of such opinion.

34. See especially, Downs, *An Economic Theory of Democracy* (1957).

Third, let it be observed that producing political influence is a particularly costly operation, and that, consequently, the costs will be assumed mainly by those who stand to gain most from it. For instance, those individuals who work in a service that is provided by government can afford to bring greater than average influence to bear upon government policy since their incomes will be particularly responsive to it. In contrast, the consumers, having interests that are spread over many products and services, cannot so easily afford to buy influence over the supply of only one of them. In particular, they will not be able to afford the information necessary to evaluate the full implications of government policy such as, for example, the true incidence of taxation necessary to pay for "free" services or the eventual effects of "free" service upon consumer choices.

The application of the maximisation hypothesis to education is not to imply that educators are prompted by motives of self-interest in any greater degree than anybody else. Every profession no doubt has its full share of benefactors and altruists. But on any realistic assessment the typical member of a profession can reasonably be regarded as having more than one motive in life. Thus, he may be prompted by the desire to help others *as well as* by the desire to help himself and his family. Predictions that relate to actual human behaviour require an assumption not about which motives are highest, but which are strongest.[35] And what people *do* is a better guide than what they *say*. It is interesting that while Horace Mann, for instance, typically referred to the teaching profession as a noble and religious calling, which demanded persons of the very highest principles, he nevertheless continually attributed to teachers the strongest of economic motives:

35. This distinction between highest and strongest motives is taken from Alfred Marshall. See *Memorials of Alfred Marshall* 310 (Pigou ed., 1925).

We want a profession which understands the laws of the intellectual and spiritual nature of man—so much more prolific of true enjoyment than any laws of property can be . . . But how can this be done, while the salaries and the social consideration bestowed upon teachers, furnish so little inducement to enter the profession, and while avenues to greater honour and emolument, constantly opening around, are seducing its members into more brilliant or more lucrative walks of life?[36]

Mann was especially sensitive to the tendency of the private sector to bid teachers away from the public:

If teachers look for more liberal remuneration, they abandon the service of the public, and open private schools . . . [37]

While we pay so inadequate a salary at home, many of our best educated young women go south and south-west, where they readily obtain $400, $500 or $600 a year . . . Others of our best educated young women become assistants in academies, or open private schools on their own account.[38]

It is merely an extension of such observation to suggest that teachers will promptly be energetic in the political arena if it so happens that the political process suddenly provides one of the easiest routes to economic gain.

To return now to the facts surrounding the emergence of a free school system in nineteenth-century New York State. The suppliers of educational services to the government, the teachers and administrators, as we have seen, had produced their own organised platforms by the late 1840s; it was they indeed who were the leading instigators of the free school campaign. Whilst conventional history portrays them as distinguished champions in

36. 9 *Ann. Rep. of Sec. Mass. Bd. Educ.*, p. 33 (1846).
37. *Ibid.*, p. 30.
38. *Ibid.*, p. 36.

the cause of children's welfare and benevolent participants in a political struggle, it is suggested here that the facts are equally consistent with the hypothesis of self-interest behaviour as described above.

This hypothesis assumes that it is in the interests of individual suppliers, whatever the setting they find themselves in, to seek out those courses of action which bring either better returns for given efforts or the same returns for less effort. The outcome, of course, will differ according to the number of obstacles that the social framework places in the way of competition. Where the benefits of improved efficiency of a competitor cannot be denied to consumers in general, the only course is for others to try to match his efforts. But, where an opportunity presents itself, it may be more profitable to concentrate upon schemes to prevent a competitor's action from being effective—that is to say upon schemes of monopolisation. The success of an efficient competitor is normally demonstrated by the actions of new customers in placing orders with him. Customers can only do this, however, if their expenditure is not tied in some way to their "normal" supplier.

Implications for the Later Nineteenth-Century Developments

By the mid-nineteenth century most parents were already considerably tied to the Common Schools because much of the finance was already preempted through compulsory taxation. If a parent transferred his child from a Common School to a competitor outside the system (that is, a private school) the only funds that he could transfer consisted of his fees. Nevertheless so long as these fees were of *some* marginal significance they remained some threat to the Common Schools.

The total amount paid in fees (rate bills) by parents in New York State in the year 1845, for instance, was $461,000. The number attending Common Schools was 742,000.[39] As it was estimated that in the same year one quarter of the population were in districts that had already made their own free school provisions,[40] this means that about 560,000 were attending schools where rate bills were payable. On this basis, the average payment was about 80 cents per child. There was, however, considerable variation on either side of this average. The charges were assessed according to the length of attendance during the year; and school attendance varied significantly.[41] Furthermore, there were wide variations in charges between districts. Parents who sent their children to school for the whole year seem to have been paying $4 or more per child in some districts.[42] One important feature of the system was that because they varied with attendance, the rate bills were unpredictable to the parents. If attendance fell, the "loyal" parents would automatically be obliged to pay more. Mr. Pierpont Potter, county superintendent of Queens County wrote in his annual report of 1846:

> I have witnessed more than one instance under the present system, where one or two wealthy individuals, from some trifling offense, withdrew their children from the common school in the vicinity, and sent them either to a select or boarding school, which act so alarmed others in the district, that they withdrew their children through fear of being compelled to pay a very high rate bill. The result of all these evils was that those who had the patriotism and the firmness to adhere to the common school,

---

39. 1847 *Ann. Rep. N. Y. Supt. Common Schools* pp. 25 and 12.
40. Finegan, *op. cit.* note 19, p. 156.
41. See the estimate for 1852 in Finegan, *op. cit.* note 19, p. 466.
42. *Ibid.*, p. 84, for the case of Westchester in 1846.

were compelled to pay *six or seven dollars per scholar for one quarter's tuition.*[43]

There is not much evidence available about fees charged by
typical private schools. Some idea of the range of charges to be
expected from competing private entrants into schooling may be
obtained, however, by considering the following estimates[44] of
total costs per pupil in attendance in the various parts of the
Common School system in 1845:

New York	$9.52
Brooklyn	9.64
Albany	5.74
Buffalo	6.03
Rochester	3.99
Troy	9.94
Utica	5.66
Schenectady	4.12
Hudson	7.04
Syracuse	3.42
Geneva	3.85

Such information does suggest, therefore, that where rate bills
were charged they were often of sufficient importance at the
margin to encourage many ordinary families to be choice conscious. In a free school system, it is usually out the question for
the majority of parents to consider transferring their children to
private schools and so "paying twice." In contrast, in a non-free
(rate bill) system of public schools, many people would be

43. *Ibid.,* p. 91. My italics. This was originally printed in *Teachers' Advocate,*
1846. Potter did not say what the "trifling offense" was. Nor did he give any
indication whether other private schools eventually catered to the less wealthy
who could not pay the high rate bills.

44. *Ibid.,* p. 93.

prompted more realistically to consider alternatives. Paying, say, "one and a half times" is more within reach than "paying twice."

Self-interest would have dictated to the Common-School employees and organisers that the best course was to campaign for a 100 per cent subsidised, that is, free school system, in order that the last traces of customer discretion be removed. Teachers in private schools stood to lose wherever the contest was transferred to the political arena since they were in a minority in the profession as a whole. Moreover, the public-school teachers had allies in the form of the growing body of administrative personnel that had a direct interest in the expansion of the public-school sector.

To what extent had the parents been using those powers of choice between the public and private sector which remained with them before 1849 and to what extent had private schools become a competitive threat to public schools? Between 1832 and 1847, according to the State Superintendent's reports for those years, the number of students attending private establishments increased from 43,000 to 75,000. Over the same period the numbers attending Common Schools rose from 512,000 to 776,000. The private institutions had thus taken over 12 per cent of the increase in school "customers" over the period.

Other states, incidentally, had similar experiences in the 1830s and 1840s. It was in the setting of competition from private schools, interestingly enough, that the very strenuous efforts of Horace Mann were made. It will be helpful to present here a quotation in which Mann not only gives evidence of the contemporary private-school "problem," but also reveals his full reaction to it. Reviewing the progress of his work from 1837 as Secretary to the Massachusetts Board of Education he stated in his Report of 1849:

Facts incontrovertibly show, that, for a series of years previous to 1837, the school system of Massachusetts had been running down. Schoolhouses had been growing old, while new ones were rarely erected. . . . To crown the whole, and to aggravate the deterioration which it proved to exist, the private school system was rapidly absorbing the funds, patronizing the talent, and withdrawing the sympathy, which belonged to the Public Schools. All these things were undeniably true, and yet the Secretary, in reporting upon our school system from year to year, might have concealed or palliated these steps of declension and prognostics of ultimate ruin; he might have conspicuously set forth whatever remained of hope or of promise, and *the general indifference of the public* would have made the imposture easy.

The other course led in a direction diametrically opposite. It counselled an energetic and comprehensive system of Popular Education, good enough for the richest, open to the poorest . . . The intelligence of the State was to be invoked to justify such a system, and its liberality to support it . . . Committees were to be informed and stimulated, that they might both know and discharge their duty. Money, for the more liberal payment of teachers, was to be won from the pockets of the wealthy by persuasion, or exacted by law.[45]

45. 12 *Ann. Rep. of Sec. Mass. Bd. Educ.*, pp. 17–19 (1848). My italics. For an interesting account of the decline of the public schools in Rhode Island at this time see Carroll, *Public Education in Rhode Island*, pp. 110–14 (1918). It is noteworthy, incidentally, that this author challenged the popular view that Massachusetts was superior because it had earlier, or more elaborate, legislation:
    "The unfavourable estimate of Rhode Island's school history, which has prevailed generally, arises largely from the error of studying school progress exclusively in legislation. The historians of the past who found general school laws in Massachusetts and Connecticut in the middle of the seventeenth century, and none in Rhode Island before 1828, reached the conclusion that Rhode Islanders were backward in providing schools, ignoring the fact that there were 193 schoolhouses in Rhode Island in 1828. It is, and has been characteristic of Rhode Island school history that progress and improvement precede legislation . . . " *(Ibid.*, pp. 34–35.)

One possible explanation of the public-school decline in the 1830s and 1840s is that, dollar for dollar, an increasing number of parents were preferring the quality of the private schools. Another possibility was that there was a high income elasticity of demand for schooling and that increased incomes were finding a more ready outlet in the private sector, the public sector keeping one step behind. For whereas expenditure on a public system, dependent as it is on political votes, is determined by the *median* preference only, under private financing the full range of *all* preferences and *all* incomes is reflected.[46] Hence significant differences are likely between the growth of public and private schools, especially when the former are not free of charge. Whatever the case, it is clear that the fortunes of the private schools could have been expected to vary in proportion to the level of fees charged in the public sector.

The Act of 1851 in New York State sought a compromise to resolve the first free school controversy. By putting more dependence on State funds it relied more upon new taxes, whose incidence was less clear than those of district taxes. By introducing a State tax of $800,000, the immediate significance of the fees (rate bills) in public schools was substantially reduced. From the economic principles so far discussed, we are led to expect that this would have resulted in a severe check on the growth of private schools. This seems to have been the case; evidence indicates that growth was slowed down, and, indeed, there may well have been an absolute decline.[47]

By the 1860s the rate bills had become confined to the rural areas. But here their importance eventually began to revive con-

46. See Stubblebine, "Institutional Elements in the Financing of Education," 32 *Southern Economic Journal* 15 (Supp. to July 1965 issue).

47. The incompleteness and undefined character of the statistics make it difficult to come to a definite conclusion.

siderably. For the year 1860–61 the State money allocated to the rural districts was $950,000. The rural district taxes brought in $500,000 and the rate bills $400,000. There was a dramatic increase in the annual revenue from rate bills to over $700,000 in 1867.[48] This was accompanied by another revival of the private-school population. Excluding Kings County and New York City (for which figures for the earlier years are not available), the statistics published by the State Superintendent show an increase in the number of pupils in private schools from 48,541 in 1863 to 68,105 in 1867. This was followed by a decrease to 49,691 in 1871 after the passage of the Act of 1867, which abolished rate bills. Notwithstanding the incompleteness of these figures, there can be little doubt that the abolition of rate bills led to a decline in the private-school share of school population.

Increasingly hostile propaganda put out by the protagonists for free Common Schools indicated the continuing competition of private schools. There was also an attempt to shift the popular image of the public school system. As was suggested above, it is consistent with motives of self-interest that special pressure groups should try to mold public opinion at the same time as they are trying to persuade the government that such opinion exists. There is plenty of evidence that this kind of strategy was employed by the teachers' associations and organisations by the middle of the nineteenth century.

The initial motive of the original legislation, it will be remembered, was to *encourage* education in order that the members of the republic become responsible voters, prosperous individuals, and property-respecting, God-fearing persons. The expressed desire was simply to aid those who were too poor to provide education voluntarily. There was no suggestion of abolishing,

48. See *Ann. Rep. N.Y. Supt. Pub. Instruction* (1867), p. 82.

hindering, or taking over existing private schools; such a policy indeed would have been in direct conflict with that of encouraging education.

Already by the 1840s, however, the special interest groups in the public-school sector were beginning to distill new ideology from the legislation. They urged the demise of the private schools and the establishment of free schools on the grounds that the State and the will of the people demanded it.[49] Among the arguments in the 1844 report of the Onondaga County Teachers' Institute (which provided the opening attack in the free school campaign) was the new assertion that free schools were especially necessary for the children of the rich:

> The children of the rich do not generally form those habits of energy or perseverance—steady, unwearied, continuous labor— without which no man can attain eminence. The Free School sys-

49. Finegan, *op. cit.* note 19, p. 305. The claim that the "popular will" demanded free schools conflicts with the evidence given in the 1850 select committee on the free school law. It is interesting to compare the experience in Great Britain in the 1860s. Active pressure groups such as the Birmingham League proclaimed themselves as representing popular wishes in their campaign for "free" education for all. Yet systematic evidence that was then available pointed firmly in the opposite direction. A massive Royal Commission Report published in 1861 (known as the Newcastle Report and written by a body that included the economist Nassau Senior) stated:

"Almost all the evidence goes to show that though the offer of gratuitous education might be accepted by a certain proportion of the parents, it would in general be otherwise. The sentiment of independence is strong, and it is wounded by the offer of an absolutely gratuitous education."

Even those in the minority who wanted "free" education in England often consisted of ordinary people who only supported it because they thought it was one practical way of being compensated for the heavy taxes they paid. For, as Senior remarked when referring to the government subsidy to education:

"A considerable portion of it, probably one-half, is paid by the labourers whose children frequent those schools. In the price of every pot of beer and of every pipe the labourer pays a portion of the expense of the education of his own children." (*Suggestions on Popular Education* [1861].)

tem . . . would benefit the children of the rich by the lesson invaluable to them, that they are just such beings as the children of the pauper, and that if they would attain greatness they must work with untiring energy and perseverance.[50]

The next year the County Superintendent of Genesee in his report complained that without sufficient public funds the Common Schools would never be made acceptable to the rich and that therefore they were witnessing the rise of "private and select" schools, "thus creating a distinction in society that ought not to exist in a community of free men, who profess to believe in, and attempt to sustain the principles of republican liberty."[51] At the height of the free schools controversy of the late 1840s, the State Superintendent told his Government:

Private schools ought not to receive the encouragement of the State, or the support of the community. They are usually sustained by those who have the ability to employ competent teachers, and the common schools are weakened by the means applied to their support. Our district schools may be so elevated, [by

50. Randall, *op. cit.* note 1, pp. 216–17. Others in the public system began to denounce the support of private schools as unpatriotic. See for instance the protest of the County Superintendent of Queens Court in his 1846 report quoted in Finegan, *op. cit.* note 19, p. 91.

51. Finegan, *op. cit.* note 19, p. 162. Horace Mann pointed to the likelihood of alienation arising from the strong tendency for wealth to become concentrated in the hands of one class. Universal education in Common Schools was necessary, he maintained, to countervail the tendency to "the domination of capital and the servility of labour." He pointed to the example of Britain where, he said, the manufacturer prescribed wage rates and reduced them under any pretext he pleased. Only in rare instances "have kindly offices smoothed the rugged relation between British Capital and British Labour." No power in the realm had been able to secure working-class children an education. See 12 *Ann. Rep. of Sec. Mass. Bd. Educ* 58–59 (1849). This is not the place to discuss the validity of the theory of the class struggle. It seems necessary, however, to point out that Mann's view of the mid-nineteenth-century educational attainment of the masses in England was wrong. The majority of English people were literate and the majority of children were receiving a schooling by this time. See above, chapters 9–10.

more public expenditure] that those who seek superior advantages for their children, can find them only in the common schools.[52]

In some instances, particularly in the case of teacher training colleges, Government had been making special grants to private establishments. Eventually those who were associated with Common Schools began strongly to oppose such practice. They called for the complete termination of what they termed the two conflicting systems of education, the public and the private. As a New York State Superintendent argued:

> If all the schools of every grade that the State to any extent supports were associated in one homogeneous system, and the appropriations of the State were confined to that system as heretofore recommended by this Department, and as repeatedly urged by the State Teachers' Association, there would be no ground for conflict.[53]

Never was there any suggestion by the operators of the State system that open competition, by spurring most schools into adopting the methods of the best, could also be to some degree effective in reducing distinctions of efficiency. Indeed, competition was openly disliked by the administrators because it was untidy, embarrassing, and disruptive of their "system." Competition between schools *within* the public system, as well as from

52. 1849 *Ann. Rep. N.Y. Supt. Common Schools*, p. 8. The argument that private schools "weaken" public schools has long been prevalent despite the fact that there is little or no evidence for its support. Even if we ignore the beneficial effects of competition that private schools bring, the argument can only be true if education resources are infinitely inelastic. Private expenditure in fact may so enlarge total educational resources (e.g. by attracting more people into teaching) as to cause an enlarged expenditure per head in the public sector. The point is developed in my contribution to *Education: A Framework for Choice* (London: Institute of Economic Affairs, 1967), pp. 78–83.

53. 19 *Ann. Rep. N.Y. Supt. Pub. Instruction* (1873), p. 39.

without, was disliked by them. Consider the following view concerning competition in the city of New York in 1850. Because the city was at that time unique in allocating the proceeds of public taxes "untidily" to miscellaneous groups: to charitable bodies, to incorporated societies, as well as to municipal schools, parents were enjoying a wide range of choice. The Superintendent protested, however:

> Scholars or parents being thus privileged to select any school they please, it is not strange that some go two miles to school; and that large [school] houses, which will conveniently accommodate one thousand scholars in the three departments, have, some of them, but four hundred, and some of them have sixteen hundred.[54]

The Superintendent's solution, which he urged continually in his annual reports and which was eventually adopted, was that of "districting" (zoning) the city:

> as is done in most other towns, or at least confining the scholars to their own wards; but this cannot be speedily accomplished, nor perhaps ever, so long as there are rival organisations of schools, overlaying one another, and each in competition for the same scholars.[55]

In one report, the Superintendent suggested that the preferences of parents were not well founded and described children going "from one side of the city to another, to attend a crowded School, passing half a dozen Schools just as good as the one they had chosen to attend."[56] But in another he suggested that the parents' choice might be based on real differences between the

54. 1851 *Ann. Rep. N.Y. Supt. Common Schools*, p. 120.
55. *Ibid.*
56. 1849 *Ann. Rep. N.Y. Supt. Common Schools*, p. 125.

schools (at least in the minds of the parents): "The disadvantages of conflicting school limits are too obvious to need much comment. One effect most observable is, that respectable people prefer to send their children to schools that are in good neighborhoods; we accordingly see schools that are well located, are filled to repletion, and those that are unfavorably located, are not half-full."[57]

The strategy employed by the administrators was to try to focus public attention on what they called the "inequity" of having schools with superior advantages outside their province (the private schools) while at the same time themselves allowing what were to ordinary people gross differences of quality within their own public system. There was a tendency, in other words, for areas of "privilege" to creep into the public system. For the erection of district boundaries to prevent parents and scholars from moving to the best areas created privileges for those who happened to reside in them. Although presenting themselves as champions of the needy, the supporters and leaders of the Common School system do not seem to have given any serious attention to the possibility that the expansion and evolution of it might thus serve to worsen, not improve, the chances of poor children. As subsequent experience has shown, where all pay taxes for the support of such a system, it often transpires that it is the poor who subsidise the middle class.[58] Being more politically active, the latter are more able to obtain and to perpetuate bigger revenues and superior provision for the districts serving their own children. Lack of money or obstacles to mobility prevent

57. 1850 *Ann. Rep. N.Y. Supt. Common Schools*, p. 125.
58. Kenneth E. Boulding has recently written: "One wonders also whether 'free' public education supported by a tax system, which is regressive as most state and local tax systems tend to be, is not really a device for subsidizing the education of the rich rather than that of the poor."33 *University of Chicago Law Review* 618 (1966).

others from moving into the superior middle-class districts to correct the imbalance. The point is more emphasised where housing also becomes, as it has subsequently become, government subsidised and controlled. For then the population tends to be distributed geographically even more strictly in accordance with income groups and becomes generally still less mobile since the subsidy cannot be transferred to other areas.

With the passing of the Free Schools Act of 1867 the rate bills (fees) were finally abolished. As we have seen, the statistical evidence indicates that this led to a check in the growth of education in private schools after the passage of the new Act. In his report of 1870, the Superintendent of Cortland County observed with satisfaction:

> Private schools, always exerting, to a greater or less extent, a deleterious influence on the public schools, do not flourish under the operation of the free school system. Most of the academies are unable to compete with free schools, and are rapidly giving place to union schools. Of the four academies formerly located in this commissioner district, but one remains. It is generally conceded that union free schools are best adapted to meet the wants of the people.[59]

The process of school monopolisation after 1867 was carried much further than was possible for any undertaking, educational or otherwise, in the private sector. For while it was possible for monopolising private organisations to charge high prices, they could not, as could the Common Schools, go further and *enforce* payment from their customers through compulsory taxes. But, unique as this particular feature was, there yet remained for the organisers of the Common Schools the possibility of securing and strengthening their monopoly still further.

59. 17 *Ann. Rep. N.Y. Supt. Pub. Instruction* (1871), p. 210.

It must be remembered that there remained one area of discretion for the customers of education; they still possessed the freedom to restrict their consumption. This meant, for instance, that in those areas where the public supply was inferior, and where the new public monopoly removed any hopes of quick improvement, it was likely that some parents would want to exercise their remaining freedom by removing their children from school at an earlier age than in those areas where better-quality teaching existed. Still bearing in mind our economic theory of politics, it is interesting retrospectively to "predict" the responses of the school suppliers in such circumstances. Especially since public money was distributed to the schools and their staffs in proportion to the numbers in attendance, we should expect that the kind of agitation that would next have been undertaken by the income-maximising teachers, managers, and other officials, especially those of average or less-than-average ability, would have been a campaign for an education that was compulsory by statute. The historical evidence is in fact compatible with such "prediction." Serious agitation for compulsory attendance built up very soon after the success of the free school campaign of 1867. "The irregular attendance of a large number of enrolled pupils is a serious obstacle," protested the Superintendent of the City of Newburgh in 1870, and he placed the blame on "the laxity and indifference of the parents." The Superintendent believed that:

> not only the true enjoyment and perpetuity of our liberties, but also the true and real progress of our national prosperity, demand an enforcement by legislative enactment, of a system of education that shall contain, among its provisions, one that will compel the attendance, at some good school, of all the children of proper age . . . [60]

60. *Ibid.*, pp. 303–304.

Thus, while before 1867 the prevailing argument had been that the main reason for lack of attendance had been the rate bills, after 1867, when these had been abolished, and when what was considered to be bad attendance persisted, the new contention was that parental indifference was the main trouble.

Curiously enough there was one dissentient voice, that of the Superintendent for the State himself. He conceded, in his annual report dated 1871, that it was rarely the case that "parents who provide for their children in other respects, wholly neglect their education." To meet the *minority* case of the children of vagrant or improvident parents, he pointed out that there was already on the statute books a law applicable to them but which had not been enforced. That law, an Act of 1853, provided discriminatory powers to rescue and care not only for their education but for their physical and moral needs as well.

> And yet, with such a statute unemployed, a demand is made for a compulsory law which could not be enforced against the destitute classes amenable to the existing law, but which would be directed against those who are not idle, nor truant, nor vagrant, nor vicious, and which might be made the means of annoyance and oppression to many well-disposed people.[61]

In effect the Superintendent was pointing out that there were two types of compulsion—universal and selective; and that existing laws already involved compulsion anyway. Where a minority class of malefactors was aimed at, the correct policy was to use a selective law and therefore a selective kind of compulsion. Government funds might be dissipated if the authorities tried the costly method of continually policing the whole responsible majority, which did not need it. To illustrate from another field, child malnutrition was an offence but it had not been found

61. *Ibid.*, p. 65.

necessary to pass universal laws for compulsory feeding of every child.[62]

It is interesting to reflect that, in an "ideal" democratic world where there was little uncertainty and where there were low costs of political participation, such legislative powers of compulsion would be less easy to establish than in the real-world case of "impure" government with its powerful lobbyists and special interest groups. This is not to say that compulsion would never be resorted to; only that the costs and benefits would be more widely and carefully scrutinized. For instance, the costs of the activities of officials operating under a new law of compulsion would be compared with the benefits of reduced (time) costs of parents in their accustomed and self-imposed task of checking that their children went to school. Among the costs to be reckoned would be the danger of undermining the feeling of responsibility in parents as a whole. Another cost to be considered would be the social cost of monopolising. A consideration of the latter would involve an attempt to measure the deterioration in the quality of schools consequent upon the reduction of competition between schools and the restriction of consumer choice. Moreover, since competition might be considered to cause a total upgrading of the quality of schooling, reliance on it to encourage a voluntary increase in attendance might be judged a preferable (less costly) policy than compulsory laws. But the State Superintendent of 1871 seems to have been an isolated voice when he raised these kinds of considerations:

> It is palpable that the prominent defect, which calls for speedy reformation, is not incomplete attendance, but poor teaching . . . I speak of the needed improvement in the particular mentioned, in comparison with compulsion, as a means of securing atten-

62. For fuller discussion of this argument see above, Chapter 13.

dance; and I contend that, before sending out ministers of the law to force children to school, we should place genuine teachers in the school-room to attract them . . .

Let the attendance at school of every child within the State be secured, and that would not improve the schools in other respects; but let the schools be made what they should be in themselves, and it is more than probable that there will be no occasion to send for pupils. In any event, the improvement in question should be made; and, in my judgment it should be made before resorting to the doubtful experiment of compulsion. It cannot be done suddenly, by legislation.[63]

On reflection, if we may digress a little, it is remarkable how readily most democratic governments, especially republican governments, have, within the last century, resorted to the general use of police power in education. In the case of America, the addition of the term "compulsory" to those of "free" and "universal" seems to the modern ear to be rooted in the same kind of sentiments as those which inspired the Constitution itself. It is interesting too, to notice how often historians rank the different states according to the dates of their adoption of compulsory laws. The first honor is usually given to the State of Massachusetts, whose laws of 1642 and 1647, in the words of one historian, "constitute the precedents upon which the subsequent universal free education program of the country has been established."[64] The fact that this type of legislation should respect such an ancestry has its paradoxes. In one respect at least, nothing could have been more alien to the spirit of the American Constitution than the early legislation of Massachusetts. For it was passed at a time when the policy of the state being that of the church, a puritan theocracy was in full power. Certainly, nothing can be fur-

63. 17 *Ann. Rep. N.Y. Supt. Public Instruction* (1871), pp. 66–67.
64. Allen, *Universal Free Education* (1934), p. 10.

ther from the spirit of the Fourteenth Amendment than the idea of compulsory religious instruction that was contained in the 1642 measure.

But to return to the particular events in New York State: the agitation by the teachers' association (and other interested groups) for compulsory laws, following the victory in 1867 of their Free School Campaign was soon rewarded. The Compulsory Education Act was in fact passed in 1874. And interestingly enough, after several years of operation this Act was declared ineffective. The Superintendent of 1890, asking for yet more legislation, complained that the existing laws were still not reaching the hard core of truant cases, those associated with dissolute families.

> It is worse than futile to assume that all persons charged with the care of children will send them to school. The great majority will. But unfortunately some parents are idlers, drunkards or criminals themselves . . . [65]

But whatever the fate of the children of the "hard-case" families, the final link in the process of monopolising had now been firmly secured in the education of all the other children. Compulsory payment and compulsory consumption had become mutually strengthening monopoly bonds and the pattern of schooling for the next century had been firmly set.

Our account of the nineteenth-century evolution of school legislation therefore draws to its conclusion with the observation that whether or not it was appropriate to apply compulsory laws unconditionally to all classes of individuals, the laws that were actually established did not in fact secure in the nineteenth century an education that was universal in the sense of 100 per

---

65. 36 *Ann. Rep. N.Y. Supt. Public Instruction* (1890), p. 35.

cent school attendance by all children of school age. If, on the other hand, the term "universal" is intended more loosely to mean something like, "most," "nearly everybody," or "over 90 per cent" then we lack firm evidence to show that education was not already universal prior to the establishment of laws to provide a schooling that was both compulsory and free.

Conclusion

Whilst propositions from welfare economics about the role of government in education might have logical appeal in themselves, the full application of our economic knowledge is not complete until we have considered the motivations and behavior of those individuals who operate in or near to the seat of government itself. Accordingly the present article has concentrated not upon such conventional matters as the question of the optimal allocation of public funds to our state education institutions, but rather upon the shape of the institutions themselves and upon the economic behaviour of those who have a personal stake in their specific form.

At least one conclusion emerges from this investigation. The familiar "trinity" in educational parlance: "universal," "free," and "compulsory," takes on quite a different perspective from that to which most of us have been led to hold. The word "universal," as we have seen, may have been used in more than one quantitative sense. Moreover, what has been intended by this term has often been not a target of universal education so much as an education that is universally in public schools—a universal system, or a system that is used exclusively to anything else. The word "free" also appears more than usually equivocal. True, average parents and scholars were eventually given a schooling that was "free," but this was largely in a technical sense. Furthermore, they were simultaneously made "unfree" in the sense that their choice became severely restricted. As for the term "compulsion," the above survey suggests the need to consider more carefully not only the exact purposes of the legislation, but also the political and economic consequences of the precise shaping of it.

Beyond this it is clear that government intervention can lead to conflict between those already established in education; to disagreement for instance between charitable society schools and to bankruptcy among private ones. And, prompted not so much by abstract welfare theorems as by motives of self-interest, it is likely that those engaged in the initiation of a Common School system to *augment* a private one will soon give reasons why the former should *replace* or *supersede* the latter.

As was shown in the introduction to this case study, there are several patterns of intervention from which government is able to choose; each of them has costs peculiar to itself and something more than intuition is needed in order to select the "right" one. The moral seems to be that economists more than anybody else should question how far *their* acceptance of particular instruments of public intervention springs from logical demonstration and how far from the successful salesmanship of those already employed in government undertakings; and how far indeed, those which we call necessary institutions are, in the words of de Tocqueville, simply no more than institutions to which we have become accustomed.

SELECT BIBLIOGRAPHY

BOOKS

Altick, Robert D., *The English Common Reader,* Chicago, University of Chicago Press, 1957.

'Annual Reports of the Committee of Council on Education', 1872–87.

Aspinall, Arthur, *Politics of the Press,* London, Home and Van Thal Ltd., 1949.

Baker, J., *Children in Chancery,* London, Hutchinson, 1964.

Balfour, George, *Educational Systems,* Oxford, Oxford University Press, 1903.

Barnard, Henry C., *History of English Education,* London, University of London Press, 1947.

Barnard, Henry C., *A Short History of English Education,* London, University of London Press, 1949.

Berlin, Isaiah, *The Two Concepts of Liberty,* Oxford, Oxford University Press, 1958.

Birchenough, C., *History of Elementary Education,* London, University Tutorial Press, 1932.

Blaug, Mark, 'Economic Aspects of Vouchers for Education', *Education: A Framework for Choice,* Readings in Political Economy 1, E. G. West, *et. al.,* London, Institute of Economic Affairs, 1967.

Buchanan, James M. and Gordon Tullock, *The Calculus of Consent,* Ann Arbor, University of Michigan Press, 1962.

Burgess, Tyrrell, *A Guide to English Schools,* London, Pelican, 1964.

'Census of Population', Education Supplement, 1851.

Chalmers, Thomas, *Political Economy in connection with the Moral State and Moral Prospects of Society,* 1832.

Choice in Welfare, London, Institute of Economic Affairs, 1963.

Craik, Herbert, *The State in its Relation to Education*, London, Macmillan, 1896.

Crosland, Colin A. R., *The Future of Socialism*, London, Jonathan Cape, 1956.

Curtis, Samuel J., *History of Education in Great Britain*, London, University Tutorial Press, 1963.

Dean, Phyllis and W. A. Cole, *British Economic Growth, 1688–1959*, Cambridge, Cambridge University Press, 1962.

Department for Education, *Choice and Diversity: A New Framework for Schools*, London, Her Majesty's Stationery Office, July 1992.

Dicey, Arthur V., *Law and Public Opinion in England*, London, Macmillan, 1952.

Dolton, Christopher B., *The Manchester School Board*, M.Ed. Thesis, Durham University, 1959.

Douglas, James W. B., *The Home and the School*, London, MacGibbon and Kee, 1964.

Eaglesham, Eric, *From School Board to Local Authority*, London, Routledge and Kegan Paul, 1956.

Finer, S. E., *The Life and Times of Sir Edwin Chadwick*, London, Methuen, 1952.

Friedman, Milton, *Capitalism and Freedom*, Chicago, University of Chicago Press, 1962.

Glass, David, 'Education and Social Change in Modern England', *Education, Economy and Society*, Edited by A. H. Halsey, Edinburgh, Free Press of Glencoe, 1962.

Godwin, William, *Enquiry concerning Political Justice and its influence on Morals and Happiness*, London, 1796.

Gregg, Pauline, *A Social and Economic History of Great Britain, 1760–1950*, London, Harrap, 1954.

Habakkuk, Henry J., *American and British Technology in the Nineteenth Century*, Cambridge, Cambridge University Press, 1962.

Halevy, Elie, *The Growth of Philosophic Radicalism*, London, Faber and Faber, 1934.

Half our Future: A Report of the Central Advisory Council for Education (England), (The Newsom Report), London, Her Majesty's Stationery Office, 1963.

Halsey, Arthur H., J. Flond, and C. A. Arnold (Editors), *Education, Economy and Society,* Edinburgh, Free Press of Glencoe, 1961.

Hayek, Freidrich A., *The Constitution of Liberty,* London, Routledge and Kegan Paul, 1962.

Home Office, *Report on the work of the Children's Department 1961–63,* London, Her Majesty's Stationery Office, March 1964.

Judges, A. V. (Editor), *Pioneers of English Education,* London, Faber and Faber, 1952.

Kay, James Philip, *The Moral and Physical Condition of the Working Classes,* London, James Ridgway, 1830.

Kay, James Philip, *The Report of the Poor Law Commissioners,* London, Poor Law Commission, 1841.

Lester Smith, W. O., *Education,* London, Pelican, 1962.

Lipsey, R. G., *An Introduction to Positive Economics,* London, Weidenfeld and Nicolson, 1963.

Lowndes, George A. N., *The Silent Social Revolution,* Oxford, Oxford University Press, 1937.

Machlup, Fritz, *The Production and Distribution of Knowledge,* Princeton, Princeton University Press, 1962.

Malthus, Thomas R., *An Essay on the Principles of Population,* London, Everyman's Library, 1826.

Marks, John, *The National Curriculum and Primary School Method,* London, Centre for Policy Studies, November 1992.

Marks, John, *Standards in Schools,* London, The Social Market Foundation, 1991.

Mill, John Stuart, *Autobiography,* New York, Henry Holt, 1873.

Mill, John Stuart, *On Liberty,* Fontana Edition, London, The Fontana Library, 1962.

Mill, John Stuart, *Principles of Political Economy,* Ashley Edition, London, Longmans, 1909.

Minutes of the Committee of Council on Education, 1840–41.

de Montmorency, J. E. G., *State Intervention in English Education,* Cambridge, Cambridge University Press, 1902.

Musgrave, Richard A., *Public Finance,* New York, McGraw-Hill, 1959.

National Union of Teachers, *The State of Our Schools,* London, 1963.

Paine, Tom, *The Rights of Man,* London, Everyman's Library, 1958.

Pakenham, Henry, *Causes of Crime,* London, Weidenfeld and Nicolson, 1958.

Parkinson, Michael, *The Labour Party and the Organization of Secondary Education,* London, Routledge and Kegan Paul, 1970.

Peacock, Alan T. and J. Wiseman, *Education for Democrats,* Hobart Paper 25, Institute of Economic Affairs, 1964.

Porter, George R., *The Progress of the Nation,* London, Methuen, 1912.

Rae, John, *Life of Adam Smith,* London, Macmillan, 1895.

Randall, George, *History of The Common School System of the State of New York,* New York, Ivison, Blakemen, Taylor & Co., 1871.

Reid, T. Wemyss, *The Life of the Right Hon. W. E. Forster,* London, Macmillan, 1889.

Report of the Select Committee on Scientific Instruction, London, 1868.

Robbins Committee—Appendix IV, London, Her Majesty's Stationery Office, 1963.

Robbins, Lionel, *The Theory of Economic Policy,* London, Macmillan, 1952.

The Royal Commission on Popular Education, *Report of the Commissioners appointed to enquire into the State of Popular Education in England,* Vol. I, 1861.

Schultz, Theodore W., *The Economic Value of Education,* New York, Columbia University Press, 1963.

Senior, Nassau, *Suggestions on Popular Education,* London, John Murray, 1861.

Sexton, Stuart, *New Zealand Schools: An Evaluation of Recent Reforms and Future Directions,* Wellington, N.Z., New Zealand Business Roundtable, 1990.

Simon, Brian, *Studies in the History of Education, 1780–1870,* London, Lawrence and Wishart, 1960.

Smith, Adam, *An Inquiry into the Nature and Causes of the Wealth of Nations,* Book V, Edited by R. H. Campbell and A. S. Skinner, textual editor W. B. Todd, Indianapolis, Liberty Fund, 1982.

Smith, Adam, *Lectures on Rhetoric and Belles Lettres,* Edited by J. C. Bryce and A. S. Skinner, Indianapolis, Liberty Fund, 1985.

Smith, Adam, *The Theory of Moral Sentiments* (sixth edition 1777), Edited by D. D. Raphael and A. L. Macfie, Indianapolis, Liberty Fund, 1982.

Spencer, Herbert, *Social Statics and Man Versus the State*, London, Chapman, 1884.

Talmon, John L., *The Origins of Totalitarian Democracy*, London, Secker and Warburg, 1955.

Tawney, Ralph, *Equality*, Second Edition, London, Allen and Unwin, 1931.

Thornton, William T., *Over Population and Its Remedy*, London, Longman, Brown, Green and Longmans, 1846.

de Tocqueville, Alexis, *Democracy in America*, New York, New American Library, 1956.

de Tocqueville, Alexis, *The Old Regime and the French Revolution*, New York, Doubleday, 1856.

Vaizey, John, *The Economics of Education*, London, Faber and Faber, 1962.

Webb, Robert K., *The British Working Class Reader* (1790–1848), London, Allen & Unwin, 1955.

Webb, Richard K., 'The Victorian Reading Public', *From Dickens to Hardy*, London, Pelican, 1963.

Weisbrod, Burton A., *External Benefits of Public Education*, Princeton, Princeton University Press, 1964.

Wicksell, Knut, 'A New Principle of Just Taxation', *Classics in the Theory of Public Finance*, Edited by R. A. Musgrave and A. T. Peacock, London, Macmillan, 1962.

Williams, Raymond, *The Long Revolution*, London, Chatto and Windus, 1961.

Wootton, Barbara, *Social Science and Social Pathology*, London, Allen & Unwin, 1959.

Young, Michael, *The Rise of the Meritocracy*, London, Pelican, 1958.

ARTICLES

Assistant Handloom Weavers' Commissioners, 'Report on the State Education in the Borough of Kingston upon Hull', *Journal of the Statistical Society of London*, July 1841.

Balogh, Thomas and P. Streeten, 'The Coefficient of Ignorance', *Bulletin* of the Oxford University Institute of Economics and Statistics, Vol. 10, No. 1, May 1963, pp. 25–30.

Bowman, Mary J., 'Schultz, Dennison, and the Contribution of "Eds" to National Income Growth', *Journal of Political Economy*, Vol. 72, No. 1, October 1964, pp. 36–42.

Buchanan, James M., 'Politics, Policy and the Pigovian Margins', *Economica*, Vol. 29, No. 3, February 1962, pp. 256–63.

Coase, Ronald H., 'The Problem of Social Cost', *Journal of Law and Economics*, Vol. 3, No. 1, October 1960.

Harris, Ralph, 'Economic Forecasting: Projections or Targets?', *Statist*, Vol. 24, January 1964.

'The Incidence of Taxes and Social Benefits in 1967', *Economic Trends*, Her Majesty's Stationery Office, February 1969.

Korner, Shirley, 'Partners or customers?', *Where?*, Summer 1964.

McLean, Martin, 'The Conservative Education Policy in Comparative Perspective: Return to an English Golden Age or Harbinger of International Policy Change?', *British Journal of Education Studies*, Vol. 36, No. 3, October 1988.

Mill, James, *Edinburgh Review*, Article IX, 1813.

Mill, James, *Westminster Review*, Vol. 6, October 1826.

Perkins, Harold J., 'The Origins of the Popular Press', *History Today*, July 1957.

Rowley, Charles K., 'The Political Economy of British Education', *Scottish Journal of Political Economy*, Vol. 16, 1969.

Shaffer, Harold G., 'Investment in Human Capital: Comment', *American Economic Review*, December 1961.

Turvey, Ralph, 'On Divergences between Social Cost and Private Cost', *Economica*, Vol. 30, No. 2, August 1963, pp. 27–33.

Webb, Richard K., 'Working Class Readers in Early Victorian England', *The English Historical Review*, 1950.

Weisbrod, Burton A., 'Education and Investment in Human Capital', *Journal of Political Economy*, Vol. 70, October 1962.

West, Edwin G., 'Private versus Public Education—A Classical Economic Dispute', *The Journal of Political Economy*, Vol. 72, No. 2, October 1964.

Wiseman, Jack, *'The Economics of Education'*, British Association for the Advancement of Science, August 1958.

RECOMMENDED READING

Anderson, G. M., W. F. Shughart, and R. D. Tollison, 'Educational Achievement and the Cost of Bureaucracy', *Journal of Behavior Organization* 15, 1991, pp. 29–45.

Becker, Gary S., *Human Capital*, New York, National Bureau of Economic Research, 2nd Edition, 1975.

Becker, Gary, 'What Our Schools Need Is a Healthy Dose of Competition', *Business Week*, December 18, 1989.

Bee, Michael, and P. J. Dolton, 'Costs and Economies of Scale in U.K. Private Schools', *Applied Economics* 17, 1985, pp. 281–90.

Bergen, John J., 'The Private School Movement in Canada', *Education Canada*, Summer 1981, pp. 4–8.

Black, David E., Kenneth A. Lewis, and Charles R. Link, 'Wealth Neutrality and the Demand for Education', *National Tax Journal*, Vol. 32, 1979, pp. 157–64.

Boaz, David (editor), *Liberating Schools: Education in the Inner City*, Washington, D.C., The Cato Institute, 1991.

Cannell, John, *Nationally Normed Elementary Achievement Testing in America's Public Schools*, Daniels, West Virginia, Friends for Education, 1987.

Chubb, John E., and T. Moe, *Politics, Markets, and American Schools*, Washington, D.C., The Brookings Institution, 1990.

Chubb, John E., and T. Moe, 'A Response to Our Critics', *Education Week*, 20 February 1991.

Cohn, Elchanan, and Terry Geske, *The Economics of Education*, New York, Pergamon Press, 1990.

Coleman, James S., T. Hoffer, and S. Kilgore, *High School Achievement*, New York, Basic Books, 1982.

Flew, Antony, *Power to the Parents: Reversing Educational Decline*, London, The Sherwood Press Ltd., 1987.

345

Frey, Donald E., 'Optimal-sized Tuition Tax Credits Reconsidered: Comment', *Public Finance Quarterly* 19(2), 1991, pp. 347–54.

Frey, Donald E., *Tuition Tax Credits for Private Education*, Ames, Iowa State University Press, 1983.

Friedman, Milton and Rose Friedman, *Free to Choose*, New York, Harcourt Brace Jovanovich, 1980.

High, Jack, 'State Education: Have Economists Made a Case?', *Cato Journal* 5, 1985, pp. 305–23.

James, Estell, and Gayle Benjamin, *Public Policy and Private Education in Japan*, London, Macmillan Press, 1988.

Lee, Dwight, 'The Political Economy of Educational Vouchers', *The Freeman*, July 1986.

Lieberman, Myron, *Privatization and Educational Choice*, New York, St. Martin's, 1989.

Lieberman, Myron, *Public Education: An Autopsy*, Cambridge, Harvard University Press, 1993.

Lott, John R., 'The Institutional Arrangement of Public Education', *Public Choice* 54, 1987, pp. 89–96.

Lott, John R., 'An Explanation for Public Provision of Schooling: The Importance of Indoctrination', *Journal of Law and Economics*, Vol. XXXIII (1), April 1990.

Lynn, Richard, 'The Japanese Example of Indirect Vouchers', *Economic Affairs*, Vol. 6(6), London, Institute of Economic Affairs, September 1986, pp. 49–51.

National Task Force on Education for Economic Growth, *A Nation at Risk*, Washington, D.C., U.S. Department of Health, Education and Welfare, 1983.

Psacharopoulos, George, and Maureen Woodhall, *Education for Development*, Oxford, Oxford University Press, 1985.

Purkey, Stewart C., and Marshall S. Smith, 'Effective Schools: A Review', *Elementary School Journal*, Vol. 83, March 1983.

Seldon, Arthur, *Capitalism*, Oxford, Blackwell, 1990.

Williams, Mary Frase, Kimberly Small Hancher, and Amy Hutner, *Parents and School Choice: A Household Survey*, School Finance Project: Working Paper, Washington, D.C., U.S. Department of Education, December 1983.

OTHER PUBLICATIONS BY E. G. WEST

BOOKS, CHAPTERS IN BOOKS AND PAMPHLETS

Adam Smith: The Man and His Works, Indianapolis, Liberty Fund, 1977.

Economics, Education and the Politician, Hobart Paper No. 42, London, Institute of Economic Affairs, 1968.

'The Economics of Compulsory Education', in *The Twelve Year Sentence,* Edited by William F. Rickenbacker, La Salle, Illinois, Open Court, 1974.

'Education and Choice', published as an Occasional Paper by the Centre for Independent Studies, Sydney, Australia, 1990.

'Education and Competitiveness', School of Policy Studies, Queen's University, Discussion Paper No. 93–02, 1993.

Education and the Industrial Revolution. London, Batsford's, 1975. Liberty Fund, Inc., plans to publish a second edition incorporating new material.

Education Tax Credits, Critical Issues Series, Washington, D.C., Heritage Foundation, 1981.

'Extra-governmental Powers in Public Schooling: The Unions and the Courts', in *Collective Choice in Education,* Edited by Mary Bowman, The Hague, Kluwer Nijhoff, 1982.

'Free Education: A Re-Examination', in *Government Aid to Private Schools: Is It a Trojan Horse?* Edited by Richard E. Wagner, Menlo Park, Calif., Institute for Human Studies, 1979.

'Literacy and the Industrial Revolution', *The Economics of the Industrial Revolution,* Edited by Joel Mokyr, Rowman and Allenheld, Totowa, New Jersey, 1985.

Non-Public School Aid: The Law, Economics, and Politics of American Education, Lexington, Mass., D. C. Heath, 1976.

'Private Versus Public Education', in *The Classical Economists and Economic Policy,* Edited by Arthur W. Coats, London, Methuen, 1970.

'The Prospects for Education Vouchers: An Economic Analysis' in *Papers on State Controlled Educational Processes*, Edited by Robert B. Everhart, San Francisco, Pacific Institute, 1982.

Readings in Political Economy, London, Institute of Economic Affairs, 1967 (with Mark Blaug, Henry Beales and Sir Douglas Veale).

Religion, Morality, Values and Education, Edited by Thomas C. Hunt, Bombay, Ann Prakasham Press, 1980 (a contributed paper).

ARTICLES

'The Assisted Places Scheme in British Education', *The Journal of Economic Affairs,* Vol. 3, No. 1, October 1982, pp. 9–11.

'The Benthamites as Educational Engineers: The Reputation and the Record', *History of Political Economy*, Vol. 24, No. 3, Fall 1992, pp. 595–622.

'Challenging the Public School Monopoly', *Reason*, Vol. 11, No. 8, December 1979, pp. 17–25.

'Classical Economic Views of the Role of the State in Victorian Education: Comment', *Southern Economic Journal*, April 1969, pp. 185–7.

'Constitutional Decisions on Non-Public School Aid', *Emory Law Journal*, Vol. 16, No. 1, April 1987, pp. 795–851.

'De Gustibus Non Est Disputandum: The Phenomenon of "Merit Wants"', (with Michael McKee), *American Economic Review*, Vol. 73, No. 5, December 1983, pp. 1110–21.

'The Demise of "Free" Education', *Challenge: The Magazine of Economic Affairs*, Vol. 27, No. 6, January/February 1985, pp. 13–20.

'The District of Columbia Education Tax Credit Initiative', Cato Institute Policy Analysis Papers, November 1981, pp. 27–33.

'An Economic Analysis of the Law and Politics of Non-Public School Aid', *Journal of Law and Economics*, Vol. 11, No. 1, 1976, pp. 101–18.

'An Economic Rationale for Public Schools: The Search Continues', *Teacher's College Record*, Vol. 88, No. 2, Winter 1986, pp. 152–67.

'Education, Alienation and Radical Economics', *Review of Social Economy*, Vol. 34, No. 3, October 1976, pp. 217–29.

'Education and Liberty: John Stuart Mill's Dilemma', *Philosophy*, Vol. 27, No. 2, April 1965, pp. 35–48.

'Education Budget Reductions via Tax Credits: Some Further Considerations', *Public Finance Quarterly*, Vol. 19, No. 3, July 1991 (with Felice Martinello), pp. 355–68.

'Education Reform: Administrative Objections Overruled', *Economic Affairs*, London, Institute of Economic Affairs, Vol. 6, No. 4, May 1986, pp. 33–40.

'Education Slowdown and Public Intervention in Nineteenth Century Britain: A Study in the Economics of Bureaucracy', *Explorations in Economic History*, Vol. 11, No. 3, January 1975, pp. 61–87.

'Education Vouchers: New Perspectives in the Eighties?', *Policy Review*, Washington, D.C., Vol. 15, Winter 1981, pp. 7–12.

'Extra Governmental Powers in Public Schools: The Unions and the Courts', *Public Choice*, Vol. 36, No. 3, 1981 (with Robert Staaf), pp. 619–37.

'Imperfect Capital Markets as Barriers to Education', *Atlantic Economic Journal*, Vol. 5, July 1977 (with Michael McKee), pp. 23–30.

'The Interpretation of Early Nineteenth Century Education Statistics', *The Economic History Review* 24, November 1971, pp. 633–42.

'Literacy and the Industrial Revolution', *The Economic History Review*, 2nd Ser. 31, No. 3, 1978, pp. 369–83.

'The Meaning of Autonomy in Education', *Economics of Education Review*, Vol. 11, No. 3, 1992, pp. 417–25.

'Nineteenth Century Educational History: The Kiesling Critique', *The Economic History Review*, Vol. 36, No. 3, August 1983, pp. 426–34.

'The Optimal Size of the Tuition Tax Credit', *Public Finance Quarterly*, Vol. 16, No. 4, November 1988 (with Felice Martinello), pp. 425–38.

'The "Opting Out" Revolution in British Education: Real versus Fictitious Opportunities', London, *Economic Affairs*, February 1993, pp. 18–20.

'Parental Choice of School Characteristics: Estimation Using Statewide Characteristics', *Economic Inquiry*, Vol. 26, No. 4, October 1988 (with Halldor Palsson), pp. 725–40.

'Parental Versus State Goals in Education: Comments on Arthur E.

Wise and Linda Darling-Hammond's "Education by Voucher"',
Educational Theory, Vol. 34, No. 1, Winter 1983, pp. 51–3.

'The Perils of Public Education', *The Freeman*, Vol. 27, No. 11, November 1977, pp. 13–17.

'Policies to Reduce Criminal Activity: Do Schools Make a Difference?', *Character*, University of Illinois, Vol. 3, April 1980, pp. 7–9.

'The Propriety of Migration Controls', *Il Politico*, 1968, Vol. 27, pp. 360–75.

'Public Aid to Ontario's Independent Schools', *Canadian Public Policy*, Vol. 11, No. 4, 1985, pp. 37–45.

'Public Education and Exclusive Territories', *Public Finance Quarterly*, Vol. 18, No. 4, October 1990, pp. 371–94.

'The Public School System and the Deterioration of Free Exercise', *Review Journal of Philosophy and Social Science*, Vol. 4, No. 2, 1980, pp. 10–15.

'Public Schools and Excess Burdens', *Economics of Education Review*, Vol. 10, No. 2, July 1991, pp. 159–69.

'Quality Trends in U.S. Public Schools', *Policy Report*, Cato Institute, Fall 1983, pp. 21–30.

'The Real Cost of Tuition Tax Credits', *Public Choice*, Vol. 46, No. 1, 1985, pp. 61–70.

'Regional Planning: Fact and Fallacy', *Lloyds Bank Review*, April 1966, pp. 35–48.

'Reply to Ehrenberg', *Public Choice*, Vol. 36, No. 3, 1981 (with Robert Staaf), pp. 647–50.

'Resource Allocation and Growth in Early Nineteenth Century British Education', *The Economic History Review*, Vol. 23, April 1970, pp. 68–95.

'Restoring Family Autonomy in Education', *Chronicles*, Vol. 13, October 1990, pp. 11–15.

'The Role of the State in Financing Recurrent Education: Lessons from European Experience', Commentary, *Public Choice*, Vol. 36, No. 3, 1981, pp. 579–82.

'The Shapiro Report on Ontario's Private Schools', *Fraser Forum*, Vancouver, Fraser Institute, November 1985.

'Social Legislation and the Demand for Children', *Western Economic Journal*, Vol. 6, December 1968, pp. 419–24.

'Social Returns from Education: Some Neglected Factors', *Canadian*

Public Policy, Vol. 17, No. 2, June 1991 (with Christos Constantatos), pp. 127–38.

'Tom Paine's Voucher Scheme for Education', *Southern Economic Journal*, Vol. 33, No. 2, January 1967, pp. 378–82.

'Tuition Tax Credit Proposals: An Economic Analysis of the 1978 Packwood/Moynihan Bill', *Policy Review*, Vol. 3, Winter 1978, pp. 17–21.

'Voters Versus the Public Schools', in *Policy Report*, Cato Institute, Vol. 1, No. 2, February 1979, pp. 9–11.

'The Yale Tuition Postponement Plan in the Mid-Seventies', *Higher Education*, Vol. 5, 1976, pp. 17–23.

SELECTED BOOK REVIEWS, 1980–93

Review of *The Economics of Education*, by Elchanan Cohn, *Journal of Economic Literature*, Vol. 11, December 1973.

Review of *The Educational Thought of the Classical Economists*, by Margaret G. O'Donnell, *Economics of Education Review*, Spring 1987.

Review of *Education and Economic Growth*, by Fritz Machlup, *Journal of Economic Literature*, Fall 1976.

Review of *Education and Opportunity in Victorian Scotland: Schools and Universities*, by Robert D. Anderson, *The Economic History Review*, Vol. 37, August 1984.

Review of *Is Public Education Necessary?*, by Samuel L. Blumenfeld, *Inquiry Magazine*, September 1981.

Review of *Public Dollars for Private Schools: The Case for Tuition Tax Credits*, Edited by Thomas James and Henry Levin, *Economics of Education Review*, 1984.

INDEX